Studying P

Palgrave Study Guides

Authoring a PhD
Career Skills
Critical Thinking Skills
e-Learning Skills
Effective Communication for Arts and Humanities Students
Effective Communication for Science and Technology
The Foundations of Research
The Good Supervisor
How to Manage your Arts, Humanities and Social Science Degree
How to Manage your Distance and Open Learning Course
How to Manage your Postgraduate Course
How to Manage your Science and Technology Degree
How to Study Foreign Languages
How to Write Better Essays
IT Skills for Successful Study
Making Sense of Statistics
The Mature Student's Guide to Writing
The Postgraduate Research Handbook

Presentation Skills for Students
The Principles of Writing in Psychology
Professional Writing
Research Using IT
Skills for Success
The Student Life Handbook
The Palgrave Student Planner
The Student's Guide to Writing (2nd edn)
The Study Skills Handbook (2nd edn)
Study Skills for Speakers of English as a Second Language
Studying the Built Environment
Studying Economics
Studying History (2nd edn)
Studying Mathematics and its Applications
Studying Modern Drama (2nd edn)
Studying Physics
Studying Programming
Studying Psychology
Teaching Study Skills and Supporting Learning
Work Placements – A Survival Guide for Students
Write it Right
Writing for Engineers (3rd edn)

Palgrave Study Guides: Literature

General Editors: John Peck and Martin Coyle

How to Begin Studying English Literature (3rd edn)
How to Study a Jane Austen Novel (2nd edn)
How to Study a Charles Dickens Novel
How to Study Chaucer (2nd edn)
How to Study an E. M. Forster Novel
How to Study James Joyce
How to Study Linguistics (2nd edn)

How to Study Modern Poetry
How to Study a Novel (2nd edn)
How to Study a Poet (2nd edn)
How to Study a Renaissance Play
How to Study Romantic Poetry (2nd edn)
How to Study a Shakespeare Play (2nd edn)
How to Study Television
Practical Criticism

Studying Programming

Sally Fincher and the Computing Education
Research Group

First published 2006 by
PALGRAVE MACMILLAN
Houndmills, Basingstoke, Hampshire RG21 6XS and
175 Fifth Avenue, New York, N.Y. 10010
Companies and representatives throughout the world

PALGRAVE MACMILLAN is the global academic imprint of the Palgrave Macmillan division of St. Martin's Press, LLC and of Palgrave Macmillan Ltd. Macmillan® is a registered trademark in the United States, United Kingdom and other countries. Palgrave is a registered trademark in the European Union and other countries.

ISBN-13: 978–1–4039–4687–4
ISBN-10: 1–4039–4687–6

This book is printed on paper suitable for recycling and made from fully managed and sustained forest sources.

A catalogue record for this book is available from the British Library.

10   9   8   7   6   5   4   3   2   1
15   14   13   12   11   10   09   08   07   06

Printed and bound in China

Contents

List of Figures

List of Tables

About the Authors

Studying Programming has been written by the following nine members of the Computing Education Research Group from the Computing Laboratory at the University of Kent. It is a work of equal authorship.

David Barnes is a lecturer at the University of Kent and has been teaching programming for nearly 25 years. He has a broad experience of different languages and programming styles and is an author of two textbooks on object-orientation.

Janet Carter teaches Mathematics, Formal Reasoning and Network Analysis to Computer Science students. Before this she taught mathematics and IT at a secondary school. Her research interests include the initial learning of programming and she runs the annual HE Academy ICS one-day conference on the teaching of programming.

Sally Fincher is a senior lecturer in the Computing Laboratory at the University of Kent where she leads the Computing Education Research Group (and gets them to write books). She is editor of the journal *Computer Science Education* (jointly with Renee McCauley).

Aliy Fowler is a lecturer in Computer Science at the University of Kent. She has taught many different programming courses – a large proportion of which have been to novice programmers. Before becoming a computer scientist she trained as a translator and before that studied art and design.

Ursula Fuller is Dean of Science, Technology and Medical Studies at the University of Kent. She teaches modules on information systems to students at all levels from the first year to postgraduates. Before she became Dean she taught introductory programming to students who were not computing specialists.

Matthew Jadud is a PhD student at the University of Kent. He studies how students learn to program, and in his spare time writes compilers for old, little languages and plays with LEGO robots.

Colin Johnson is a senior lecturer in Computer Science at the University of Kent. He has teaching experience in many different areas in computer science and mathematics. In recent years his teaching has particularly focused on programming and software engineering. He is also actively involved in research, with particular interests in the application of computing to understanding biological and medical problems.

Bob Keim has been in classrooms most of his life. He currently lectures in computing at the University of Kent-Medway. Elsewhere, his students have included American pre-schoolers and graduate students, Japanese elementary pupils and university students, and Croatian businessmen. He holds postgraduate degrees in philosophy, TEFL and Computer Science.

Janet Linington has worked with computers and in education for many years. Currently a lecturer in the Computing Laboratory at the University of Kent, she has also worked as a teacher of maths and of computing in secondary schools and for the Computing Service at the University of Cambridge.

Part One
Getting Started

1 Who is this Book for?

▶ Getting acquainted

Since you have opened this book we guess you have some interest in computer programming, even if it's just curiosity.

As authors, we cannot be sure exactly who you are but we might guess that you are a student either taking a programming course or thinking about taking one? Alternatively, you might be the parent of such a student, or maybe you teach programming? Still not right? Then perhaps you are just someone who is interested in finding out what programming is all about. Whichever of those groups you belong to, you are one of the people we are primarily writing for: students in the final two years of school, in Further Education colleges or the first year of university; and those who support such students. But we hope this book might also be useful to others outside those boundaries.

This book is about how to go about learning programming effectively. We should stress at this early stage that it is not a tutorial for a particular **programming language**. Instead, it focuses on some of the skills, attitudes and techniques required to study programming successfully. We won't assume that you know anything about programming already, but we'll begin by telling you what programming is and how to get started. We'll also explain how studying programming may be different from studying other subjects, what pitfalls to avoid, and much more.

The naming of programming languages

You'll find boxed sections like this throughout the book. We use them to give short additional explanations of things like new words and ideas.

If you are not already familiar with any programming languages then you will soon learn that there is a bewildering number of them, most with strange names – Algol, APL, **BASIC, C, Fortran, Java, Scheme** – to name just a handful.

Do the different names mean anything? Some do and some don't! For instance, Algol stands for Algorithmic Language and Fortran stands for Formula Translator. On the other hand, Java gets its name from the coffee drunk by its designers!

Throughout this book we will make use of lots of different languages. Remember that we aren't trying to teach you any particular language, but just to give you a feel for the ways in which programming languages support the task of programming. If you want to learn a specific programming language – as part of one of your courses, say – then you will find that there are plenty of textbooks available that will give you an in-depth guide to all the commonly available languages.

Who are we then, and why did we write this book? We are all computer scientists and teachers of programming. We enjoy programming and enjoy introducing it to others. When we were sitting around discussing our teaching, we discovered that even though we were teaching different programming topics, there were ideas and techniques that we all discussed with our students. These were common to all the programming courses but were different from what was needed in other subjects. When we looked around for a book that covered the material we were surprised not to find one; and so we set about writing this.

▶ Picking your route

Many books are designed to be read straight through, from page 1 of Chapter 1 to the end. You would not normally read a novel any other way, for instance, unless you are one of those who peek at the last page early! But, of course, books are rarely written in a linear fashion, and most novels have multiple themes that run through them, with characters or plots that come and go to provide variation of pacing and interest.

We hope you will find that there is a variety of ways you could read this book. If you wish, you can read each chapter in turn, from Chapter 1 through to Chapter 16. On the other hand, you might like to take the chapters in a pick-and-mix fashion – following a route that fits in with your existing knowledge and your individual approach to study.

In our minds there are some recurrent themes that run through this book – rather like the warp and weft fibres that run through a fabric. You can think of the book as being structured into five parts, each of which consists of

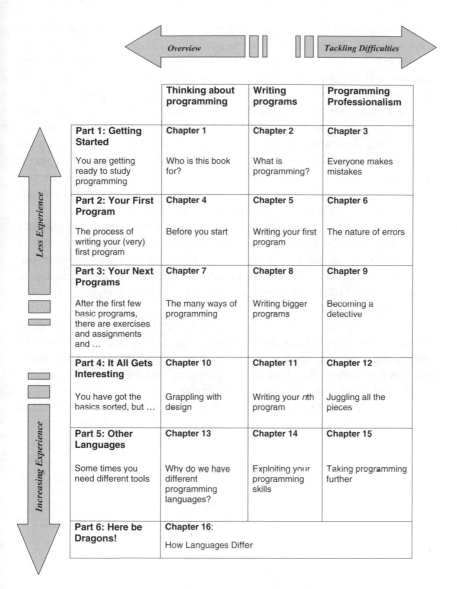

Figure 1.1 This book

three chapters. Each part relates to a stage in the development of a **programmer**, from *Getting Started* (Chapters 1–3), to moving on to *Your First Program* (Chapters 4–6), then exploring *Your Next Programs* (Chapters 7–9), to find that *It All Gets Interesting* (Chapters 10–12) and then learning about *Other Languages* (Chapters 13–15). These parts make good sense if read in order but each can also be read independently of the others. For instance, if you've already written quite a few programs, you might want to start with *Your Next Programs* or *Other Languages*. You can dip in at the point that suits you. Whatever your level of experience you will probably find that there are ideas that you haven't come across before in most of the chapters.

Another way that we have structured the book is to use three themes that recur in each part: 'Thinking about Programming' (Chapters 1, 4, 7, 10 and 13), 'Writing Programs' (Chapters 2, 5, 8, 11 and 14) and 'Programming Professionalism' (Chapters 3, 6, 9, 12 and 15). So if you want to spend some time just thinking about programming issues you can dip into the first chapter of each part. Or you could focus on practical programming issues and take the second chapter in each of the five parts.

We have tried to capture the essence of these structures in the diagram shown in Figure 1.1. As you can see, the final chapter, 'Here be Dragons!' is a little different and stands outside the other structures. It takes you into the land beyond regular programming tasks and explores the fascinating world of programming **paradigms**. If you want to know what they are, you could even make that your starting point.

The recurrent themes we have highlighted serve to illustrate an important principle about any subject, not just programming: as you learn more and more about a subject, you will find yourself again and again revisiting topics that you have already encountered, and refining and deepening your understanding of them. You will never stop learning.

So, that's it with the first overview. We hope you enjoy the rest of the book!

2 What is Programming?

One of the things about programming that can make it appear difficult or inaccessible at first sight is the languages that are used to write **computer programs**. We are going to remove some of this mystique. Many programming languages are odd mixes of mathematical symbols, **punctuation** marks and ordinary words. In fact, programming languages are actually very simple in nature – far simpler than any human language – but this simplicity is obscured by our lack of familiarity with them. We are going to find a way through that obscurity by looking at everyday human activities and see how they are similar to, and different from, programming. By seeing the similarities between everyday life and problems we would use a **computer** to solve, we will begin to understand how computers are programmed and, hence, why programming languages often look like they do.

▶ What it means to be programmed

If we say that someone or something has been 'programmed' then we usually mean that they will do something slavishly – without thinking – possibly doing it over and over again. That idea fits quite well with the concept of computers being programmed. Computers cannot think for themselves; they can only do what they have been instructed to do, and they cannot vary from the instructions they have been given.

Most of the time, this predictability is a good thing. It means that the miniature computer that controls a washing machine goes through its cycles in the right order, and turns our dirty clothes into clean and rinsed clothes; that banks keep an accurate record of credits and debits on our accounts; that aircraft carry us safely on holiday and back again; that word processors don't scramble our files.

However, sometimes that lack of an ability to think for itself means that a computer will go ahead and carry out its programmed task even when it isn't appropriate. For instance, a washing machine will go through its cycles even when are no clothes in it. A person would see that this is pointless, but a computer in a washing machine does not.

Much of the skill in programming is about creating a set of instructions that will tell an otherwise mindless computer what you want it to do. That is a very powerful idea, because computers are much better at doing some things than we are. If we can find an appropriate set of instructions for a problem we want to solve or a task we want to perform, then there is a good chance that we can hand that task or problem over to a computer and let it get on with it for us. That is one reason why computers have become so common in everyday life. In order to successfully give instructions to a computer, we need to understand what kinds of instruction a computer can deal with. That means we will need to discuss 'programming languages' – languages used to program computers.

However, before we do that, let's explore a little more about the nature of 'programming', because we shall see that most of us already know a good deal about it, even if we have never consciously been involved with computer programs before.

▶ Task-oriented languages

For centuries people have been creating 'languages' to express solutions to tasks, or to capture descriptions of things, in such a way that other people can reproduce them accurately. A non-computer programming language familiar to most people is musical notation (Figure 2.1). Even if you cannot read music, you will probably be aware of the look of a piece of music. For hundreds of years, musicians have used various forms of notation to communicate what notes to play, what order to play them in, how long to make each note last, whether to repeat a particular section, and so on. Such notations have proven to be very effective because anyone who can understand the notation and has sufficient skill on an appropriate instrument would be able to reproduce a composer's tune.

Of course, to music lovers and *aficionados*, the dots on the page really only communicate a part of the story. What they don't describe effectively is any

Figure 2.1 Musical notation

```
Using 3.25 mm needles cast on 40sts and work 20 rows K1,
P1 rib.
Work 8 rows st st,
Inc 1 st at each end of the next, and every following 4th
row 6 times, then every 7th row 9 times.
```

Figure 2.2 Knitting notation

sense of emotion or artistic expression, and two musicians playing from identical manuscripts may well create two significantly different performances. Once again, we have an example of the difference between slavishly following a set of instructions (as a computer would) and the way that people can think beyond the bare notes on a page. Nevertheless, for our purposes, musical notations provide a convenient analogy for computer programming languages, in the way that they capture a set of instructions that those familiar with the notation can understand and '**execute**'.

Notice that we have talked about 'notations' in the plural because there is more than one way to describe music, just as there are lots of different computer programming languages. An interesting difference, however, is that most musicians will only ever learn a single notation, whereas many programmers are familiar with more than one language – some may be fluent with a dozen or more. As you make progress with your own programming you might like to reflect on why that difference might be.

A set of non-programming languages that may be less familiar to you, but which are equally as effective as musical notations, are those to do with knitting (Figure 2.2). These tend to be simpler and less structured than music or computer languages, but that does not prevent them from being widely used as a means of conveying instructions sufficient to enable people to create accurately all sorts of items. Knitting languages describe the different types of stitches to use, how many stitches are required in each row, how many rows to knit, and so on.

The principles are the same with both music and knitting: the instructions match the task in hand (musical notes or types of stitches) and anyone who understands the instructions and has the ability (skill) to carry them out can perform the task that they describe.

One further language: the language of heraldry
This is a little bit different from music and knitting languages. Those notations both describe actions to be performed – playing an instrument or making a garment. Some languages have been created in order to describe what things look like. A particularly old example of this is the language of *blazon*, originally used to describe heraldic bearings or coats of arms. Figure 2.3 shows the arms of Canterbury in England.

Figure 2.3   Canterbury's coat of arms

We might try to describe what is shown in the arms by saying that it shows three birds on a white background in the bottom part, and a yellow lion on a red background in the top part. This kind of description is too informal and imprecise to enable someone to reproduce accurately what we have seen if they haven't seen it themselves. So, over the centuries, people known as heralds have developed a much more precise way of describing how a coat of arms should look. The blazon for Canterbury is, in fact, 'argent, three cornish choughs proper, on a chief gules a lion passant guardant or'. The words used precisely describe, for instance, the colours (argent, gules and or), the animals (cornish chough, lion), the shape of the animals (proper, passant guardant) and the areas they occupy (chief). The full language allows a highly complex arrangement of colours, shapes and objects to be described in a way that can be easily reproduced by someone who understands it.

As we shall see later in this book, there are computer languages with similarities to the language of blazon. **HTML (HyperText Markup Language)**, for instance, is a language that allows you to describe the way in which text and images should be arranged within the window of a **web browser**.

As a summary, we can say that programming involves at least two key interconnected elements: having a language that allows us to describe precisely what we want to do; and writing down a set of instructions in that language that accurately describes what we want to do.

In the next section we are going to look at some of the ways in which we piece together 'instructions' to accomplish a task or solve a problem.

▶ Programming tasks in everyday life

Everyday life is full of 'programmed' tasks. When we wake up in the morning, it will often be because an alarm clock has gone off. The alarm clock goes off because we programmed it to do so. This is quite a simple programming task; we input a time and then wait for the alarm clock to reach that time. The clock does most of the hard work.

Having got out of bed we will probably think about getting washed and having some breakfast. We can't do both things at the same time so we will have to make a decision about which to do first. If we are sharing a house with other people, the bathroom might already be occupied, giving us the further choice of either going back to bed and waiting until it is free, or getting on with breakfast.

Having eventually made it down to the kitchen for breakfast maybe we decide to have coffee and toast. We could make the toast first and then make the coffee, but then the toast is likely to be cold by the time the coffee is ready. So we are more likely to make both at once – put the kettle or coffee machine on while the toast is heating up. That is quite a sophisticated piece of programming – doing several things at once – but humans are quite good at **multi-tasking**.

After breakfast we might realize that we haven't done any washing-up for several days and the dirty plates and cutlery are piling up. With friends coming around this evening for dinner, we need to get things cleared up. Washing-up is a boring and repetitive task but it has to be done: plate in the bowl, wash it off, place it in the drainer, and then do the same with the next one, until they are all clean. Repetitive tasks such as this are another key feature of programming.

By the time we have left the house in the morning, we have probably 'executed' a considerable number of human programs, with many more to execute over the course of a whole day. You might not consider these activities really to be programs, but imagine an alien visiting your house one day; would they know how to make breakfast or do the washing-up? Probably not; but you can do them almost without thinking (something that is often essential early in the morning!) because you have learned how to do them – you have the required instructions stored in your mind and body, whereas the alien does not.

As we shall see as this book unfolds, the sorts of operations that a computer performs are very similar in nature to those that you perform, and programming languages provide us with a way to write down those instructions so that they can be stored in a computer's **memory**.

▶ The elements of a computer

When we looked at task-oriented languages and notations we saw that the elements that made them up were all directly related to the particular activity with which they were associated. For instance, the language of music involves musical notes, the language of knitting involves types of stitches and the language of blazon involves colours and animals. This point might seem fairly obvious, but appreciating it will help us to understand why programming languages are as they are – it is because we use them to control computers. For our purposes, we don't actually need to know much about the way that computers work, but a little knowledge will be helpful so in this section we will look at the basic elements of a computer. Don't worry, though! We aren't going to talk about soldering irons and electrical circuits. We don't need to know anything at all about those sorts of things to be able to program a computer.

The two most useful things you need to know about how computers work are:

- They have some memory.
- They have a **processing unit**, which is sometimes called a **CPU (central processing unit)**.

We can ignore pretty well everything else: disk drives, printers, networks, mice and so on. These are all basically concerned with getting information into and out of the computer's memory.

Computers use their memory to store things:

- The instructions that make up their programs.
- **Data** values, which represent the information we are working with. These are just numbers, but can represent other things (words, pictures, sounds) by converting them into streams of numbers.

A computer's processing unit is what executes the instructions and allows the computer to perform calculations (like adding two numbers together).

Computers lead a very simple life. Hour after hour, day after day, year after year (if you are lucky!) the processing unit works its way through the instructions in its memory, getting data values out of other bits of memory, processing the data values and then storing the results back into memory, and that is pretty much it! Sometimes the processing unit will skip over some instructions, and sometimes it will repeat some instructions that it has executed previously, but that is about the only light relief it gets from constantly executing one instruction after another. Despite this simplicity, computers are very powerful because they can perform enormous numbers of instructions per second. A computer running for just a few hours might easily be capable of performing tasks that it would take a human more than a lifetime to perform.

A problem for us is that this very simplicity could make computers hard to program, because the solutions to the tasks we want to solve would have to be broken down into millions of very simple instructions.[1] That is where computer programming languages come to our rescue. They have been designed as a compromise between the problems we want to solve, and the capabilities of the computer. They are more sophisticated than the basic 'low-level' instructions of the computer, but not as sophisticated as ordinary human language. This explains the rationale behind many of the features we see in programming languages, and why they often appear to be a mix of English and mathematical notation.

▶ The essential features of most programming languages

Computer programming languages enable us to write down ways to solve problems using a computer. In order to overcome some of the simplicity of low-level computer instruction sets, designers of programming languages have found it helpful to identify several key *language structures* that capture common ways of doing things when using a computer. In fact, we encountered most of these earlier in the chapter when looking at programming tasks that occur in everyday life. The three structures that we will concentrate on in this chapter are:

- Sequences of instructions.
- Making choices or decisions over which instructions to execute or skip.
- Repeating instructions.

Most programs are built by using these structures around other elements that reflect the low-level features of a computer's processing unit: getting data values out of memory, performing calculations on them, and then storing the results back into memory. Some further structuring techniques commonly found in programming languages are **modules**, **recursion** and **concurrency**, but we will leave discussing these until later in this book.

Many of the most obvious differences between the various programming languages are simply in the ways that these structures and memory operations are expressed, using different words or symbols as chosen by the languages' designers. In this chapter we will give you a flavour of some of the most common ways of expressing these language structures, in a range of different programming languages.

Memory operations

In the low-level language of a computer, memory locations are referred to by number – their numerical 'address'. A typical computer will have millions or billions of memory locations, and numerical addresses are not very convenient for humans to remember. So programming language designers allow programmers to give names to memory locations, and to use those names instead of the numbers. In fact, it is rare for a programmer to have to deal with numerical memory addresses. This means that we can give a name like `birthday` to a memory location that stores a date, or `mileage` to one that stores a distance. Such names are typically called **identifiers**, and identifiers for memory locations are called **variables**. Most programming languages allow us to create quite long identifiers (as long as they don't contain spaces) so we could even use a name like `my18thbirthday` if we wished.

Here are some examples of the way in which variables are used in different programming languages to take the value in one memory location (count) and store that value increased by two into another memory location (result):

```
LET result = count + 2        (BASIC)
result = count + 2            (Java)
result := count + 2           (Pascal)
```

Code 2.1

Sequences of instructions

The next step on from manipulating the values in one or two memory locations is to put together a sequence of instructions that are meant to be executed one after the other. We typically call an instruction such as

```
result = count + 2
```

a **statement**. If we want to write a sequence of statements then we have to separate the individual statements from each other. Some programming languages use the end of a line to mark the end of a statement. Others use a semicolon **symbol**; for instance

```
result = count + 2;
count = count + 1;
average = total / count;
```

Code 2.2

represents a sequence of three statements. It is important to appreciate that these statements will be executed in the strict order in which they are written. Only after the value of `result` has been calculated will `count` be increased by one, and only then will the value of `average` be computed. This order matters, because if `count` is increased before `result` and `average` are computed then different values will be stored in them. The same sorts of rules apply in everyday life. If you put butter on bread before it is toasted, you get a different result from putting it on when it has popped out of the toaster, and if you lock the stable door before the horse has bolted, you are likely to be happier than if you do so afterwards.

The simple instructions we have used as illustrations here have all involved simple mathematical calculations. Many of the examples we will see later will involve non-mathematical tasks, but the principle of lists of instructions being executed in sequence will apply just the same.

Making choices

We can get quite a lot done with simple sequences of instructions, but sooner or later we will find that we need to choose between alternative sequences. For instance, a charitable organization sending out mail shots asking for money might send letters with one sort of wording to people who have contributed in the past and with a different wording to new contacts. For an existing supporter they will do one thing, otherwise they will do another. Those two actions are mutually exclusive; no person will receive both letters. We call a language structure that allows us to phrase alternatives such as this a 'choice statement' or an '**if statement**'. If statements have several components:

- A word indicating that the programmer is using a choice statement. Pro gramming languages typically use the word `if` for this.
- A test that gives a positive or negative answer. We usually say that the result of this test will be either true or false.
- An action (or several actions) to take if the test was positive.
- An action (or several actions) to take if the test was negative. It is not uncommon for there to be nothing to do if the test was negative, and this part is sometimes left out.
- One or two special words that mark where the positive and/or negative actions start. Programming languages typically use the words `then` and `else` or `otherwise` for these.

Here is an informal version of how we might phrase an if test:

```
if the person is an existing supporter
then send version 1 of the letter
else send version 2 of the letter
```

Here is an if statement written using the C programming language to test the **relationship** between the values stored in two variables (studentMark and passMark) and store different values in the grade variable as a result.

```
if (studentMark >= passMark) {
    grade = PASS;
}
else {
    grade = FAIL;
}
```

Code 2.3

Notice that C doesn't use the word 'then' to mark the start of the positive action – this was simply the result of a decision made by the language's designers. The capability to make choices in programs is a powerful one, and you will find yourself using them a lot as you learn more about programming.

Repeating instructions

Having to do things over and over again can become tedious very quickly, which is one reason why making pupils write 'lines' was used once upon a time as a form of discipline in schools. Computers, on the other hand, never become bored by doing things again and again. If we have a lot of data to be processed, that is a useful property. So programming language designers have devised language structures that make it simple to describe actions to be performed repeatedly. Various special words are used in languages to denote repetition: repeat, do, while and for are the most common. Structures using these words are often called **loops** and the process of repeating statements is called **iteration**. Loops have two main components, in addition to the words used to indicate them:

• An action (or several actions) to be repeated.
• A way of stopping the repetition so that it doesn't go on forever.

Arranging to stop the actions being repeated once the iteration has started is probably the hardest part of writing a loop correctly. We won't go into the details here, but it is worth saying that repetition is controlled with a true or false test just like choice statements are controlled. The big difference, of course, is that the actions in a choice statement are only executed once, but the actions in a loop might be executed many, many times.

Here is an outline of how we might send different letters to everybody on a mailing list:

```
while there is another person on the list do
begin
        if the person is an existing supporter
        then send version 1 of the letter
        else send version 2 of the letter
end
```

Notice the way in which we can mix different types of statements together to implement solutions to quite sophisticated tasks. Here we have a choice statement **nested** inside a loop. The idea is that each time around the loop, a decision is made as to which type of letter to send to the next person on the list. This process is repeated again and again until a letter has been sent to every person on the list.

▶ Chapter summary

In this chapter we have begun thinking about the ways in which special languages and notations have been developed over the centuries to communicate ways of doing things, or representing things, so that other people can accurately reproduce musical tunes, knitted garments, coats of arms, and so on. You have also seen that computers are very good at doing simple things very fast. Putting those two things together, you can start to think about the ways in which programming language designers have sought to devise ways to allow people to express ways of solving problems so that computers can find those solutions. Typically, programming languages provide support for programmers by allowing them to express sequences of instructions, to make choices between alternative sets of actions, and to cause actions to be repeated over and over. Given these fundamental features, and a little more programming language understanding, you will find that you are able to write your own programmed solutions to problems that you want to solve.

▶ Code explained

Code 2.1

```
LET result = count + 2
                    (BASIC)
```

What the code does: These **code** fragments take the value of count, add two to that value and store the total in result

```
result := count + 2
                  (Pascal)
result = count + 2  (Java)
```

Code 2.1

Both result and count were chosen by the person who wrote this code. They should help us understand the code more easily.

As you probably expect, the + sign here represents addition of numbers. The equals sign is used here as part of a way to tell the computer to do something.

LET . . . = in BASIC, := in Pascal, = in Java are used to tell the computer to assign (count + 2) to result.

```
result = count + 2;
count = count + 1;
average = total / count;
```

Code 2.2

Code 2.2

What the code does: The first line of this code takes the value of count, adds two to that value and stores the total in result. The second line takes the value of count, adds one to it and stores that value back in count. The third line takes total and divides it by count and stores the result in average.

In a similar way to Code 2.1, result, count and average were chosen by the person who wrote this code to help make the code more easily *understood*.

In this code the '/' sign represents division.

Code 2.3

```
if(studentMark >= passMark){
    grade = PASS;
}
else {
    grade = FAIL;
}
```

Code 2.3

The terms if and else are part of the language core. So the code says: if studentMark is greater than or equal to passMark, make the grade be PASS. Otherwise (indicated here by else) make the grade be FAIL.

It is important to get used to noticing things like punctuation. For example, it means different things when brackets are used (here in the first line), when curly brackets are used, and when semicolons are used. In this code the brackets mark off a single statement that can be true or false. The curly brackets mark off short blocks of code. The semicolons end single statements.

3 Everyone Makes Mistakes

Have you ever burnt the toast when making breakfast, or dropped a plate while washing up? Who hasn't! Mistakes are common in everyday life and usually turn out to be no big deal – everybody makes them and we learn from them. It is important to realize this because it is also easy and extremely common to make mistakes during the initial stages of learning programming. Indeed, the unexpected results you get from early programming mistakes actually add to your understanding of how things work. Just as we all burn the toast from time to time, the programmer who doesn't make mistakes hasn't been born yet!

We are going to look at the kinds of programming mistakes that you might make and their implications if encountered by a computer. Then we are going to look at some large-scale engineering and computing mistakes that have been made in the past. Some have been disasters, some have been rectifiable, and some have led to better products. But all have been learnt from.

▶ Little mistakes

Computers do exactly what you tell them to through your programs, and this is not necessarily what you intended them to do. Therefore, a computer may appear unforgiving when a program does not run at all, or runs but produces the wrong **output**. Simple slips in instructions can lead to unexpected effects. The feeling that the machine must have got it wrong (and getting over that feeling) is intimately connected with the process of learning to program!

Recall the example from Chapter 2 that decides whether a student's mark is a pass or fail. If the pass mark is 40 per cent then a student obtaining a mark of 40 per cent or above should obviously pass, and this is correctly encoded in the following instructions (see Code 2.3):

```
if(studentMark >= passMark) {
    grade = PASS;
}
else {
    grade = FAIL;
}
```

However, what happens if you make a mistake in the code and omit the '=' symbol from '>='? The code would read as follows:

```
if(studentMark > passMark) {
    grade = PASS;
}
else {
    grade = FAIL;
}
```

This looks very similar to before but its effect may be significantly different. Now a student obtaining exactly the pass mark will be deemed to have failed. If you were that student you would not be happy!

If you challenged the grading of 'fail' you would win your case and probably be told that the reason for the mistake was a 'computer error'; this phrase is used often. Computers rarely make mistakes unless there is a genuine technical fault. Most 'computer errors' are actually likely to be either data input errors or programmer coding errors – both the result of human error. As we stressed earlier, making mistakes is simply part of human nature. The process of learning about programming gives you a chance to understand how they often come about, and to learn some of the ways to avoid making them.

▶ The kinds of mistakes you might make

Here we are going to look in more detail at some examples of programming-like tasks and the kinds of errors that can arise from them. It will prepare you for thinking about first programs in Chapter 5 and the nature of errors in Chapter 6; if you are aware of the kinds of errors that are commonly made you should be less demoralized by the mistakes you will inevitably make when attempting your first few programming tasks. In fact, if you don't make any mistakes, how will you learn?

We will explore issues that may cause mistakes or unexpected outputs. For example, when following a knitting pattern, what happens when the wrong-sized needles are used, or the wrong type of wool? If the pattern is followed correctly the garment is likely to be too big or too small – you must have heard plenty of jokes about sweaters knitted as Christmas presents by grandmothers.

Heraldry in days of old

During the Middle Ages, knights used coats of arms to identify themselves. One man in armour looked a lot like another, so the coat of arms was used to distinguish knights from each other in battle. 'Emblazoning' is the drawing of the shield and 'blazoning' is the description in words. Here we are going to look at the errors that could occur with a simple misrepresentation of the blazoning. Let's assume that the emblazoning of our shield is something simple, such as 'Sable a lion rampant guardant argent' – a silver (argent) lion standing on its hind legs facing the viewer (rampant guardant), on a black (sable) background (Figure 3.1).

Imagine that you work for the knight to whom this coat of arms belongs and your job is to acquire a new shield. Suppose that you cannot read or write but you must pass the blazoning on to an emblazoner who will produce another shield with the same coat of arms. If you recall the blazoning correctly and pass it on correctly to the emblazoner then all is well; another shield with the correct coat of arms is produced. What if things don't go quite as smoothly?

If you cannot read or write then you would have to rely on your memory to get the description right. Knowing what the shield looks like you might say to the emblazoner, 'An argent lion on sable.' Although you have used the right sort of words, they aren't in the right order and at least one is missing. The rules of blazon are very strict and the emblazoner won't let you get away with breaking the rules like that. He would probably tell you to go away and come back with the right description. In programming, we call this sort of error a **syntax error**. Computers check our programs for syntax errors and won't allow them to be run if any are present.

Suppose that you return the next day to the emblazoner, having carefully learned the description and repeated it to yourself over and over on your way there. You say, 'Sable a lion rampant argent.' This time the emblazoner is satisfied and creates the shield for you (Figure 3.2). To your horror you discover that the lion is facing the wrong way; the shield of a different knight! What went wrong? The description you gave was perfectly valid (no syntax errors) and the emblazoner followed your instructions. The problem is that you missed out a word – *guardant* – but the blazon still made sense. In programming we call this a **semantic error**. You meant one thing but communicated something different.

It is apparent from these examples that care must be taken both to ensure that you know the instructions you must convey, and that you convey them correctly. Here your blazoning is the program and the emblazoner is the computer that is interpreting your program to produce the results. The computer did exactly what you told it to – it just wasn't what you should have asked it to do.

Figure 3.1   Sable a lion rampant guardant argent

Figure 3.2   Sable a lion rampant argent

In today's world

Here are three everyday examples of the kinds of errors described above and the ways in which we either cope or experience problems due to them.

Eats, Shoots and Leaves is the title of a book about punctuation by Lynne Truss.[1] Truss explains that the title is supposed to represent the (incorrect) wildlife manual entry for a panda. She does this by means of a joke:

> A panda walks into a café. He orders a sandwich, eats it, then draws a gun and fires two shots into the air. When the confused waiter asks 'Why?' the panda throws a wildlife manual at him. The manual entry for 'Panda' states 'Panda. Large black-and-white bear-like mammal, native to China. Eats, shoots and leaves.'

Did the comma in the manual appear as a **typo** (a syntax error), or did the writer mistakenly believe that it was required (a semantic error)? The two types of error have the same outcome, so when we don't know which type of error has occurred we call it a **grammatical error** – a person reading the text has no way to determine whether the comma is there by accident or design.

Most of us would know that the manual entry referred to the food that pandas eat rather than their actions, but computers do not have the capacity to interpret based upon context; they take their input literally.

'Desert'/'dessert' is another context-sensitive spelling mistake that is often made. **Desert** is a large expanse of sand, whilst **dessert** is something sweet to be eaten after the main course of a meal. A friend sends you an email inviting you to a meal:

> Are you coming to the BBQ on Sunday? Could you bring a desert rather than a bottle?

If you received this email suggesting that you bring a desert you are unlikely to make the mistake of bringing several hundred square miles of sand with you to the meal. If you notice the mistake you know what is meant and take a gooey cheesecake with you, but you may not even notice the mistake at all – you know what it should say and may read the sentence accordingly. However, if a computer receives the above invitation, you ought to bring your bucket and spade along; it knows no better and will attempt to take the sand.

Following directions is a slightly more problematic proposition if mistakes occur, whether they are those of the author or the follower.

> turn right at the traffic lights, then take the third turning on the left. After this, Acacia Avenue and the second turning on the right.

Suppose it should have been the second turning on the left and the third turning on the right – following the directions means you could end up in Elm Drive instead. What if you miss a small turning on the left and actually turn into the fourth road? You could be in Swan Close and there may not be a second turning on the right. It is also possible that the directions are correct but that you have entered the town from an unanticipated direction. Turning right at the traffic lights might take you the wrong way, or you may even be at a different set of lights.

Spelling
Accuracy in spelling is more important in programming than it is in real life:

> Aoccdrnig to rscheearch at an Elingsh uinervtisy, it deosn't mttaer in what oredr the ltteers in a wrod are, the olny iprmoatnt tihng is that the frist and lsat ltteer are in the rghit pclae. The rset can be a toatl mses and you can sitll raed it wouthit a porbelm. Tihs is bcuseae we do not raed ervey lteter by istlef but the wrod as a wlohe.[2]

This is not the case when writing a computer program – you need to be careful to spell everything correctly and consistently for the computer to interpret the code that you write. Naming something 'wibble' and then trying to call 'wbible' or even 'Wibble' will result in an error. Unlike humans, computers do read every letter, rather than just the word as a whole.

The ideas above should have given you an insight into the problems a computer can have in understanding the code of a program. At the outset of learning to program you are bound to make mistakes; most of them will be trivial, but the computer will not be able to error-correct your input in the ways that a human can. Learning from these early mistakes is possible – it is just as easy to accidentally miss a semicolon when you are an experienced programmer as it is to not realize you need one when you are a beginner. Knowing the **error message** that goes with a particular mistake is a vital part of your progress, and is only going to be gained by experience. How these types of error can affect your programming is discussed in Chapter 6, and how to detect and correct them can be found in Chapter 9.

Types of error

Syntax refers to the spelling and grammar of a programming language. If you misspell a **command**, it is a syntax error. Computers are inflexible machines that understand what you type only if you type it in the exact form that the computer expects. The expected form is called the syntax.

Semantic is the term used to denote the meaning of an instruction (as opposed to its format). If you enter a syntactically correct command that is not what is actually required in your code, it is a semantic error. They can be as simple as incorrect **operator** usage (+ instead of –), missing out a step, forgetting to manipulate some data, or trying to use the wrong file.

▶ Big mistakes

As you gain experience and move from small coding tasks to bigger ones you may begin to work as part of a group rather than alone. The processes involved in working as part of a team introduce whole new strata of potential error cases to add to the ones we already know about.

Mistakes are also made in the world outside computing; they always have been and always will be. The mistakes that are discussed here are examples of the kinds of errors that are likely to be encountered in large projects regardless of their discipline – construction, computing, manufacturing etc.

Today, houses are designed by architects and built using prescribed materials in specific ways to keep them from falling down. Until Victorian times houses did fall down from time to time. Lessons learned from trial and error, along with increasing knowledge of materials, mean that these days new designs of building rarely collapse. We understand the strengths and weaknesses of materials. For example, it is well known in the building trade that if a load-bearing wall is removed from a building then an RSJ (rolled steel joist) is required to take the load. A professional builder would certainly get this right, although a well-meaning amateur might not. Nevertheless, engineers can still make mistakes, particularly where new situations or innovative designs are involved.

A bridge too far

Bridges are complex engineering structures whose design is still not fully understood. A group of mathematicians once calculated that the strongest possible bridge structure would contain square-sectioned rails spanning the gap; this would indeed have produced a strong bridge. The flaw in the idea only became apparent once construction began. It proved impossible to construct the bridge in practice because the rails were only strong when anchored at both ends – during construction one end was unanchored and the rails were too weak to manipulate. This was a learning experience and from that point onwards engineers began to look at construction *methods* as much as finished results.

The Tacoma Narrows Bridge[3] in the USA and the Millennium Bridge[4] in the UK are two bridges that were completed. They are two obvious examples of engineering mistakes with different consequences: the Tacoma Narrows Bridge collapsed, while the Millennium Bridge simply required remedial design. The Tacoma Narrows Bridge collapsed in 1940, but what makes it so famous is that somebody managed to film the collapse, leaving a permanent record of the disaster.

The Tacoma Narrows Bridge was a suspension bridge. At the time it was hailed as being revolutionary in its design, which was part of its problem. It collapsed due to wind-induced vibrations. Until the Tacoma Narrows Bridge collapse, suspension bridge designers had been on a quest to build ever more slender, graceful and artistic bridges. The bridge across the Narrows had taken this design artistry to new levels, being lower and more slender than any previous construction. The shape of the bridge was like that of an aircraft wing, and ever since it opened late in the spring of 1940 the bridge had a tendency to sway in windstorms; it became known as 'Galloping Gertie'. The windy conditions on 7 November generated enough aerodynamic lift (which aeroplanes use to stay in the air) to make the bridge unstable and to cause a severe and catastrophic failure – a suspension wire snapped and the bridge collapsed, killing a dog.

The bridge was technically a failure – it did collapse – but it was also an excellent learning experience for bridge designers. The designer, Leon Moisseiff, was not new to bridge construction. He had been a designer and consultant on nearly every large suspension bridge built in America before 1940, including the San Francisco Golden Gate Bridge, which still stands today. This collapse caused engineers to realize that new research was necessary in order to understand and predict the aerodynamic forces acting upon bridges. New mathematical theories of vibration, aerodynamics, wave phenomena and harmonics, as they apply to bridge design, arose from these studies. They learnt from the experience!

The Millennium Bridge opened in London in June 2000, the first new pedestrian river crossing over the Thames in more than a century. The bridge was designed to be a radical and unusual suspension bridge; it is six times shallower than a normal suspension bridge. It looked the part, being an interesting modern shape spanning the river. Problems were noticed because it began to sway sideways when more than a few people tried to walk across it at the same time. The bridge had to be closed whilst the cause of the swaying was investigated. The synchronization of pedestrians' footsteps when walking in a crowd had generated slight sideways movements of the bridge. It then became more comfortable for people to walk in synchrony with the bridge movement, thus making it worse. The more people walked in rhythm with the swaying the more the bridge swayed. (This is a positive feedback effect.) There was obviously a design problem, but fortunately it was a rectifiable one. After analysing the problem and its causes the engineers added dampers (similar to shock absorbers) to minimize the sway. This was a more feasible option than stiffening the bridge to change its frequency, or dismantling it and rebuilding in a more conventional and tested style. The lessons learnt from Tacoma were insufficient to prevent the failure of the Millennium Bridge, and this is unlikely to be the last bridge-building disaster.

Rocket power

It isn't only engineers who can have extremely embarrassing and expensive problems when they make mistakes. Programmers can too. In the summer of 1996 the European Space Agency's rocket, Ariane 5,[5] exploded less than 40 seconds into its maiden flight, scattering itself and four highly expensive and uninsured satellites across French Guiana. Why did it happen? The guidance system computer tried to convert one of its readings from a large stored number into a space for a smaller one – the number was too big to be stored and the program could not handle the output. There was a backup system, but it contained the same **bug**. The programmers of the new rocket had reused parts of the program from the older and slower Ariane 4 rocket, where it had been assumed that this particular value could never be large enough to cause trouble. It never had been for Ariane 4. Unfortunately, Ariane 5 was a faster rocket than its predecessor, so the number could become larger than its allocated storage area. Nobody had checked this section of the program because it had worked fine in the past. One simple assumption that was fine when the program was used for its original purpose led to an expensive disaster when used in a new situation. The moral of this story is not that we should always write everything from scratch, but that we should try to avoid unnecessary assumptions and limitations. And if you reuse a legacy program in a new situation you must test it thoroughly in its new context.

1 km = 5/8 mile

Sometimes mistakes are really stupid. There are some mistakes that can only be made when people are working in teams. If team members don't talk to each other, or make assumptions that their collaborators aren't aware of, then things can go horribly awry, just like they did in 1998.

In December 1998 an international collaboration of US and European space scientists sent the Mars Climate Orbiter off on its mission to become the first interplanetary weather satellite orbiting Mars.[6] After nine months of complicated journey from Earth to Mars the Climate Orbiter arrived on schedule; quite an achievement. Things were obviously going far too well, because this is the point when everything went wrong! Europeans and the international scientific community use metric units (for example, torque is measured in Newton metres), but the USA still uses its own version of imperial units (the unit for torque is foot pound-force), and the project was an international scientific one. . . . You can probably guess what went wrong.

The safe altitude above the planet for the Orbiter was calculated by one part of the team to be 50 miles, which converts to 80 km. However, this had been programmed by the other part of the team as 50 km, a discrepancy of some 30 km (just under 19 miles). Once the orbiting thrusters were fired the Climate Orbiter was never seen or heard from again. The cause of this catastrophe was simply the failure to convert from miles to km when reporting the calculated safe altitude. Oops!

Y2K – year 2000

The Y2K problem, also known as the Millennium Bug, generated a great deal of hype. Its cause was simple – the inability of some computers and computerized products to identify dates past 1999. Back in the 1960s and 1970s, the turn of the century seemed so remote, and memory and disk were so expensive, that most programs stored only the last two digits of years. Consequently many programs recognized only the last two **digits** of a year and assumed that the first two were '19'. This meant that '99' was read as 1999, with an anticipated problem arising when the year 2000 began. In programs that were not corrected, when '00' was read it would be identified as 1900 instead of 2000.

When nothing untoward happened as the clocks turned from 31 December 1999 to 1 January 2000 the press decided that there mustn't have been a problem at all. Alternatively, perhaps the advance warning and the preparation of many thousands of programmers actually fixed the problems and avoided the catastrophe.

A sticky problem

Let's finish with something a little more positive. All mistakes may be a learning experience, but not all end up as disasters. Sometimes people encounter problems and turn them into opportunities. Sometimes mistakes lead to something good. Everyone knows what the Post-it® Note[7] is. Not everyone knows that it came about because of a failed attempt to make something else.

During the early 1970s a research chemist, Spence Silver, working for the 3M office-supplies company, was trying to create stronger glue for sticky tape. Instead, he managed to create a weaker one. He discussed his failed experiments with colleagues, including Arthur Frye. Whilst sitting in his local church congregation Frye was playing with his hymn book rather than listening to the sermon when he realized that it would be possible to make a bookmark with the weak adhesive that would stick and remove without damaging the book.

A prototype bookmark was created, and when it was ready, he attached one to a research report, and then wrote a note on it. His manager later wrote his answer on the bottom of the bookmark and attached it to an item he was returning to Frye. 'It was during a coffee break that afternoon when we both realized that what we had was not just a bookmark, but a new way to communicate or organize information.' The Post-it Note was born, and Silver's failed adhesive became the key ingredient of what today is 3M's best-selling product.

What can we learn from mistakes?

The mistakes mentioned here have all had a major impact upon the project they occurred within – mostly devastating. They all have similarities with, and implications for, large group projects within computing. If you don't want your project to collapse like a bridge then you need careful design and plenty of **testing**. If you don't want your Climate Orbiter to disappear then you need to make sure that all members of the team are working to the same **specification**, and test the program thoroughly before launch. If you don't want your rocket to explode then you need to test your legacy programs to ensure that the assumptions made in the past hold for your own situation. What is the lesson to be learnt from this? Testing, testing . . .

Let's put all this into context before we move on. Any problems you may be about to encounter as you embark upon learning programming are nothing compared to what has been described here. You have to become an expert before you can be in a position to make that kind of mistake!

Bugs

You may have heard the word 'bug' used to describe a fault. It has the same meaning in programming, too. Finding and removing the 'bugs' in a program is called '**debugging**'.

There are rumours that a woman called Grace Murray Hopper invented the word 'bug', but the word has been around for centuries. Debugging, however, is unique to computing and has been around for a much shorter amount of time. This is how Grace and her team became credited with naming the technique for removing the bugs from programs.

Back in 1947 computer programs were written as patterns of punched holes in thin cardboard. The card was 80 columns wide, and each column held one **character** of the program. The punched cards were fed into a computer. One day the program that Grace's team were trying to run would not work as expected. Upon investigation a moth was found inside the computer blocking some of the holes in the punched cards of the program. To make the program work again they had to remove the 'bug' from the computer. Grace claims, 'From then on, when anything went wrong with a computer, we said it had bugs in it.' Grace and her team did not coin the word 'bug' (that is just a piece of computing folklore) but they did put out the word that they had 'debugged' the machine, thus introducing the terminology 'debugging a computer program'.

▶ Tips to take away

- We all make mistakes.
- We learn from our mistakes.

- The bigger the project, the bigger the potential mistakes.
- Little mistakes can have big consequences.
- Some mistakes lead to better things.

▶ Chapter summary

Computer programming isn't about producing a perfect program from scratch when we sit down at the computer. You will make mistakes in your programs, and it is important to understand what kinds of mistakes you can make and how to spot them in your programs. In this chapter we have talked about different kinds of mistakes, both in programming and in other aspects of the world. Later on in the book we will return to these ideas and give you some tips for finding errors in the programs you write.

Part Two
Your First Program

4 Before You Start

How can we get started on the right foot to learn to program? The first step is getting clearer about what programming is like, what to expect from programming classes, programming lectures and programming textbooks. Then it is key to learn how to make the most effective use of these learning resources. There will also be a range of informal learning resources available to you: time spent thinking about the topic, practising the ideas and discussing them with fellow students.

▶ Learning about programming

Let's focus on the skills that you will need to develop to learn programming effectively. That is, not on the skills of programming itself, but on the skills you will need to make the best use of the teaching you get, the resources available to you, and the time that you have for private study.

What is learning to program similar to?

What is learning to program similar to? Is it like learning a list of historical dates? Is it like learning a practical skill such as driving a car? Is it like learning to write a **natural language** such as French or German? Is it like learning how to construct a historical argument?

Learning to program isn't quite like any of these but there are a lot of similarities to the kinds of learning you have already done in other subjects. By working on these other subjects, you will have already acquired study skills that will be useful when you start to study programming. If, later on, you are finding some aspect of programming difficult, you might find it useful to think about your other studies – how you managed to study successfully in those areas and how those successes can be transferred to your study of programming.

How is programming like learning a practical skill?

Some aspects of learning to program are like practical skills such as learning to drive a car or play a musical instrument. In order to master a practical skill you have to practise it! This might sound obvious but many people attempt to learn programming by reading large sections of a textbook and then attempting to write complex programs from scratch. Practical skills are best learned by a *cycle* of trying something within your capabilities, then extending it to something a little harder, thinking about what went right or wrong about that attempt, and looking up relevant bits of background or theory before you try again.

Another aspect of practical skills is that you can't always break them down into separate skills that can be practised in isolation. When learning to drive you cannot learn steering, braking, using the gears and using the accelerator on their own; you have to begin by doing the whole thing badly, and gradually improve in all aspects. Sometimes programming is like this: some aspects of programming languages, for example graphics systems, are large and unified.

Some practical skills also require care and precision otherwise the results will be very different from what you intended to achieve. Consider a very practical skill such as setting the video: typing in one wrong digit can mean that you record the 10 o'clock news programme rather than the 11 o'clock film, or that you record the programme on BBC2 rather than BBC1. This level of precision is important in programming computers, too. If you make a semantic error in programming that nonetheless is acceptable in the computer language, then the computer will carry out the instructions that you have put in. Computers have no sense of what you are trying to achieve by writing a program: they just do what is written in the program, regardless of whether it is correct or not.

How is programming like learning to do maths?

Some people think that you have to be good at maths to be a good programmer. This isn't the case, but there are some similarities between programming and solving mathematical problems. When you solve a mathematical problem, particularly a 'word problem' where a situation in the real world is described in words, you have to do some things that are similar to programming. In particular, you have to convert the problem from an informal, verbal description into a precise version, using formal notation. You need to decide what things are important, what sort of things they are, and give them names so that you can manipulate them using mathematical techniques. You might say that x is the length of a hockey pitch, y its breadth and a the area of a piece of turf. In each of these you are giving a name to something in the problem and saying what **type** of thing it is. This is similar to the creation of *variables* in computer programming.

Another similarity with mathematical problem solving is in breaking down problems in some structured fashion. When we begin to solve a mathematical problem, we think about how that problem breaks down into simpler problems, then look at each of those in turn, and repeat this until we have reached problems that are simple enough to solve by applying standard techniques that we are already familiar with. A similar process is used in programming, where we break down a complex problem into smaller problems, until we get down to simple sub-problems that we can solve easily in a computer language.

How is learning to program like learning a natural language?

Computer languages are called **languages**. Is there any comparison to be made with learning human languages such as French or Spanish? One interesting aspect of learning a natural language is that we usually think of it as four skills: reading, writing, listening and speaking. It is tempting to think that learning to program is largely about learning to *write* in a language. However, an equally important skill is to learn to read programs. Often this is not taught directly, but is something that you are expected to pick up as a side-effect of learning to write. Learning to read programs is particularly useful because many practical programming tasks involve understanding and modifying someone else's program and not simply writing your own from scratch.

Learning a computer language is not always similar to learning a natural language. For example, when tackling a foreign language you need to learn long lists of vocabulary. By contrast, although there is new 'vocabulary' associated with programming languages, the number of words you will need to know for a particular computer language is very small. This is because computer languages build up solutions to problems out of a small number of basic ideas combined in interesting ways. This is a bit like learning useful phrases in a natural language, and then substituting alternative words or verb tenses as required to fit different situations.

Natural language

Human languages such as English or French are often referred to in computing lectures and textbooks as natural languages. This is to avoid confusion with computer languages; if you talk about a 'language' in computing, the first thing people tend to think about is a computer language.

How is programming like creative design subjects?

There are some similarities with subjects in which you have to design objects before you make them. For example, in design and technology subjects you don't start making a new object from scratch with tools and wood; you spend time designing what the object is going to look like and how it is going to work before you start making it. Similarly you don't sit down to write an essay without making a plan first. These subjects spell out an important lesson that is useful when it comes to programming: you should spend some time planning out a program before sitting at the computer to create the program itself.

▶ Getting the most out of your teaching

If you are studying programming at a university, college or school you will be involved in different kinds of learning situations where you come face to face with your teacher. There are skills you can develop to make the most of these formal sessions and, in particular, discover how such sessions on a programming course might differ from those in other subjects. Even if you are studying without a teacher, you should find some of these ideas useful.

Some general guidelines apply to all sorts of teaching. In particular, you will get most from all forms of teaching by going through a pattern of 'prepare, attend actively, follow up'. For example, consider how to get the most out of a lecture:

1. *Prepare.* At a minimum you should have some idea of what the lecture is about before you turn up, and where it fits into the course as a whole. *Is it building on what was talked about in the previous lecture or is it introducing a new topic?* Programming is a subject area where new ideas build closely on ideas from previous lectures. By contrast, lectures in History or Literature, say, may be structured into historical periods that can be studied independently. *Is it giving examples of ideas that have been discussed in general in previous lectures?* A common structure for lectures in programming courses is to introduce a general concept and then illustrate it with specific examples of how this concept is used in a particular programming language. These examples are likely to be of program code that you can run for yourself after the lecture. *Is it summarizing the material from previous lectures?* There is usually some material available in course handbooks or web sites about the lectures on a course: this might at a minimum consist of a list of which topic is being covered each week, or it might consist of a summary of each lecture, or sometimes the lecturer might provide the slides that they are going to use for the lecture in advance. This can all be useful material for getting prepared to get the most out of the lecture time.

2. *Attend actively.* Clearly attending lectures is useful! However, it is even more useful if you pay active attention to what is going on. You will find

it useful to develop a style of making notes during lectures. This will vary from individual to individual: however, the two opposite extremes of writing nothing at all or attempting to write everything from 'Good morning', to 'Are there any questions?' are probably not a good idea. Are you the sort of person who finds it easy to remember whole ideas when reminded by a keyword or two? If so, you might want to make fairly 'bare' notes with just a few keywords. By contrast you may find that these are not sufficient to help you recall and use the ideas discussed in lectures. Alternative techniques include adding your own notes to copies of the slides that lecturers may make available, or using spider diagrams which show the relationship between ideas.

You should find out what material is going to be provided by the lecturer before or after the lecture. Programming lecturers sometimes provide handouts containing the lecture slides in advance, in which case you can bring these along and add notes based on what the lecturer is saying. His or her asides are one of the main things that make the difference between attending to the lecture and reading through the handouts, so try to capture their essence in your note taking.

Programming lectures often revolve around the discussion of example programs. If the programs used as examples in the lectures are made available after the lecture on a web site, you needn't spend lots of your time in the lecture writing down the program code. A good skill to develop in dealing with these programs is to think of data of your own – particular values – and to work out what the program will do with them.

Another aspect of attending actively is asking yourself questions as the lecture progresses. How does what the lecturer is saying fit in with what else has been taught on the course? Is it similar to something that you have learned already? What is this material going to lead on to next? If the lecture consists of a lot of theoretical ideas, can you come up with specific examples that show how these ideas can be used? If a lot of seemingly disconnected examples are being given, then why? It is unlikely that the lecturer is giving these examples at random – what is the underlying theoretical idea or technique that is being demonstrated? If the answers don't emerge you may be able to ask a question during the lecture. If not, jot down the questions in your notes so that you can follow them up afterwards.

3. *Follow up.* Much research into learning shows that our ability to remember the material we have been taught drops rapidly within a short time – as short as a single day. However, if we revise the ideas soon after we have seen them for the first time, then our ability to recall and use the ideas is much better, even if we only spend a small amount of time over

them. If you can spend some time on such 'revision' you will save a lot of time in the long run because you will not need to relearn material later on. Try to build this into your day in some structured way: for example, ten minutes going over the day's lectures before dinner.

Another good way to follow up on lectures is to run the programs that have been discussed. Try them with different input data. Test out small changes to see what effect they have. See if you can predict what effect your changes will have even before you make them.

You should also notice that the follow-up that you do from a lecture is likely to be good preparation for the next lecture because, when you are learning to program, concepts used in early lectures are built upon in subsequent lectures.

Getting the most out of various kinds of teaching

This structure of 'prepare, attend actively, follow up' can be applied to most kinds of classes that you will encounter. Here are some thoughts on the particular types of teaching used in programming courses in universities and colleges.

Practical classes

Most programming courses have some kind of practical classes, usually in large rooms with rows of computers. Sometimes these are supervised by the course lecturers, but they are often taken by other tutors, such as post-graduate students. Being prepared is of particular importance here: a one-hour practical class is not long to try out a substantial set of problems, so you will get a lot more from it if you arrive with some question to ask. In particular, we have noticed that a lot of practical classes are very quiet for the first half hour or more, and that there is a rush of questions towards the end, meaning that a lot of questions fail to get answered or get a hurried response. Clearly you will benefit in this kind of situation if you have questions that you can ask early on, as you will get the attention of the staff when they are otherwise unoccupied.

Lectures

One thing to remember about lectures is that there is often little communication from the rows of students to the lecturer. From the point of view of the person standing at the front, rows of heads staring blankly because they already know the stuff and are bored look remarkably similar to rows of heads staring blankly because they are understanding nothing. Most lecturers would like to know if this is happening. It is worth finding out early on what the 'ground rules' are in your lectures – for example, whether it is acceptable to interrupt to ask a question – but remember that these 'rules' might vary from lecturer to lecturer. Many lecturers welcome questions during a lecture and it is worth taking advantage of this opportunity. If it becomes clear to a lecturer that something they have said hasn't been understood, then they can adjust their pace, or bring in more examples to keep things clear. You can be fairly confident that if *you* don't understand something then plenty of other people will be in the same position, so it is worth asking about.

Seminars/problem classes/revision classes

The final main kind of class is the small to medium-sized class held in a room without computers. Some programming courses make a lot of use of these: for example, to teach students that it is important to design programs away from the computer rather than plunging in and typing straight away. Other programming courses don't have anything like this. Again the 'prepare, actively attend, follow up' pattern is useful here: you will get the best from this type of class if you go along knowing what it will be about, and having done any preparatory work that has been set. Active engagement is the norm here so have the confidence to speak up. Afterwards, follow up by thinking about what the material taught in the class was designed to help you with and how it fits into the course as a whole.

▶ Using programming textbooks

This book is not a book about learning to program: its aims are to help you to learn about learning to program, and to give a general overview of the ideas that you will meet when you take a programming course. To learn the details of a particular computer language it is likely that you will use a textbook of some kind.

Typical programming textbooks are large ('10-pound doorstops') with a mixture of explanatory text, examples and exercises. Although their size might seem intimidating at first, they are large because they contain not only theory, but lots of practical examples for you to try. A few programming textbooks are short; these can often be good, and are particularly suited to people who find it easy to make up their own examples when engaging with the material. Another kind of book is the programming reference book; this contains lists of definitions and explanations, e.g. a dictionary of all the commands in a programming language. This is useful when you want to look up something that you have seen in a class, from a friend or in a textbook, but it isn't designed to teach you the language.

Some textbooks are available online, e.g. on the web. These may be essentially the same as printed textbooks and may seem attractive because they are free. However, they can be less convenient to use because it is difficult to read lots of text from the screen, and because it is harder to read the text and work on a program at the same time. Some online books contain a lot of additional, interactive material, such as quizzes that you can try out and get marked instantly.

Reading a textbook differs from reading other kinds of books. Furthermore, reading a programming textbook differs from reading textbooks in other subjects. Here are some suggestions for making good use of programming textbooks.

1.   **Programming textbooks are designed to be used interactively.** Reading a programming textbook is not like reading a novel. It will contain *some* explanatory text that can be read continuously, but it will also contain information that you will need to engage with more actively. For example, programming textbooks contain fragments of programs that can be typed into the computer. You can take the program fragments that are in the book and try out small variations on them to check that you have understood what they are doing. Does a small change to the program do what you had expected it to? You can look at a program in a book and try to work out what it does before you sit down at the computer. That way, you can get a better understanding of the details of the program – developing a reading skill. You can try to make up an example program before it is provided in the text, or make up examples where there aren't any. Sometimes a long explanation will precede an example, or follow it. You are meant to use each to help understand the other, and you will need to look back and forth between the explanation and the program before you fully understand what is going on.

Another big contrast with most other books is that you may take a long while to understand a particular part of a program or an explanation. Other sorts of books, like novels, are written to be read at a steady pace. In a textbook you will read some pages easily but others require you to spend minutes (or longer) working out how one line of text relates to the next. You might want to scribble in the book: explanations, connections between programs and the main text, questions that you are uncertain about, etc. Some people like to use a highlighter pen to mark important sections – you should beware of getting carried away and highlighting most of the book, but highlighting can help if done in moderation.

Reading programs is a special and valuable skill. One technique that can be useful in reading programs is to work through one with a particular set of input data and see what the program does with that particular data; then you can think about whether that behaviour is typical for all data, or whether there are other examples that would cause the program to behave in a different way. Programs cannot normally be understood by reading from one end to the other; when a program is running the computer will jump between parts of the program, and you will need to follow these possible jumps when you are working out what the program does.

2. **The exercises are part of the book.** Most textbooks contain exercises. These exercises are very much part of the book and a following chapter might depend on ideas that have been introduced in the exercises as well as in the main text. It is tempting to flick quickly through the exercises on the assumption that you can do them all. A good check, if you think this is the case, is to attempt one of the later exercises in the section first, as they are typically ordered by difficulty. Some textbooks have many exercises; clearly you need to use your judgement to decide how many of these are worth doing for a particular topic.

3. **Textbooks carefully use typographical and visual material.** `What is unusual about this sentence?` It was written in a different **font** from the rest of the paragraph; the words look as if they have been written on an old-fashioned typewriter rather than being typeset for a book. Programming textbooks use different fonts to distinguish between the informal natural language used to discuss programs, and formal programming languages that are used on the computer. For example, in a discussion of the concepts you need to understand in order to be able to **print** from a program, the word 'print' would be in the normal font. But if the book goes on to discuss how the word `print` is used in a computer language, it might be set in the typewriter font because that word has a significance in the language. Code samples are also normally distinguished from the surrounding text.

   Sometimes a style such as *italics* is used where you are meant to substitute some text in the book by something specific to you. Here is an example that illustrates all of these ideas.

   To print your name you might use

   ```
   System.out.println("My name is " + "name");
   ```

   You will often find a discussion of the meaning of the various fonts being used in the introduction to any programming textbook.

4. **Some sections will make more sense in the light of later sections.** Sometimes it will help to read ahead to make sense of what has come before. Seeing earlier material *used* in different ways will often help you to understand it. Don't feel that you have to fully understand everything about one topic before moving on to the next. It can be good

to plough on, trying to get a broad understanding, and then return to the earlier sections and go through them in detail.

5. **You may need to read the same text a number of times.** One strategy that works well is to read a section of a textbook and then leave it for a few days. You might feel that you have failed to understand much from the first reading; when you return to it later you are likely to find that some of the ideas have 'fallen into place'. You might, for example, have made subconscious links between the material that you have read and lectures you have been to, exercises that you have tackled or other things that you have read in the meantime.

6. **Sometimes you should just read the book offline.** Earlier we have said that textbooks are designed to be used actively. This is true, but there are times (for example when you are attempting to get a mental summary of a chapter) when it is valuable just to sit and read through a section of the book away from the computer.

7. **Programming textbooks often come with CDs or online material.** In contrast to books in most other subjects, programming textbooks often have some computer-readable material to accompany them: a CD-ROM attached to the book, or a companion web site. These are of varying value: sometimes they contain useful supplementary material (for example, computer-based tutorial programs, programming environments aimed at the beginner, programs that help you to visualize complex aspects of programming), sometimes they just repeat the material in the book, and sometimes they contain additional material that has little relationship to the main book at all.

Often found on such CDs and web sites are listings of the program **source code** for the examples in the book. This is both a blessing and a curse: the blessing is that you don't have to type the programs in yourself; the curse is that it is tempting to download the programs, compile and then run them without understanding them at all. You can make proper use of these programs by reading them carefully to ensure that you know how they work before running them and by trying out variations on them.

▶ Studying programming by yourself

Most courses expect that you will do some study outside the timetabled class times. Sometimes this is stated directly: for example, in our university the student handbook suggests that each student should spend five hours per module per week in general private study over and above classes and coursework.

What you need to do may follow directly from the teaching on the course. For instance, you might be set work in a lecture and be expected to have done it in time for the practical class later in the week. You may also be set coursework that will be marked and count towards your grade, to be done in your own time. It is a mistake to let your self-study be too strongly guided by your coursework: the latter is designed to be an end-point. If you are struggling with a topic, rather than plunging straight into the coursework associated with it you might decide first to master the skills required by working up to it through easier exercises.

One idea that has proved useful is to make your work *active*, particularly when you are stuck on problems with coursework. Staring *passively* at a program for hours on end in an attempt to spot what is wrong is seldom successful. Asking *active* questions, which lead to you doing something with your problem statement or program under development, is much more likely to produce a solution. Active questions include:

- How can I try out some variations on the problem that I am stuck on? What is it similar to?
- How can I simplify the problem?
- How can I do some exercises on simpler problems that lead to my getting the skills required to understand the current problem?
- How can I implement part of the current problem?
- If my program isn't working, which part of it isn't working?

Balancing work done at the computer against work done away from the computer is another important skill when working outside timetabled classes. Some tasks, such as designing programs, are best done away from the computer: you might want to turn off your computer or go to a room without computers in the library to help you focus. Even when you are engaged in detailed programming work, some time away from the machine can be useful. For example, try printing out parts of your program that are not functioning correctly and working out what they are doing on the printout. This can provide a fresh perspective, particularly as you are able to scribble over the printed code.

In the end, learning to study by yourself is a matter of finding ways of working that suit how you prefer to work and learn. Some students find that setting a fixed period of time aside for daily study is useful, especially if it is tied into the structure of the day in some way (last lecture always finishes before 4 o'clock, and dinner is from 6 o'clock, so the time in between is set aside every day as study time). Others find this kind of structuring useless, and prefer to work when they feel attentive and inspired; this can be fine, as long as you feel inspired often enough! Some people like to do a bit every day, others to work in intensive stretches when coursework deadlines are looming. Some people work best at night, others in the middle of the day, others early in the morning. With all of these things it is usually a matter of experimenting with different patterns to see which works best for you.

► How do I cope with the amount of material?

People studying programming commonly complain at the sheer amount of material that needs to be studied. You should expect to go through some periods when the amount of new material seems overwhelming, and you appear to be being expected to learn it before you have had much chance to master earlier stuff. Sometimes this ties into the nature of computer programming as a unified skill. In this way programming is like learning to drive: you can't learn to steer, brake, negotiate traffic, etcetera, separately; you have to do it all at once. Sometimes the complexity of learning to program ties in with the need to see a piece of the computer language used in several different contexts before you fully understand it. Even though you might be able to use particular features of a computer language when you are told which one is appropriate, being able to choose the right feature for yourself is much harder.

In our experience some students reach a 'sticking point' a few weeks into learning to program, where the amount of new material is increasing yet they have not quite mastered the 'basics' of programming. Persevering through this point is important; most of these students only get bogged down for two or three weeks, after which it seems to get easier! Some more strategies for getting past this sticking point are discussed in Chapter 9.

Learning to program can be thought of as a spiral process. You begin with a simple knowledge of a small amount of a computer language and a small number of examples of the use of that language. You then apply this to solving problems; then you discover that there are some problems which you cannot solve using your existing knowledge of the computer language. This encourages you to learn more features of the language, which in turn means that you are able to tackle larger or more complex problems, and so on.

► Getting the programming toolkit

Finally, before you can run your first program you will need to check that your computer is set up to handle the language you are going to learn. When you buy a computer 'out of the box', typically the software provided does not include a programming language. You need to be sure which language you are going to learn and then obtain a copy of the programming toolkit for that language. In your toolkit you will need a **compiler** and some means of entering and editing the program code.

Sometimes you will need to buy this software. For some languages, however, a free copy of the software will be available. Having got the software, you will need to install it on your computer and set it up to work in a way that you find convenient. If you are studying on a course then information should be available as to how to set up for the language you are going to learn.

▶ Chapter summary

Studying programming is similar in some ways to studying other subjects, and different in other ways. To learn programming effectively you can draw on study skills you already have from other subject areas but you also need to develop new study skills that are specific to programming. You may even need to read programming textbooks in a different way from other textbooks. In this chapter we have seen the kinds of skills you will need both for taught sessions and for studying by yourself.

5 Writing Your First Program

In popular culture, there are many images of what 'the Programmer' looks like (the loner, the social recluse) but rarely are they characterized as someone who simply delights in challenging and creative activity. For example, we don't have any images on television or in the movies of a programmer who enjoys rock climbing, singing in the choir, playing squash and (even though it is their full-time job) programming.

Programming is fun. We think learning to program can also be an enjoyable experience, but starting with the right tools is a critical first step – or, at the very least, figuring out how the tools you do have work is critical. So before we write the next great computer game that will take the world by storm, we should figure out which end of the hammer we hold, and which end we hit things with.

▶ Keeping it simple

We think the first few programs beginners encounter should be like rollercoasters: they'll have unexpected twists and turns, but someone else should do the steering for you. In this way, we keep the process of writing our first program as simple as possible. The simplest way we can think of is to copy your first program from a textbook. Just as we all learned to write by copying individual letters and words, copying your first program means there is less to think about, and fewer opportunities for mistakes. Traditionally, people often begin with some form of **'Hello, world' program**, so called because all a 'Hello, world' program does is write out the message 'Hello, world' on the screen (Code 5.1).

```
int main(void)
{
   printf("hello,world\n");
   return 0;
}
```

Code 5.1 A 'hello world'
program in C

Understanding Code

The program here simply prints 'hello, world'.

main refers to a special **function** in C that is the program's starting point.

int immediately before main says that the program will **return** an **integer** number to indicate whether the program ran successfully.

void means you don't have to put anything into the program to make it work. In this particular case, that also means that the program will do exactly the same thing every time it is run.

printf tells the computer to print the text that has been provided. The '\n' character pair is a way of telling the computer's output to end the line and be ready to start a new one, like hitting return on your keyboard.

return tells the program to return the number zero as an 'exit code' from the program to indicate that everything went fine.

Such a program has all the components that are essential for it to work and to demonstrate (e.g., by producing output) that it has worked. You can find more explanation, together with examples of 'Hello, world' programs in every computer language you are likely to have heard of and many others, in the **Wikipedia** entry for the 'hello world' program.[1]

Usually there will be a simple program in your learning materials to copy and run, together with instructions on how to make it work. The instructions will need to be followed exactly. Now is not the moment for being ambitious or doing something grand and exciting; even experienced programmers sometimes start with a 'Hello, world' program when learning a new language. This enables them to check that they have understood the basics of the language and that they have set up their computer system correctly to run the program. To provide a bit of guidance, we'll take a look at the critical pieces you need to have in place to write your first program.

▶ Tools of the trade

Writing your first program requires a few critical tools. If you are learning to program as part of a course in your school, college, university, or other classroom setting, these tools are often provided for you. While we can't predict exactly what kinds of tools you'll be using for writing your programs, we can guess that they will probably include a **text editor** of some sort (for writing your programs), and a compiler (for turning your programs into a form that the computer can run).

Editing programs: not just Word anymore!

Programming languages use a small vocabulary of special words (for example, `if`, `else`, and `for` are used in many programming languages), names made up by a programmer like yourself (these could be things like `bookAuthor`, `getValue`, `System`, `println`) and punctuation symbols like brackets, full stops, commas and semicolons. We can see examples of all three of these in Code 5.2, another 'Hello, world' program, this time written in **Pascal**.

When we encounter programs in textbooks, or work with them in a text

```
(* Print a friendly
 * greeting to the user.
 *)
program Hello(output);
begin
   writeln('Hello, world!')
end.
```

Code 5.2 A 'hello world' program in Pascal

Understanding Code

The first three lines of this program provide a comment letting fellow programmers know what the code that follows is supposed to do. Line 4 begins the code for the program the programmer has called `Hello`. The single code block is marked off by a `begin`/end pair. The code in this block means, 'Write a single line saying, Hello, world.'

editor, we often find a monospace font has been used; this lets us see how things line up in our programs more easily. Furthermore, we can immediately see that the program is not indented or punctuated like plain English (or Spanish, French, German, or any other language we might be familiar with). The choice of font and way programs are indented are two ways we attempt to make our programs more readable to people – including ourselves.

Furthermore, when we sit down to write our programs, the tool we use can make a large difference. You are probably familiar with a **word processor** called 'Word', produced by Microsoft. While you may be comfortable writing essays and letters using Word, it is important to note that Microsoft Word is not a text editor – it is a word processor. This may sound like an odd distinction, but a word processor lets *you* do all kinds of sTRaNGe things to your text, and is intended for producing printed content (like you might find in a book, or write in a letter to a friend overseas). A text editor, on the other hand, doesn't let you change the look of the programs you are writing, but instead helps you focus only on the content – the program – you are trying to write. We point this out, only because you simply *must* have a text editor for writing programs; you cannot write computer programs using Microsoft Word.

On Windows-based computers, there is a program called Notepad. This is a text editor. On the Apple Macintosh computers, there is a program called TextEdit; this is a text editor as well. These are both tools you could use for writing your first programs. However, as we will discuss in a moment, there may be better tools available to us, or you might be recommended to use a particular text editor if you are taking a programming course.

Emacs *vs.* vi

There is a long, rich history to text editors. One of the first text editors was called 'ed'. It can still be found on many computer systems today, even if no one in their right mind uses it. It is small, simple and certainly lets you edit text . . . but not in any powerful or useful way.

In the programming world, there is a mighty argument that has been in the making for 20 or more years: **Emacs** *vs.* **vi**. Emacs and vi are both text editors that provide the programmer with tools for indenting their programs, highlighting errors, finding and replacing text, and a host of other things useful to programmers. In fact, the text editors themselves can be programmed by the programmer!

So, if you ever find yourself in a programmer's pub (you know, a pub where disreputable programmers hang out after they finish . . . erm, programming), you should be very, very careful if someone casually asks: 'You look like you're new here; are you an Emacs user, or vi?'

Start backing away from the bar slowly but clearly in the direction of the door. The rivalry between Manchester United and Manchester City fans is nowhere near as epic. Proceed with caution lest you end up another casualty of the editor wars!

Making things go: the compiler

Let's say we were to open up Notepad, and copy the 'Hello, world' example from Code 5.2; we've now written a program in Pascal! Well, that's not exactly correct: we have copied the source code for a program in Pascal, but that doesn't make it do anything. Before we can run any program that we write, a special tool must be used to convert our source code (that humans can read and understand) into something the computer can read and understand. This is called a **compiler**.

A compiler takes program source code and transforms it into a program that can be executed by a computer. When you run the right compiler on your code (the 'right' compiler is the one designed to work with the language you are programming in), one of three possible things will happen. The first possibility is that your program compiles successfully. You are likely just to see a short message saying something like 'Compilation succeeded'. If you look in the right place (usually but not always the folder where you saved your source code), you will find that a new file has been created – this is the **executable** version of your program, the thing you run. You should probably follow the instructions in your textbook or learning materials at this point.

If the executable version of your program runs successfully, you will see its output on the screen. In the case of our 'Hello, world' program, the words

Hello, world!

should appear.

We said just now that there are three possible outcomes when you give the command to compile a program. Apart from success, there are two ways in which it can fail. The first one, which often troubles new programmers in a language, comes about because you have not set your system up correctly to run the compiler. If you see a message telling you that the command or the file is not found, you either need to be more careful about following the instructions available to you for setting up your system, or ask a friend who is more experienced in this kind of thing for some help. Remember: this is sometimes frustrating stuff, and it's perfectly acceptable to ask more experienced people for help. Someday, you'll be on the other side of the question, and you'll remember what it was like to be stuck with the computer spitting bizarre error messages at you!

The other kind of error we are certain to encounter as programmers is a message saying that compilation failed because of an error in the program. The compiler will provide information about what went wrong and where it thinks the error is. This means that we probably didn't match all our {}, ( ), and [ ] correctly, or perhaps we misspelled something (`prnit` instead of `print`, perhaps), or any of a host of other possible mistakes. Once we have identified all the mistakes in the program, wrestled with fixing them, and the compiler says that everything went well, we're well on our way to becoming the world's next great programmer!

Compilation

Compilation is the process of taking a program written in source code and turning it into executable code. There are several steps. The first is to split the text of the program into its constituent parts (*tokens*) such as **keywords**, identifiers, arithmetic operators and so on. The second step checks that the program is syntactically correct and can be converted into executable code. If it isn't, this step produces error messages for the user. The final step is to produce a file of executable code, but this step is only taken if the program is syntactically correct. This form may be **machine code** that is specific to a particular type of machine. Alternatively it may be in a form that can be executed by a **runtime system** for that language on any machine.

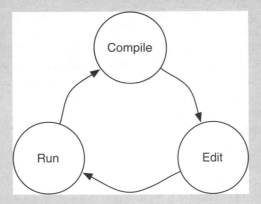

Figure 5.1 The edit–compile–run cycle

Edit–compile–run

The process of writing and editing our programs, running a compiler on the code, and then executing what the compiler produces, is commonly referred to as the **edit–compile–run cycle**. As a beginner, you are likely to spend a lot of time in the 'edit–compile' part of the cycle, because of the number of errors you will encounter when you first start programming. This is just part of the game; don't let it discourage you. It gets easier the longer you do it, and you eventually start wrestling with more challenging and enjoyable problems, instead of trying to figure out where a '{' went missing!

This cycle is true for most **general-purpose** programming languages. However, there is a small family of languages called **scripting languages** where this compilation step is absent, or at least hidden from the programmer. If you are learning one of these, your interaction with the code will be different. There's a section on scripting languages in Chapter 16.

One-stop shopping: the IDE

Text editors and compilers are not about to go away; they have been used for writing programs since the 1960s, and they will continue to be used for years to come. However, the repetitive nature of the edit–compile–run cycle has lead to the development of tools that make this task easier. These tools, called **integrated development environments (IDE)**, combine the editor and compiler, giving us all the tools we need to write programs in one place.

Pictured in Figure 5.2 is **BlueJ**, an IDE designed for beginning programmers who are learning the Java programming language; it is freely available for everyone, and runs on the Macintosh, Windows and Linux environments. BlueJ gives the beginner two views of their program: a structural view (on the left), and the source code (on the right). If we look more closely at the text editor that comes with BlueJ (Figure 5.3), we see that some handy features are right there, ready for us to use. The BlueJ text editor provides tools for us to copy, paste and undo while we're programming: this is handy. Also, it has a nice, big 'Compile' button built right into the text editor. This way, as we are working on our program, we can just click this button and find out if we have any mistakes in our code, as well as run the results of our efforts. Any IDE that you make use of will provide features similar to this; BlueJ is not unique in this respect.

If you decide that you really need something more sophisticated than a basic text editor, one recommendation we would make is that you try and find an IDE designed specifically for beginners. BlueJ is an example of an environment designed for programmers starting out in Java; **DrScheme** was written for students studying Scheme, and Squeak is an environment with resources available for students studying **Smalltalk**. We do not mean to imply that these tools cannot be used by experienced programmers – they

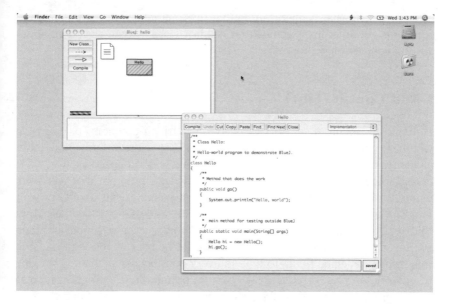

Figure 5.2 An integrated development environment

```
000                           Hello
Compile  Undo  Cut  Copy  Paste  Find...  Find Next  Close          Implementation        ⬍

/**
 * Class Hello:
 *
 * Hello-world program to demonstrate BlueJ.
 */
class Hello
{
    /**
     * Method that does the work
     */
    public void go()
    {
        System.out.println("Hello, world");
    }

    /**
     *  main method for testing outside BlueJ
     */
    public static void main(String[] args)
    {
        Hello hi = new Hello();
        hi.go();
    }
}
                                                            saved
```

Figure 5.3 The BlueJ text editor

often are – but what is important is that these simplified development environments get rid of many things that will be useless to you as you go about writing your first few programs.

▶ Did I get it right?

Perhaps the toughest question when you start programming is knowing whether – after working through the compiler, syntax errors and other challenges – the program you wrote does what it is supposed to.

To know without doubt that you have written a program that will work without fail all the time is very difficult. For example, you might try your program out with a number of different inputs, and see whether the output that you get is what you would expect. However, even a simple program such as a miles to kilometres converter would be near impossible to test in this fashion: imagine trying to type in every possible distance and checking whether it converts correctly. Now consider trying to test a program such as a word processor (inputting all possible combinations of words!) or a complex game (trying out all different strategies). Clearly this 'exhaustive' testing of the program is impossible.

However, there are techniques through which we can be reasonably certain that our programs work well. The first stage in this is to make certain that we understand how our programs work. This seems like a simple statement at first: how can we write programs without this kind of understanding? However, it is often tempting to try and write bits of programs without a full understanding; for example, if you think there are only a few ways of doing something, by writing them all and choosing the one which appears to work, without really understanding why it does so.

Another problem is with the compilation process that converts your program text into the internal language of the computer. Some beginners program in the following way: write a program, try to compile it, take out those bits of the program that cause trouble with the compiler, then try to add back in the functionality removed in order to get the program to compile. This inevitably leads to incomprehensible programs. Just as writing a good essay often requires planning and careful thought so that the essay 'flows' from one paragraph to another, so your programs need to be planned in the same way. If you get too excited about cutting and pasting things all over the place, you'll end up with something that neither you nor your tutor will understand!

The second strategy is to test your programs carefully. You are never going to be able to do a complete test for anything but the simplest programs. However, you can choose a number of inputs that are typical for the ways in which users will interact with the program. This, for example, is how computer games are tested. A number of people play the games, carrying out the various strategies which a player might adopt: the first time the program is tested, the character is moved round the left-hand side of the building; the second time round the right-hand side. This is better than someone just randomly playing the game and missing out whole sections.

▶ Writing your second program

Our first programs are typically copied from books, or perhaps examples that we modify in an attempt to understand how other people's programs work. This is how everyone starts out – even people who have been programming for years but are now learning a new language. However, we all come to the point where it's time to start thinking about writing some code of our own – our 'second program', so to speak.

Writing a program 'from scratch' is as creative a process as sitting down on a rocky coastline at sunset with a set of watercolours, or trying out scales and chords in preparation for a solo in your jazz quintet. Writing a program from scratch can also be every bit as challenging, depending on the task you've chosen for yourself. The challenge lies in turning an informal description of a problem in English into ideas that can be written in a programming language.

Although we may be eager to stretch our wings and soar like eagles, the truth is that our programming skills at this stage probably still put us in the same category as penguins. Mind you, penguins are excellent creatures: they live in remarkably harsh climates, and are excellent swimmers . . . it's just that they don't fly so well. Or at all, for that matter.

Even when you're ready to start flexing your programming muscles, don't be afraid to go looking for inspiration in the world. There are many examples you can (and should) make use of on the **Internet** that can help get you going when you decide you're ready to tackle writing programs of your own design.

Kelluretill?

Learning to program is not so different from learning other languages. When learning a language we often learn how to say whole sentences, and only later are able to work out what the individual words mean, or how those words can be combined into new sentences. For example, if we were studying French, we might learn that something sounding like 'kelluretill' means 'What time is it?' Only after we have learned a little more do we see that 'kelluretill' is actually 'Quelle heure est-il?' – it is a sentence, not a single magic word we use to ask what time it is. Once we have learned this, we might modify the phrase (e.g. 'Quel jour est-il?' – 'What day is it?'). Similarly, when learning to program for the first time we will often work with programs that already do something, and it may be our task to make them do something slightly different. As we spend time modifying and exploring these programs, we begin to see how the larger ideas of the program fall together.

▶ Getting ready to read code

Sometimes we find ourselves reading code to learn about the programming language in which it has been written. Sometimes we are reading code to understand the code itself – trying to understand how it works, or because we are hoping to use ideas from the code in something we are doing. Sometimes our purpose is to fix something that is broken.

The example we will look at is some code written in Java (Code 5.3). A slightly more detailed version of this code can be found in Chapter 11. The purpose of this code is to capture the general characteristics that a book might have. As the code stands it says a book will have a title, an author and some number of pages:

```
class Book
{
    String title;
    String author;
    int numberOfPages;

    Book(String t, String a, int nop)
    {
        title = t;
        author = a;
        numberOfPages = nop;
    }

    // other details omitted
}
```

Code 5.3 Part of a Java class definition

If we just look this code over, we find it contains punctuation such as brackets, curly brackets, semicolons and commas. There is a symbol ' = '. There are some English words and some non-words; words like 'class', 'Book', 'String' and 'title'. There is 'numberOfPages' made up of words but all joined together. And finally there are non-words like 'nop' and 'int', and a few letters that appear just on their own. Finally, it is spaced out over several lines on the page.

The uses of punctuation

Punctuation is used to indicate the starting and ending parts of bits of code. In a language like Java, a semicolon ';' is used to end a statement. This allows the compiler and us to see that there is a sequence of separate statements. In Code 5.3, pairs of curly brackets like '{' and '}' are used to enclose statements into a group. Brackets are also used to group and enclose other smaller language pieces, and the pair of slashes '//' is used to mark the beginning of a **comment** (that is, a part of the program designed to be read by people who are working on the program, rather than by the computer).

```
class Book
{
    String title,
    String author;
    int numberOfPages;

    Book(String t, String a, int nop)
    {
        title = t;
        author = a;
        numberOfPages - nop;
    }

    // . . .
}
```

Code 5.3(a)   Punctuation highlighted

Punctuation with these functions is found in most languages, but they may be accomplished in different ways. One of the first things you will encounter when you start learning to read and write a programming language are the ways it separates and blocks out code.

Predefined words and symbols

At the start, it is not always easy to tell from the code what expressions are part of how the language is regularly used and what expressions have been chosen by the programmer to be used just in this specific program. As your experience of the programming language grows, this will quickly become second nature. In the code we have been looking at, the highlighted expressions below indicate basic parts of the language itself and its regular usage:

```
class Book
{
      String title;
      String author;
      int numberOfPages;

      Book(String t, String a, int nop)
      {
            title = t;
            author = a;
            numberOfPages = nop;
      }

      // . . .
}
```

Code 5.3(b)   Java words and symbols highlighted

The word `class` is a special word that is used in the language to say that what follows will provide a general concept of something (here a general notion of a book). A **String** is used to store an arbitrary sequence of characters. An `int` is an integer (a number like 2 or 3, or −5 or 0).

Programmer-chosen words and symbols

The programmer who wrote the code of `Book` realized that it was easy to associate 't' with `title`, 'a' with `author` and 'nop' with `numberOfPages`. Practical judgement and knowledge of the conventions of use make code easier to read and understand.

```
class Book
{
      String title;
      String author;
      int numberOfPages;
```

```
Book(String t, String a, int nop)
{
    title = t;
    author = a;
    numberOfPages = nop;
}
// . . .
}
```

Code 5.3(c) Programmer-chosen words highlighted

If you are looking at a piece of code there is often no way to tell, just by looking, whether an expression is defined as part of the language itself (a keyword or a common expression) or whether it is an expression made up and used by a programmer. To help learners and to help all programmers, textbooks and IDEs use different colours and/or fonts for the different language elements.

There may be rules concerning capitalization, but often choices are dictated by the conventions of programmers. However, like driving on the same side of the road, these conventions need to be followed. In Code 5.3, there are a number of conventions used – the word Book begins with an **upper-case** letter 'B' followed by **lower-case** letters. The other terms in this code are all completely written in lower case. And these, in fact, reflect the standard conventions used by Java programmers.

The order in which things are presented sometimes makes a tremendous difference and sometimes does not matter at all.

White space
White space (the 'gaps' at the beginning of lines for example) also helps to make programs easier to read. Programs are *indented* (i.e. different parts are placed at different distances from the left-hand margin) to make them easier to read, especially by making the chunks more obvious. Compilers don't pay much attention to code indentation but it certainly helps human readers, like us. It would be much harder to read code if it looked like this:

```
class Book {String title; String author;
int numberOfPages; Book(String t, String a,
int nop) {title=t; author=a;
numberOfPages=nop; } // . . .
}
```

Code 5.3(d) Omitting white space that is unnecessary
to the compiler

▶ Chapter summary

Getting started with writing our first program is probably best carried out as an exercise in copying programs from books or web pages where we know the programs are correct. Even if we get it right the first time, there are still the challenges of setting up and running the compiler on the programs we write. An IDE can simplify the process of writing programs by putting all the tools we need – text editor and compiler – in one place. In the end, getting started with our first programs is challenging, sometimes frustrating, but almost always rewarding in the end.

Useful vocabulary

Compiler A computer program that turns a computer program written in one language (the source language) into an equivalent program written in another language (the target language). The target language is usually one that the computer can directly execute.

Source code A computer program in the source language for a compiler.

Editor A piece of software that allows the user to edit files. The term 'editor' is usually reserved for software that allows users to edit plain-text files, to distinguish it from a word processor, used to edit formatted documents.

Executable code This is a computer program in a language that can be directly converted into actions by a computer. It is not intended for human readers.

6 The Nature of Errors

A couple of the keys to making progress with programming are, firstly, to understand the different situations in which errors arise, and, secondly, to learn from the early errors you make so that later errors become much easier to correct.

The kind of mistakes you encounter will depend on the stage you are at in the edit–compile–run cycle. In other words, the mistakes you make and the messages you get as a result will be different depending upon whether they are from the computing environment, the compiler or the runtime system. This is true even if you are using an IDE, because this is really just a system that bundles all three of these components together.

Mistakes made in the computing environment are usually to do with file handling and naming. For instance, you might want to edit a file but mistype or misremember its name, and the editor gives you a message about an unknown or missing file. Another example would be trying to save a file when your disk is full. This will also produce an error message, although you haven't done anything wrong. These sorts of mistakes and error situations are really generic computing errors and not specific to programming, so we won't spend any more time on them in this chapter. Instead, our focus will be on the different types of errors that occur when writing programs.

▶ Right and wrong programs

Beginning students often think that programming problems have a single correct answer and that there is only one right program that will give the answer. In fact, this is never the case! There are lots of different ways of writing even the simplest program, which is great because it gives you a lot of scope to be creative when writing programs. Creativity is fundamental to programming and as you learn to program you will develop your own style. This also means that you shouldn't assume that your program is wrong just because it looks different from someone else's. As long as both programs do the right things and produce the same answers, both are right. However, what primarily interests us in this chapter is knowing what to do when our programs don't work. There are two circumstances in which you can be sure that your program is wrong: if it will not even run, or if it runs but gives the wrong answer. Such programs must contain one or more errors that need to be corrected.

We know from other subjects that it is possible to make different sorts of mistakes. For instance, if you write an essay you might make errors of fact, make grammatical errors, misunderstand a key theory, or even miss the point of the question and write about the wrong topic. When your essay is marked you receive feedback in which these errors are likely to be pointed out. You will then try to avoid them in your next piece of work. Programming is very similar in many respects. One big difference, however, is that with programming you don't have to wait for a human marker to give you feedback, which might take many weeks. When you write a program, the first step is to get it checked by the compiler. The compiler is a bit like a proofreader, which checks for spelling mistakes and grammatical errors. If the compiler isn't happy, then you won't even be allowed to run your program, which means that you won't be able to tell whether the program gives the right answer. We always have to follow two separate error-checking steps when programming: ask the compiler to check for errors; then, when the compiler is satisfied, run the program and check that it works as it should. Making sure that each program gives the right answers is a key part of learning to program, so you have to keep reworking the program until you are satisfied that it is correct, just as you will often draft, proofread and redraft an essay until you are happy with it.

As Chapter 5 made clear, dealing with errors is a major part of programming and can be a cause of huge frustration to novice programmers. This chapter tries to limit the potential for frustration by helping you to distinguish between **compile-time** and **runtime errors**, describing how common errors arise that prevent your programs from compiling or running, and how to deal with them.

▶ Types of errors

Errors within your program can be divided into two types, **syntax errors** and **semantic errors**, as defined in Chapter 3. Syntax errors are notified to you by the compiler, because they occur where you write something that the compiler cannot understand, for instance if you miss or mistype a piece of punctuation, such as a semicolon. Syntax errors show up when you try to compile your program; they always produce error messages. A program with syntax errors cannot be run.

Semantic errors do not show up until you have satisfied the compiler and can actually run the program. These errors are what are commonly known as **bugs**. They represent errors in the program's logic. What is slightly tricky about **logical errors** is that they are not always easy to spot. Whereas syntax errors *always* elicit an error message from the compiler, only some logical errors result in error messages when a program is run. Logical errors produce error messages when your program attempts to make the computer do something impossible or inappropriate. For instance, it does not make sense to divide a number by zero, and a program that does this will fail because of a logical error and produce an error message.

Logical errors that do not result in a runtime error message are more subtle and harder to spot than those that do. They occur when the program runs successfully (no obvious logical errors) but the answer it produces, or the task it carries out, is not what you intended it to be. Of course, spotting these errors assumes that you will always be able to spot when what the program has done is incorrect. This is not always as easy as it sounds. As an example of a hidden logical error, suppose you had to write a trivial program to add two numbers and print the result on the screen. Your code should have a section with the calculation x + y and the result for a particular pair of numbers might be supposed to be 10. If you had a momentary brainstorm and typed x - y instead, the result will almost certainly be incorrect. However, the computer will not realize that you have made a logical error, so there will be no error message. It will be up to you to spot the error by noticing that the result printed is something other than 10. This means that you have to look carefully at your output every time you run a program. While this approach is fine for small programs, or those that produce small amounts of output, it doesn't scale well to larger programs. For that, we have to be more thorough and systematic. There is more about this in Chapters 9 and 12. The bottom line for logical errors is that you can never assume that the lack of an error message guarantees that everything is correct.

▶ Spotting and fixing errors

Recognizing that there is an error

On the whole, computers do not tell you when you have done things right. At the most you will get a brief confirmation – perhaps something like 'Compilation successful'. However, if you do get an error message there *must* be something wrong, even if you were totally confident that you had done everything right. This means that if you get a message you really must make sure you read it, and be clear what it is telling you. This is the single most important part of spotting and fixing errors. Code 6.1 shows a typical error message from a compiler:

```
SimpleServer.java:27: cannot resolve symbol
symbol: variable clientCount
location: class SimpleServer
          while(clientCount < maxClients) {
                ^

1 error
```

Code 6.1   A Java compiler message

The next thing to do is work out where the error message came from. The error message might come from the compiler or it could even come from the environment. If the compiler cannot find your file you have probably mistyped the file name or are in the wrong folder. Alternatively you may have mistyped the name of the command to compile or run your program.

Once you have found the source, you are in a position to track the error down and correct it. This sounds simple but your experience of computers might tell you that it won't be simple at all. Nevertheless, you can make it as easy as possible by using a systematic approach.

Tracking down syntax errors
Let's deal first with programs that will not compile. Before you go any further, it is worth checking that you have tried to compile the latest version of your program. One of the many common gotchas that trip people up is making changes and forgetting to save them before trying to compile the program again.

Now that you have eliminated that possibility, have a good look at the error message or error messages. If there are lots, do not panic. It could be that there are lots of mistakes, in which case you can sort them out one at a time. On the other hand, it is quite common for one simple syntax error to elicit several error messages from the compiler. This happens when the compiler gets very confused and ends up unable to make any sense of a chunk of your program at all. These errors are known as **cascading errors** and once you have sorted out the root cause they will all go away with one simple correction. Starting a string with a quote mark and then forgetting to put the closing quote mark at the end is a very easy way to produce cascading errors.

. . . and understanding them
A compiler usually includes in its error message the part of your code that it thinks is in error, and marks the spot where the error was detected. More

often than not, the spot that it marks is indeed the place where you need to make the changes. So, you need to find the first error message and locate the place it refers to in your source code.

Before you take any action, it is essential to work out what is wrong and why. It is tempting to guess but you should resist the temptation. At first you will find the error messages hard to understand but with practice you should be able to interpret most of them with ease. Code 6.2 illustrates the potential for confusion. The error message says that a semicolon is missing, but the line shown *does* contain a semicolon. The explanation is that the semicolon is missing from the previous line, but the compiler has not been able to work that out until it reaches the following line. The error indicator has been positioned just before the next statement in an attempt to indicate that we need to look one line above.

```
SimpleServer.java:31:  ';' expected
       clientCount++;
     ^

1 error
```

Code 6.2 A potentially confusing compiler error message

There are two reasons why the error messages are confusing to begin with: because you are unfamiliar with the terminology they use and because automatically generating helpful error messages is extremely difficult. Human beings are very inventive when it comes to making mistakes, so it is easier to train programmers to understand error messages than to write a compiler that can diagnose every mistake exactly and explain in simple language what is wrong.

Compilers actually have a limited set of error messages that they use over and over again for each program. This turns out to be very useful for us because over time we can build up experience of error messages and what they are likely to mean in terms of the code we have written. In the early days of your programming experience it will be very helpful to you to keep a logbook of the compiler's error messages you see, and what you had to do to fix the problem the compiler was indicating. A single error message won't always indicate the same problem, but you will gradually build up a catalogue of things that could be wrong in each situation, and that will soon make it easier for you to fix your errors.

If you get compiler errors after typing in an example from a book, you probably made a typing error so go back to the book and make a careful comparison between the two versions. (However, be on your guard, because syntax errors do sometimes creep into examples in books; there might even be some in this one!) Read the error message carefully and try to work out the relationship between the mistake and the message. This will make it easier to spot that kind of mistake in future.

Research shows that the vast majority of compiler errors are caused by typos. The most common is misspelling words and not being consistent in the spelling of names (remember that bookAuthor and bookauthor are likely not to be interpreted as being the same in many languages). The next most common error comes from getting the punctuation wrong or missing it out. It is remarkably difficult to spot when you have typed a ':' (colon) instead of a ';' (semicolon). Brackets are another fertile source of errors. Do opening and closing brackets match? Missing brackets are hard to spot in a complicated mathematical expression and one way to check is to count the number of opening brackets and make sure that it is the same as the number of closing brackets. Different types of brackets also cause confusion. '[ ]', '{ }' and '( )' have different meanings, so double-check that you have the right kind. Starting and ending quote marks around strings, and the characters used to show where comments start and end, are also very easy to leave out. They produce error messages referring to unterminated strings (or comments). In summary, most syntax errors come from trivial mistakes that can be remarkably hard to spot, so it is sensible to check for them before you look for bigger mistakes.

Fixing syntax errors

A methodical approach to fixing syntax errors (errors identified by the compiler) is important. Start with the first one, correct it in the source file, save the file and then recompile. Don't try to fix all the errors in one go. This approach is particularly important if you have cascading errors, or multiple errors that have the same cause, such as a misspelled identifier. If that has not solved the original problem you need to think again about the root cause of the error message.

In general this approach, of making a small change and checking whether it did what you expected, is a very sensible one. However, it is most effective if you know why the change you have just made is likely to work. Some novice programmers carry this approach to extremes. Instead of doing any proofreading they just compile whatever they have typed, thus using the compiler as a proofreader. Code 6.3 shows a genuine example of where this has been done. It contains more errors than lines of code. In this particular case, the compiler was actually able to make a fairly good diagnosis of the individual errors when corrected one at a time.

```
int largestValue(ArrayList ls) {
        Iterator it = ls. iterator();
        int temp = 0
        while (it hasNext()) {
            Integer intTmp =(Integer) it.next:
            int num = intTmp. intValue ();
            if(num >temp); temp = num;{
                return temp;
            }
}
}
```

Code 6.3 Source code with many errors

Is this approach a good idea? Well, the compiler will certainly flag up everything that is a mistake. The difficulty, as already mentioned, is that it may not always explain very well what the mistakes are. This can lead to you taking corrective action that takes you further from the solution rather than closer. Provided that you can cope with this, it may work well for you.

The real problem comes if you do not think carefully about what the causes of the error messages are, and how to fix them. Just making changes at random, in the hope that if you make enough something is bound to work, is *not* a good method. Monkeys hitting the keys of a typewriter at random might theoretically produce one of the plays of Shakespeare but it would be an incredibly slow process. Worse, it would be just as slow to produce the second play because the monkeys would have no more knowledge of play writing at the end than they did to begin with. Making mistakes and working out how to fix them is an essential part of learning to program. If you adopt the monkey method and just make changes at random, you will not learn much. Working out what the error messages mean is hard work but it pays dividends when you come to write bigger programs.

A better strategy is to focus on making relatively small changes to a program before checking it over with the compiler. If you start from something that already compiles – this might be a program outline given to you as part of an assignment, or an example from a book – and then make small changes or additions, you are likely to be able to focus on just the new parts if you receive a compiler error message. If you fix that problem before adding anything new, you will once again be in the position of being able to focus on a relatively small part of the program (and probably just one or two errors) when trying to sort out problems.

Logical errors

Once your program has compiled successfully you can run it. Now you can focus on checking your program's logic and that it does exactly what you intended. Any logical errors reported by the system will have to be fixed. The approach here is similar to the approach you use with compiler errors. You will usually be given an indication of where in your program the error was spotted, and that is the place to start looking in order to fix it. Make sure that you understand what the error message means and try to relate it to the error location. Of course, once you have attempted to correct a logical error, you will have to ensure that the program compiles before you can run it to confirm that the logical error really has been fixed.

Remember, too, to check for unreported logical errors. Compare any output you get to the output you expect and be suspicious of any inconsistencies. If you are not sure what the results should be – perhaps because there is too much data to work them out for yourself – try running your program with smaller amounts of data that you can check more easily. Tracking down unreported logical errors sometimes requires detective work because there are no error messages to help you know where to look in your program for the problem. Chapter 9 describes a number of useful approaches but a good first step is to print out the program on paper and read through it carefully. Such a walk-through often shows up where the problem lies so that you can fix it. Don't assume, too, that because the program gives the right results with one set of data, that it works in every case. The logic of most programs is such that different paths through the code are followed with different sets of data. Try out different values to build up your confidence that your program really is doing what it should. Later chapters give more detailed advice on testing, test cases and test sets.

▶ Avoiding errors

Of course, the one way to make errors easier to deal with is to try to avoid them in the first place! Being human, we won't be able to avoid mistakes entirely, but some simple pieces of advice that might help are:

- When developing a program, always try to work from a program that already compiles. Even if you are starting a new program, you can start with an absolutely basic working one, perhaps from your learning materials.
- Make one change at a time, and then recompile.
- Type carefully (maybe even learn to type?!).

- Keep a version that works under a different name so that if your experiments result in errors you cannot fix, you can always go back to the old one if necessary.
- Try to learn from past mistakes by keeping a logbook.

Typos and brainos

These are colloquial terms for mistakes most of us make all the time. Typos are silly slips in typing, where a finger hits two keys or where letters somehow get themselves typed in the wrong order. **Brainos** are sudden lapses of thought causing things you know perfectly well to somehow get themselves muddled up or disappear altogether.

Punctuation

When we write English, we use a lot of words and not very much punctuation at all. Most people are rather vague about the rules for using commas and don't have a clue what to do with semicolons and colons. Do you even know the difference between a colon and a semicolon? By contrast, punctuation is heavily used in programming and getting it right is absolutely essential. So if you didn't know that ';' is a semicolon and ':' is a colon, now is the moment to learn. Programming languages use a very wide range of punctuation marks, whose proper names are not at all well known, like solidus for '/', or not known at all, such as '{' '}' which just get referred to as curly brackets.

Programming languages typically use punctuation for marking the ends of program statements, indicating comments, bracketing groups of statements, enclosing expressions, and separating items in lists.

► Chapter summary

Much of your time spent programming won't be spent writing programs, but will be taken up with correcting errors in the programs that you have written.

In this chapter we have explained the different kinds of errors you will find, and strategies for avoiding, finding and fixing such errors. In particular you should remember that some errors will be picked up by the computer when you compile your program, whilst some will affect the program's behaviour, and you will need to track back from the erroneous behaviour to where the error actually is in your program.

▶ Code explained

Code 6.1

```
SimpleServer.java:27: cannot resolve symbol
symbol: variable clientCount
location: class SimpleServer
      while(clientCount < maxClients) {
                 ^

1 error
```

Code 6.1   A Java compiler message

Let's go through this error message in a little more detail. The compiler found a problem in source code contained in `SimpleServer.java`. The problem was found on line 27. It could not figure out what 'clientCount' was. It then shows the context where it had the problem. Usually when something like this happens the variable `clientCount` has not been **declared**.

Code 6.3

```
int largestValue(ArrayList ls) {
   Iterator it = ls. iterator();
      int temp = 0
      while (it hasNext()) {
         Integer intTmp =
                  (Integer) it.next:
         int num = intTmp. intValue ();
         if(num >temp); temp = num;{
              return temp;
           }
}
}
```

Code 6.3   Source code with many errors

```
int largestValue(ArrayList ls) {
   Iterator it = ls.iterator();
   int temp = 0;
   while (it.hasNext()) {
      Integer intTmp = (Integer) it.next();
      int num = intTmp.intValue();
      if (num > temp) {
         temp = num;
      }
   }
   return temp;
}
```

Code 6.3(a) Corrected source code

You might want to compare the code between these two examples. There's not much different – a word space here and there, some punctuation in different places, but compilers are designed to be finicky and only syntactic correct code will get through them. Of course, a person can take the Code 6.3 and turn it into 6.3(a), code which will compile.

Code 6.3(a)

What the code does: The code provides a method called `largestValue` that finds the largest number in a collection.

An **ArrayList** is a kind of collection and the terms: `int ArrayList`, `Iterator`, `iterator()`, `hasNext()`, `next()`, `intValue()`, `if` and `return` are parts of the Java programming language itself or parts of commonly used libraries; whereas `largestValue`, `ls`, `it`, `temp`, `intTemp`, and `num` were chosen by the programmer who wrote this code.

How the code works: The code uses an iterator to go through a collection item by item. The specific iterator that is created in this code is called 'it'. A storage place called 'temp' is provided and it starts at zero. As the iterator goes through the collection, if a number bigger than `temp` is found, `temp` is changed into that bigger number. When all the collection has been completely gone through, the method produces `temp`, by that point the biggest number in the collection.

Part Three
Your Next Programs

7 The Many Ways of Programming

When faced with a programming assignment, there are many different ways to get started. What should come first? What are good ways to continue after starting? Let's look at an example from outside the world of programming to illustrate this.

Imagine you are working in an office over the summer break. Your boss has set you the task of sorting and filing the correspondence she has received about a new project. This is a simple enough task, but you will need to *ensure that you understand what is required.* Do you sort by alphabetical order, by category, or by date? You find out that the post is to be sorted alphabetically. Other questions must now be answered – should it be ordered by the name of the person who sent it, or by the name of the company? In addition, if there is more than one letter from the same company, should you sort them by date? As you look through the correspondence, you find there are some tricky questions about sorting the letters into alphabetical order. There is a letter from a company called '1-2-3 Cleaning'; where will numerals go? Another problem you find is that there is a letter from a company called Robert's Insurance (with an apostrophe) and a letter from another company called Roberts Autos (without) – how should these letters be filed?

The essential first step when writing a computer program is to be sure that you understand exactly what is required. Exercises and assignments are usually written so that what is needed is made clear, but if you aren't sure then don't be afraid to ask for clarification.

Once you are clear what the end result must be you will still find that there will be further questions to answer along the way to a solution. At each of these points you will need to choose specific procedures and ways of organizing your materials. To continue the example above, in sorting the letters you are likely to realize that there are different ways of managing the physical task of sorting.

1. You could create a space on the floor with 26 places – one for each letter of the alphabet (or 27 to include the letters from companies such as 1-

2-3 Cleaning). Then you sort through the piles of correspondence placing the letters from companies beginning with A into one pile, those beginning with B into another, and so on. After you have placed all the correspondence on the correct pile, you can sort through each of the piles alphabetically by the second letter of the company name, and so on.
2. Alternatively, you could pull out all the correspondence from companies beginning with Z, and put these in a pile. Then go through and do this for the letters from companies beginning with Y, and so on. Eventually you sort everything into its proper pile, and then sort each pile by subsequent letters of the company names.

Is either of these necessarily better than the other? Sorting is a basic programming task, and detailed procedures have been developed for efficient sorting. Detailed sets of instructions for carrying out tasks such as this are called **algorithms**. You will find it useful to use algorithms when you need your programs to manipulate data.

The spaces on the floor are an everyday example of a way of holding and organizing data while working on it. In computing terms these are called **data structures**. Whole books have been written on both algorithms and data structures, and you might find that they are covered in detail in later parts of your course. What we can see from even these two simple approaches to sorting letters is that one requires more floor space than the other, but one is likely to be quicker than the other. Which you choose to use will depend upon how much time and floor space you have, and we often have to make similar decisions in choosing between alternative computer algorithms.

This example of sorting letters illustrates two key principles: be as clear as you can before you start about what you have to do; and be prepared to discover new things about the task as you work your way towards a solution. In the following sections we consider some of the different ways you might approach the issue of creating a solution and the process of discovery.

▶ What to do and when to do it

Different people do things differently and there are many different effective ways of successfully developing programs. Successful programming involves thought, good design and careful coding, but the ordering and combination of these components may vary. It is often good advice to plan out what you intend to do before you begin to code, but there are also times when it may be helpful to proceed differently – for example, by discovering what needs to be taken into account whilst you are in the process of programming. Let's explore some of these basic strategies.

The way of divide and conquer

One basic problem-solving strategy is 'divide and conquer'. Using divide and conquer, you break down a single large complicated task into smaller component tasks. These smaller tasks are simpler and more straightforward to accomplish than the original, but together they solve the whole task.

Look at a large problem and figure out what steps you need to take in order to reach the solution. Then look at each of these steps and break them down into even smaller steps, and repeat this until you reach a point at which you can see how to do the whole of a small step. At this point you can begin to perform the necessary tasks.

This approach requires that you already know or can easily find out the information you need to get started. It also presupposes that you know how to split complex tasks into smaller components.

We often follow this strategy when a group of people want something done quickly. Someone assumes the role of organizer and assigns tasks to different members of the group. Then each person breaks down their individual tasks into smaller subtasks and works through these until all the subtasks are accomplished and the entire job is complete.

The way of planning and executing

Before doing anything else, you plan out in detail what your whole program should do and how it works – then you write it. This method works well if you have a fairly good idea of how to make things happen in the programming language you are using. Some programming teachers may recommend that this is the best way to proceed.

In this way of carrying out a programming assignment, first you think through what you want to do and how you want to do it. Then you plan the various steps. You may have used this strategy when preparing for a party, and many people use this strategy when planning weddings or arranging holidays.

The way of working through a problem incrementally

You start by getting one very simplified version of your program to work. Then you add a bit more functionality to it and get this new version to work. When this is working, you build another refinement and get it to work. In the early stages, you don't worry about each little detail reflecting all the complexity that needs to be handled; you just focus on getting some appropriate code to work. By repeating this process many times, your program grows into a program that does its intended job complete with all its complexities. Sometimes this way of programming is called 'iterating' or 'building in cycles'. Notice how this fits in with the principle of always moving on from something that you know to be working.

The way of playing – learning by exploration and discovery

This is how children learn, but it is also a way that adults can learn new things. Many computer users learn their way into new **applications** like this. If they see a likely icon, or an interesting menu item, they try it out. They fiddle with this and tinker with that, trying things out and seeing what happens; and so they come to understand how the application works and what it does.

You can also use this approach to help you learn to program, especially when you want to get a feel for the way a language works. It can also be helpful for exploring different possibilities when you are not sure how to proceed. You can use 'play' to try out hunches and test different hypotheses to see which one works best. It is an exploratory, hands-on, 'no rules' approach that can help you get a better sense of the tools available. Important in this approach is not to be afraid of what might happen if you try out this or that.

The way of hacking

Just sit down at the keyboard and begin to write code. Once you have enough to work from you can see if it will run. While this way is frowned upon in some circles, it does have a place. If all you want or need to do is something simple and straightforward, this may be an option – if you know how to fit your programming skills to the task at hand. However, if what you have to do is rather complex and complicated, it will be unlikely to work. It is a 'quick and dirty' approach that may not be suitable for big tasks. If you use this approach to explore the solution to a problem, you should be prepared to throw away what you have produced at the end of the exploration, and start again from scratch using a more systematic approach.

Hacking

To non-programmers 'hacking' usually means breaking into and attacking computer systems. It's quite disreputable and usually illegal.

However, as originally used in computing circles, **hacking** means something quite different. Amongst programmers the term 'hacking' refers to a particular approach to writing programs. Hackers are clever and knowledgable programmers who write code quickly with the goal of getting the job done with apparent ease. They are good at getting lots of the details right, but overall any code that is written this way can be a very messy jumble, hence the need to be willing to throw it away and start over again at the appropriate point.

► Which strategy works best?

It depends.

It depends on who you are, how you work effectively, and what your assignment is.

Not everyone is the same. Different people learn, work and solve problems in different ways. Of course, whoever you are and however you prefer to work, you must in the end produce programs that meet what is required of them.

It can be helpful to think through some basic questions, such as: Why am I writing this program? How is this program going to be used? How much time do I have to complete this work?

Think about why you are writing the program

Am I writing this program to learn about the programming language? Your earliest programming exercises have been designed to help you understand the language itself and to help you develop your programming skills. Your goals in writing the code may be just for your program to be syntactically correct and perform a simple task. At this stage, explore – try different ways, look over solutions that are provided. The way of play can be useful for learning what you need to complete your exercises, but it can also be useful after you have completed them for broadening and consolidating your ideas, and again even later when you are doing revision. Asking yourself, 'What happens if . . .', can be a great way to learn more about the language. Some people find it helpful to think through in detail what they expect to happen and then try it out, but those of a different temperament may prefer just to plunge in and do it.

Am I writing this program to learn how to write more complex programs that involve handling many issues at the same time? Well, if you know the language pretty well, then incrementally building your program may be just the ticket. Or you might want to follow the way of plan-and-execute.

Later, when you are working on a large-scale project (it could be a final project at the end of an academic programme or it could be in a professional capacity), your target may be to build something that is correct, efficient, robust, easily maintainable, and reusable by other programmers. And, of course, there are serious responsibilities for developers of **safety-critical** programs on which people's lives may depend (see Chapter 13 for a discussion of the issues).

Looking for *the* solution
You have completed a programming exercise and looked at the sample answer provided. Your program is quite different.

'Oh no!' you may think, 'I've approached this problem quite differently. I didn't get the solution. Where did I do wrong?'

You probably did just fine. Any programming exercise will have many possible correct solutions. There is never just one definitive right answer. Perfectly appropriate solutions will differ both in detail and in the general approach followed.

You can learn a lot from looking at alternative approaches, and it is a very good idea to study any sample answers provided, but bear in mind that your own approach may be different without being wrong.

Think about how the program will be used

A program you have written may be just an exercise or it may be something you revisit again and again. Is it something to solve a small problem for another piece of work you have been doing – will you run it once and forget it? Is it a program you have written to test out some ideas that might be incorporated into a larger project? If so, you should ensure that you include accurate documentation.

Will other people be running this program? Will you be running this program again at a later date? In these cases, you need to think about who is going to be running the program and what they need to know in order to use it effectively.

Sometimes you may need to write a program to perform a task that needs to be done in a hurry. Hacking may be effective when you have a small task to do very quickly. In general, while a particular strategy may work well for one purpose, it may be quite inappropriate for another.

Think about how much time you have

We all have difficulty sometimes in completing a programming project by the deadline. One reason is that programming exercises and assignments can take longer (sometimes a lot longer) than expected. Things might go wrong. Something might not work. You might run out of ideas. Give yourself plenty of time.

It is easy to underestimate the complexity and difficulty of tasks, especially when we haven't done anything similar before. Assume everything is going to take longer than you expect, then double the time. Expect that writing and **debugging** a program will take more time than you expect. Besides simply writing your code, you will need time to test it to make sure it does what it is supposed to in the way that it should. Anticipate that things may go wrong (computers sometimes crash, disks sometimes become unreadable, printer queues become long around deadline times, access to the Internet and email may fail). If everything goes to plan you will have a pleasant surprise, and if it doesn't you won't need to panic.

It's going to take *how long*?

A rule of thumb that some professional programmers use when providing an estimate of how long a task will take is:

- Estimate how long it will really take.
- Double the estimate.
- Round up to the next unit (from hours to days).

So two hours becomes four days!

If you discover a bug, it may only take a short time to fix, but the problem could be deeper than you thought, and sometimes fixing a bug can highlight problems in other (totally unrelated) places. If this happens, do not despair – it is a common pattern.

Don't get too greedy – it is often tempting to try to make your code do more and more. Many programmers will get their code to work and to work well, but keep pushing it further. This can be a good thing, but it can keep you from completing your assignment if you focus too narrowly on minor details rather than the problem that was set.

Don't wait until the last moment to begin. The adrenalin rush when trying to finish a project really close to the deadline can be a source of inspiration, but the only way to ensure that you complete your work appropriately and on time is to get started early! Doing a great deal at the last minute usually leads to hasty coding and broken programs.

For assignments, projects and coursework, it is not simply a matter of right or wrong. Doing a solid careful job will always earn you credit even if your work is not perfect.

Think about the goals you have for your program

Some solutions are better than others . . .

- One program can be *more efficient* than another, in the sense that it runs faster and uses less memory. However, it is actually difficult to tell whether one program is *significantly* more efficient than another, so don't waste lots of time heading down the blind alley of supposed efficiency.
- Some computer programs are *easy to maintain*, allowing a programmer to adapt and change the program to altered situations, whilst other programs are extremely difficult to change successfully.

- A *robust* program will successfully handle irregularities. For example, if there is no file of the right name in the right place, or if a user interacting with the program has entered the wrong kind of information, a robust program will gracefully deal with the situation, possibly reporting a helpful error message.

There are trade-offs between these different goals. More efficient code can be more difficult to maintain. It may initially take longer to write code that is easy to maintain.

Think about yourself

What time of day and in what surroundings do you work most effectively? How do you respond to pressure? How do you respond to the lack of pressure?

Follow several different methods – a meta-strategy

It can often be quite a good idea to follow several strategies simultaneously (well, not literally at the very same moment, but 'multi-tasking'). Follow one strategy for a while and then switch to another and then back to the first or possibly on to a third.

Let's take an example. Suppose you have a programming assignment that will take you a while to complete, and that has a deadline some way into the future. There may be aspects of the programming language that you do not understand well; you may have been asked to do things that you do not yet know how to do. Nevertheless, it is important to think through the overall structure of the code you will have to produce. You might need to learn some more about the language (the way of play might be good for this), but you will also want to plan and develop a coherent overall design. It is probably a good idea to start small and then increase the functionality of code that is already working (the way of working incrementally). You will also need tests to determine if your code is working successfully. You are doing a number of things and following a number of strategies at the same time.

Another useful, but quite different, 'meta-strategy' that will help you in the long run is to develop good programming habits. Programming is like everything else. Good habits have a way of always paying off in the long term, and quite often of paying off in the short term. But just what are good programming habits?

▶ Good habits that can help you program

Keep a record

Your work can be helped if you keep a record of your thoughts and actions, and it can make your job easier. We recommend you use a logbook, in which you write down things you have tried and what the results were. It really should be a bound book (not a loose-leaf file or a spiral notebook) that holds a permanent record of what you are doing and why.

As a bare minimum, keep a record of what you are working on in this book. You should include: what you are trying to do; how you are doing things; the mistakes that you have made; and how you tried to overcome these mistakes. It gives you a place to write down on a regular basis: what still needs to be done; what gaps there are in your work; and what your ideas are on how to fill in these gaps. It is also the place for writing down ideas whenever they come to you. In this way, you have a place where all your programming thoughts are kept. If you are stuck for ideas, this is a place to visit. If you are having problems debugging a program, this is a record of what you did when you had a similar problem in the past, and when the time comes to write up a project, the log provides a crucial record of the decisions you have made and the reasons why you made them.

Don't be limited to just writing in the logbook; some people think visually, so use doodles and sketches to help you express yourself and crystallize ideas. A logbook doesn't have to be neat, it just has to be useful to your thinking and working processes.

It is also a good idea to go a bit further and include evaluation, reflection and self-assessment in your logbook. By doing this, you can gain insight into the ways you learn and the ways you are productive.

In industry, programmers, and other members of development teams, are often required to keep logbooks so that, if someone becomes unavailable (holiday, illness, move to another job), others on the team can use their logbook to continue where work was left off.

Like many good habits, this one isn't the easiest for many of us to acquire. It is really easy to just sit down at the computer and begin writing code, but this is one of those habits that really will pay off in both the short and the longer term.

Talk about programming

Talking to other people about what you are doing can start you thinking about the problem in a different way. Explaining what you are doing to your non-programmer friends and family can provide new perspectives and insights. It can also help to make programming a part of who you are. Other learners are especially good to talk things over with; and, of course, you can learn a lot by listening to what they have to say.

Read programs

Good programmers are good readers of programs, and reading lots of programs is the only way to become fluent at reading programs. You can glean ideas of how to do things from reading code. It also has other advantages: you may see **patterns** in the way that other people solve problems, and you may develop your own 'programming style'. Of course, on an even more basic level, reading the code fragments in programming textbooks is likely to help you understand what you need to do to complete the exercises and projects in that book.

Help other learners

Helping another learner can be a great way of combining talking about programming and reading programs. A word of caution is important: writing code for other people, or giving them your code to copy, is **plagiarism** and this is completely unacceptable. It is not plagiarism to give people advice and suggestions. There is nothing wrong with discussing common difficulties and problems with your assignments. Quite the contrary, it is a sound and helpful strategy. It is not plagiarism to read the code in your textbook or in online resources and learn from it and adapt what you have learnt to your situation.

Visualize

Imagining different parts of a program as being different parts of a diagram can be a great help. As the programs you write become more complex, it can be difficult to gain an overall sense of how the different parts relate to each other. Drawing diagrams can be a very useful way of gaining a sense of the interactions between the various elements of your program that need to be brought together. A **flow chart** can represent complex sequences in a step-by-step manner and an **interaction diagram** can help to see how different parts relate to each other.

Diagrams can help you when you are reading and trying to understand programs. Being able to create a diagram of what is happening often shows you have understood how the code you are reading works.

UML

Code visualization can be so helpful that programmers have developed special ways of doing it. A well-known visualization tool is **UML – the unified modelling language**.

UML is a widely accepted standard for the graphical representation of the internals of software systems – it provides a range of different ways of representing aspects of software. It is an important tool to help developers to visualize, model and document.

Several kinds of diagram are included in UML to represent important relationships – **use-case diagrams**, for example, represent how 'actors' will interact with the system.

Write code that people can read

Code is not written only for computers. People also have to read the code you write. As a student, your teachers will read the code you write for assignments, and when working on group projects other students will have to read your code. They will probably have to take your code and adapt and modify it to accomplish the objectives of the group project; you will have to do the same to theirs. If you work as a programmer, other programmers will have to read and rework your code when you are no longer around. For example, changes in business practices can lead to the need to rewrite code to accommodate new laws, business environments, and the simple passage of time. The impacts of this can be enormous, as with the case of the Millennium Bug at the turn of the century, which is discussed in Chapter 3.

For your code to be readable by others, you need to ensure that you choose sensible and understandable names. For example, suppose you want something to represent the current rate of interest. The computer doesn't care what you call it. As long as it is of the correct syntactic form the computer will handle it just fine – $x2$ or 'R' will do. But, to help people, calling it `rate_of_interest`, `rateOfInterest` or something similar is very helpful.

The readability of code also depends on the comments you put into it – they say what something is supposed to do and how it is supposed to do it. It is especially important to comment on how you have done something if what you're doing is unusual or complex.

Comments are not only for other people – they can help you too. When you return to a program some time after you first wrote it, it can be difficult to remember what something does or how it does it unless you've included descriptions in your code.

Comments

Comments are parts of programming code that are there only for people. They are specially separated from the other parts of the code as a signal to the computer to skip over them. Comments have no effect on how a program runs, but they can provide a record of what the programmer was thinking when she wrote the code.

Comments can tell you what a piece of code is supposed to do. Comments can also include information about what the various variables are intended to mean. If you comment your code well, you will be able to understand it when you return to it later, and if someone else reads your code, your comments will help them to understand it.

A word of caution; comments should not simply repeat what can easily be seen in the program code. Typically, you should document *what* your code does rather than *how* it does it.

▶ Tips to take away

- Ensure before you start that you know what the program you will be working on is supposed to do.
- There are many ways to approach programming assignments.
- You need to be aware of how *you* work best on programming tasks.
- You need to think about the specific assignment to determine which approaches are best suited to the problem. Following a few different approaches can often be helpful.
- There can be many different correct programs for any one assignment
- Giving your work to others, or taking others' work as your own is plagiarism and is not acceptable. Some people try to disguise plagiarism by changing a few variable names or similar features. Don't be one of them. Such changes are easily detected with automatic tools.
- Good programming habits include: keeping a logbook; talking about and reading about programs; giving and receiving help; visualizing what is going on; writing code that people can understand.

▶ Chapter summary

There are many ways in which you can go about programming. Different approaches are relevant to different problems. In this chapter we have explained some ways in which you can go about programming, and given you advice about how to choose the programming strategy you will need for the part of the programming task you are looking at.

Finally we discussed various techniques that you can use to keep track of the process of creating a program. These become more important to you as your programs get bigger.

8 Writing Bigger Programs

The nature of 'bigger'

Scene: the lunch table, where our intrepid trio meets every day to discuss classwork, parties, and the ins-and-outs of daily life. Today, they're discussing the assignment that they submitted yesterday.

Ralph: What an assignment! How long was your solution to problem 7?

Miguel: Wow . . . at least 300 lines.

Ralph: No kidding! Mine was 400. What about you, Ed?

Ed: [*Pauses.*] 20 lines.

[*Miguel and Ralph are silenced by this.*]

Ralph: But, that problem took me, like, 8 hours to write . . . how'd you do it in 20 lines of code?

Ed: It took me three days to write, during which time I took neither food nor water . . . I wore out two pairs of shoes as I paced my room, contemplating the deeper nature of what you call 'problem 7'. At the end of this time, the twenty lines flowed from my fingers, without error, in a hunger and sleep-induced mania. When I was done, I knew it was Good.

We can always say that one program is 'bigger' because it has more lines of code than some other program: this is obvious, simple and true. But when setting out to write programs of our own, we quickly discover that it isn't actually the length of programs that makes our lives difficult – it is *other* kinds of complexity that challenge us as programmers.

▶ What makes a program bigger?

It is very easy to think that a program that is 5000 lines long is bigger, and therefore necessarily more complex, than a program that is only 1000 lines long. Indeed, counting the number of lines (often referred to as **source lines of code**, or **SloC**) is a common metric used in the software industry for estimating the complexity of software.

It is natural for us to think about complexity this way: more lines of code means more stuff to keep track of. The previous paragraph is still fresh in your mind, but if you were to try and recall the contents of page 28 of this book, you'd have a hard time remembering exactly what it contained. Keeping track of large amounts of code is just as difficult. However, size alone is not all it takes for one program to be 'bigger' than another. In this chapter we explore what it means for one piece of code to be bigger than another, and how we can manage the complexity of these bigger programs effectively.

Large programs

It is common to hear programmers discuss how they might design for **extensibility**. This means the programmers are planning for change: they want to be able to add new features to their software in the unforeseeable future. Extending, or growing, a piece of software is only one facet of a larger problem faced by all programmers: the maintenance and upkeep of their software.

Longer programs are often harder to maintain than shorter programs; if we've just finished writing a program that is 1000 lines long and we discover a bug, it will be harder to find where it is than if the program is only 100 lines long. There are two things we can add to our code in working towards making it more maintainable: *comments* and *pictures*.

Comments

Everyone says we should comment our code. At this point, nausea is probably starting to set in because so many people have insisted that good code must be well commented. Unfortunately, there are still people who think comments aren't important, and for that reason we have to keep on saying it.

Comments can be done poorly, and they can be done well. It's hard to describe the difference between the two, but let's look at the Comment Hall of Fame. Which of the comments in Figure 8.1 are good comments with respect to maintainability, and which are useless?

If you thought that none of these comments were useful, you were right. Hall of Shame! These comments are taken from a selection of **open source projects**: they exist in real software used by real people (most likely thousands of people). The first two are pointless comments, reflecting how the

```
// Apple is stupid.
// Sun is stupider.
// Eh, that shouldn't happen.
int i; /* General counter */
```

Figure 8.1 The Comment Hall of Fame or Hall of Shame?

programmer felt about the way Java works on Sun and Apple computers. The third is the worst kind of comment: it sits at the end of a list of successive if/else statements handling various error conditions. If everything goes wrong, the code falls into the last else and . . . the only thing there is a comment – and *nothing happens*! The final comment falls into a class of 'useless comments' – it tells us something about the variable i, but it certainly doesn't tell us anything that helps us understand the role of the variable i in the larger context of the program. Compare the comments in Figure 8.1 with the comment shown in Figure 8.2. Don't worry about understanding what it means, but note that it provides information both for the programmer who wants to call the particular function being described, and for the programmer who wants to understand what the function does.

Good comments should tell a story. They orient someone who has never seen our code, informing them as to why we, the programmers, made the choices that we did. Or, perhaps more importantly, comments are there to remind us of what we were doing when we first wrote the program. It's easy to walk away from a piece of code for a few weeks or months, and then come back to it wondering, 'Why did I do that?' Good comments help jog our memory when we've been away from the code for a while.

```
/* Process the argument letter
 * and its associated value.
 * This function processes arguments from
 * the command line and from an argument
 * file associated with the -A argument.
 *
 * An argument  ofile.pgn would be passed in as:
 *      'o' and "file.pgn".
 * A zero-length string for associated_value
 * is not necessarily an error, e.g. -e
 * has an optional following filename.
 * If the associated_value is to be used
 * beyond this function, it must be copied.
 */
void process_argument(char arg_letter,
        const char *associated_value)
```

Figure 8.2 An informative comment

When commenting, there is always a balance to be struck between providing too little information (or information of poor quality) and providing too much. It is not necessary to comment every single statement of a program. Most program statements can be understood on their own without additional commentary. A good rule of thumb is to ensure that every function (method, procedure, **subroutine** – whatever the terminology happens to be in the programming language you are using at the time) has a good explanatory comment describing what that function does, what **arguments** it takes, and any result it returns. Don't worry about describing *how* the function does what it does, because that can usually be discovered by reading the code. With a good explanatory comment, little else should be required in the body of the function if it has been kept short and simple. Where there is a particularly tricky piece of code, or something you want the reader particularly to bear in mind, a short comment will usually suffice.

Pictures

Pictures are a second simple way of clarifying code for future readers. While we can't put pictures right down in the source code, we can store diagrams of the program design with the source code, perhaps in some kind of electronic format. There are many 'official' kinds of diagrams we might create: for example, in **object-oriented** languages programmers often create class diagrams using **UML, the Unified Modelling Language** (Figure 8.3). This is a graphical way of expressing how the components – called **classes** – in a program relate to each other. It might be that a program has 10 different

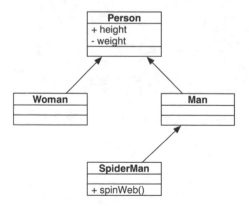

Class diagrams are a simple and useful way of expressing relationships between parts of our program in an object-oriented language.

Figure 8.3 A UML class diagram

classes, each of which are between 200 and 400 lines of code; if we printed all the source, it would be the size of a small book! However, a class diagram would easily fit on one page. Usually used as a design tool, before code is written, a class diagram provides a map of what is otherwise a large and complex landscape of code.

There is certainly much more to managing large programs than adding comments and drawing pictures; indeed, there is an apparent paradox here. Adding comments will increase the number of lines of code in our program, and adding diagrams will create more files that we need to keep track of. Both of these things make our program 'bigger'. However, they actually make it bigger in a meaningful way. These additions make our program easier to understand, both for ourselves and for others.

Tricky things

It's common for programmers to worry about how *fast* their programs will run. In fact, novices (which we mean here to be people who have spent fewer than five years as a professional programmer) will often make poor choices regarding the languages they think are useful, important, or otherwise the best choice for some project, simply because they think their choice of language will result in their program running *faster*.

In 1965, Gordon Moore made one of the most famous predictions in computing:

Moore's Law
'The pace of microchip technology change is such that the amount of data storage that a microchip can hold doubles every year.'

He revised this in 1975 to state that 'on-chip transistor density doubles roughly every eighteen months'. This was an incredible prediction, and continues to hold true today, 40 years later. The fact is that technological advances quickly make last year's computers obsolete.

This has implications for programmers because they can work as hard as they want making their programs 'go fast', but in 12 months' time they will likely be able to buy a new computer that is twice as fast as the one they have now – therefore doubling the speed of the program they've written today. This also has implications for the languages we choose to write our programs in.

Writing a program so it runs very quickly usually involves doing tricky things.[1] Often, if we write a program that is tricky, not only will other people not understand it, but when we come back to it in three weeks' time, we probably won't remember how the tricky bit worked. While our program may not have grown in terms of the numbers of lines of code, by trying to 'make it faster', we've instead made it more complex – and that's another type of 'bigger'.

Mel and Bill

I once worked for a software company that employed two programmers, Mel and Bill. Bill came in at 9 a.m. and left on time; he dressed neatly and ate healthy lunches he brought with him. His code started at A, went to B, and everything in between was commented. At the weekends he went camping. Mel was different. He came in early (or late), got stuck into problems and sometimes didn't go home at all; he ate junk food at irregular times, and he *loved* to code. He didn't just want to write code that worked, he wanted to make it efficient and fast and pretty and clever.

One weekend I was called out to a client whose software wasn't working. I can't remember why, but it was critical that the system ran before their office opened on Monday morning. And as I sat there, in the dark, with a terrible deadline in front of me, my most desperate wish was that it'd been Bill who'd written this program, instead of tricky Mel who expected you to follow his fireworks and applaud how clever he'd been.

While making programs go fast is typically not important to programmers just starting out, it can be surprising to learn that 'teaching' languages are often also fast languages. The lesson here, for keeping the complexity and size of a program down, is to remember that programming languages are just tools. Each different programming language provides a different way of expressing ideas in the form of code. When we become comfortable programming in one language over another, we can write programs more quickly, at which point we can ask the obvious question: is it more important that our program runs just that little bit faster, or is it more important that we get the job done quickly in a language we know and understand?

One program, many computers

Lots of people use Microsoft's Windows **operating systems**; so many, in fact, that it's easy to think that making sure our programs run on a Windows computer is the only thing that matters. However, some people use Apple computers, and some people use **platforms** like Linux. There are many programs that are critical to the functioning of the Internet (web servers, email handlers) that are written so they can be run on *any* of these operating systems. We refer to a program that can run on more than one operating system as being **portable** across those different operating systems.

Writing programs that can run on more than one operating system can be hard. Even in languages like Java, where programs are supposed to execute the exact same way on a Windows computer as they do on a Mac, there are problems. For example, simple (but obvious) differences often appear in interfaces, because buttons in the graphical interface are often different sizes on the two platforms. Getting things to work the same way on multiple operating systems, regardless of whether our program is running on a brand-new desktop computer or an old Palm Pilot, is very difficult.

Making our software portable may not mean increasing the number of lines of code, but it certainly makes things conceptually 'bigger'. Writing portable code often means that we have to separate the program out into parts that we know will work everywhere, and parts that we know will need to be changed when running on one platform or another. This way, we know where to look when things that worked just fine on our Macintosh start going wrong on a friend's computer running Windows.

One program, many versions

There are no magic tricks to handle programs that grow progressively larger. However, a good thing is to use some kind of **version control** or **code management system**. These are typically special pieces of software that help by automatically storing copies of each stage of our program as it evolves and changes. More importantly, this software allows us to go back a version, or 'undo' many changes at once. Ask any professional programmer and you'll find they use some kind of version control.

While it is true that having multiple versions of our program will add to the complexity of our software, this notion of 'bigger' is managed in part by the revision control system. By keeping track of the changes we make, we give ourselves the ability to 'undo', as well as a clear history that makes it easier to look back at what we've done: it's all part of managing how our program grows 'bigger'.

The computer that never crashes

There's a joke about the president of a large software company who compares his operating system to your average car. The joke is that if cars were made like computers, they would have a number of undesirable character-istics, including:

> **If cars were like computers . . .**
> For no reason whatsoever, your car would crash twice a day.
>   Occasionally, a manoeuvre (such as a left turn) would
> cause your car to shut down and refuse to restart. To fix it,
> you would have to reinstall the engine.
>   The airbag system would ask, 'Are you sure?' before
> deploying.

The joke goes on and on, but the point is clear: we accept the fact that computers crash. However, product recalls on cars because of critical failures *in their software* are less funny. While we think of cars as being mechanical, they are rapidly incorporating computers everywhere. For example, a small computer controls the anti-lock brake system in most cars. More than once, huge recalls of hundreds of thousands of vehicles have taken place because of bad software controlling the anti-lock brake systems of these cars; when the software breaks, the brakes don't work.

To put a scale on this sort of issue, Mozilla is an open-source web browser that is freely available for Windows, the Mac and Linux, and has around one million lines of code.[2] It is a remarkably stable piece of software. Compare this to the amount of software found in modern cars: there are easily 10,000,000 (ten million) or more lines of code in a car today, scattered throughout as many as 100 microprocessors.[3] That is a lot of code.

Now, despite Mozilla being a fine web browser, it still crashes. There are hundreds of people working on Mozilla, and thousands of people reporting bugs in the software so they can be fixed. If Mozilla has bugs, and it's only one million lines of code, how many bugs are there in the software in your car? And how many bugs do there need to be in the anti-lock brake system before people start to die? Perhaps you'll walk to the shops next time instead of driving, no?

Unfortunately, there are no good ways to guarantee we've written reliable software, but one thing to do is to get into the habit of *testing*. It is very good practice to program in a 'test first' fashion: that is, before you write the code, write the test that will give you confidence it's working correctly. You have to do this on fairly small pieces of code: it's hard to write a test for a whole system. This is often called **unit testing**. We will have more to say about testing in later chapters.

Of course, if we write a unit test for each piece of code then our program will end up being a lot 'bigger' than before. It will probably also have taken us a lot longer to write. But when we are done, we will have more confidence in the quality of our programs, and they will have a better chance of working the way we intend them to.

Usability

People will sometimes talk about software being 'incredibly usable,' or 'intuitive'. There is a saying: 'No software *is intuitive*'. This means that no matter how simple you think your program is to use, someone sitting down at a computer for the first time will probably have no idea how your program works. They may be able to figure it out, if they think about it and try and think the same way you do – but they won't magically 'get it' because your software is 'obvious'.

Creating usable software involves a lot of work – it isn't just a matter of throwing some buttons and text fields together. In fact, usable programs don't typically happen by working all by ourselves: if we want a program that is usable by many different people, we need to involve many different people in the process of creating our software.

Step one in creating usable software is to talk to lots of people about what your software is going to do. We often start with friends of ours who we know write programs. However, be warned: these are not normal people! Anyone who can write their own computer programs is not a typical user – unless, of course, you're designing your software to be used by programmers.

Step two: make **prototypes**. It's hard for people to imagine what a user interface will look like, but they can easily work with pictures and diagrams in front of them. These diagrams don't have to be fancy: sit down with some scissors, crayons and some glue to 'mock up' or prototype an interface. Armed with this mock-up, we can bug all our friends (programmers and non-programmers alike) and start discussing how our software will work, and whether it makes sense to them. These simple prototypes are often called **low-fidelity prototypes**; **high-fidelity prototypes** look like the final product, while low fidelity prototypes are often lacking detail and look as if our three-year-old brother did the artwork. Once our software has been discussed with a number of people, and it seems as though it's on the road to being easy to use, we might take the next step in usability: how do we make our software so anyone can use it, including (for example) someone who is blind?

Spending time and effort on the user interface will make our program 'bigger' While it won't change the functionality of your code, it should mean that more people will be able to use it.

▶ Managing the software process

Complexity comes in many shapes and sizes. Writing *bigger* programs could mean that your software:

- has more lines of code?
- has more people who will use the resulting program?

- has more programmers who will use the code in their own programs?
- will be used in finance- or life-critical applications?
- will need to be error-free?
- will be expected to run very, very fast?
- will be expected to run on any operating system currently produced?
- will be written by a team of 20 people? 200 people? 2000 people?
- will need to run reliably for the next 2 years? 2 decades? 2 centuries?
- will need to be easy to update and maintain?
- will operate on very complex data? Constantly changing data?
- will need a very simple, universal user interface that anyone can use – including people who cannot read, cannot hear, or have limited motor control?

All of these things (and more) add to the complexity of a piece of software. Obviously, someone has learned how to deal with all this complexity, as there are billions of lines of computer code running inside toasters, space shuttles, racing cars, cash machines and video games all over the planet.

Part of managing this complexity is simply being aware of what makes software complex; another way is to build software to accommodate that complexity. As programs get larger, it becomes important to manage the development process. This can be true for individual programmers but is especially important when working as part of a team.

Many techniques have been devised to support the process of writing bigger programs. We'll look at three techniques: the **Personal Software Process**, the **Waterfall Model** of software development and **Extreme Programming**.

The Personal Software Process (PSP)

As developing programmers we should learn to become aware of what we can code, what we do quickly and well, what we need to complete the job, and how long it will take us. The difficulty in answering these questions is coming up with real numbers in answer to each question. How quick is quickly? How many lines of code can we write in an hour? A day? A week? Watts Humphreys developed a method to help individuals track and understand their own work habits and personal productivity with the Personal Software Process.

> The Personal Software Process helps individual engineers to improve their performance by bringing discipline to the way they develop software.[4]

It is tempting to think that when we just work on our own, we don't need any rules or discipline. Victor Putz writes about why this simply isn't the case:

> Some time ago, I developed some applications for MS-DOS, then the dominant operating system for small home computers. The applications (a graphics and sound framework intended for simple animation and multi-media, and a small game using the libraries) were received well enough for an amateur effort, and even brought in a little cash and the thrill of seeing my game on the 'cheapware' racks at the local software store. Near this time, Windows '95 had just been released, and both my publishers and myself felt that this 'new' operating system might well be a dominant player in the games market (here in late 1999, with the dominance of Windows as a personal computer OS fairly well established, this was apparently a wise prediction!). As a result, we decided that a quick 3–4 month rewrite was in order.
>
> It is now nearing 2000, almost four years after the original planned rewrite – which still is not complete. While many other things have impacted this – several moves, the decision of the publishers to stop producing games, many additional time commitments – the fundamental problem has been a lack of personal engineering practices.
>
> Even in one of the simplest of software development environments – a single developer on a single project – I could not predict with any degree of reliability the size of a development task, or the cost in time and resources to complete it; I had little comprehension of basic **software engineering** processes; my environment was very much what Steve McConnell refers to as 'code-and-fix development'.
>
> (From 'The Personal Software Process: an Independent Study')[5]

The discipline that PSP requires isn't about doing things differently: it's still about a person programming software. The discipline is in writing down – sometimes in a great deal of detail – everything about *how* and *when* we write programs. By investing this time into a documentation process, we can begin to make accurate predictions about how long a program will take us to write as well as what parts of the process we are likely to spend the most time on. There is the additional benefit that we can identify the tedious and routine parts of programming and structure them so they are easier to get done.

Getting started using a methodology like PSP takes commitment. One way we might recommend getting into PSP is to try using it on one or more coursework assignments. When you get them back, you can begin asking simple but useful questions: Did I get better grades when I spent more time designing my solution in advance? Did I spend more or less time coding on projects where I did well? How much time did I spend coding when I did poorly?

While PSP is a wonderful model for the lone programmer, bigger programs are often written by many people. When programming, we have found there are differences between working as an individual and working as part of a team. There are several ways people have addressed the challenge of programming as a team, and we'll look at two very different models used for managing this complexity. First we'll look at a long-established software development method – the Waterfall Model – which involves a good deal of 'planning ahead'. Then, we'll take a look at Extreme Programming (XP), which is a more **agile**, or flexible, method that involves less planning ahead and more 'just-in-time', iterative planning.

The Waterfall Model of software development

The Waterfall Model of software development was one of the very early ways of managing software production. It was 'borrowed' from other disciplines and practices, such as industrial product design and, closer to home, hardware design. It provides a simple way of characterizing the process of designing and implementing a piece of software. It separates the software production process into phases, and development proceeds linearly through the phases of **requirements** analysis, design, **implementation**, testing (validation), **integration** and maintenance (Figure 8.4).

The Waterfall Model has been much criticized because, while it might be good for producing hardware, it doesn't reflect the practical manner in which

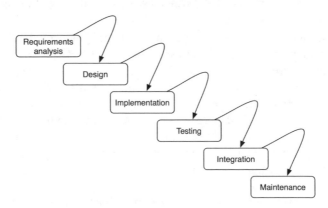

Figure 8.4 The Waterfall Model

software is built. Rarely is *all* the analysis carried out before design work is begun, nor is all the design done before implementation, and so on. To address these weaknesses, Barry Boehm characterized a **spiral model** of software development that supposes incremental development, using the Waterfall Model for each step, with the aim of managing risk. In the spiral model, developers define and implement features in order of decreasing priority.

Extreme Programming (XP)

The most recent ideas regarding how teams create software productively and efficiently are a family of techniques called **agile methods**. These methods attempt to take into account the fact that needs and requirements will probably change over the life of a project. The most well-known example is Extreme Programming, or XP. If you were to compare Waterfall and XP you'd say the former was like a train, fixed in its track and unwavering in its course, while the latter was like a motorbike, dodging through the traffic, making the most of every gap and opportunity. Which will suit you best and get you where you need to go depends on the nature of your journey.

XP starts with stories from users about what they want from the software. These stories are turned into requirements, and they become part of the plan for the next release (Figure 8.5). To keep things flexible, a 'requirement' for a release never requires less than one week of work or more than three weeks of work; clearly, as we noted when talking about PSP, programmers need to know how much work they can do in that amount of time! Releases are working versions of the software, and in XP there are supposed to be many small releases, so the user can interact with their software as it evolves.

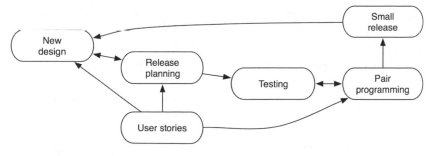

Figure 8.5 Extreme Programming

As this happens, users may realize how the software could better meet their needs, and things evolve and change.

One way XP programmers deal with this ever-shifting set of needs and requirements as they develop code for customers is to practise **pair programming**. Pair programming means that no one ever writes code by themselves: two people sit side by side, watching each other for mistakes, or perhaps helping to answer questions that come up during development. This results in higher-quality code, and means that no programmer has 'just their bit' of the system.

Another way to produce high-quality, reliable code in changing conditions is to make extensive use of unit testing. XP is strongly test driven – before any piece of code is written in an XP project, the code that tests it is constructed. In this way, a piece of code written a day, week or month ago is constantly being tested and retested as new software is being written and old software is being modified. If anything changes that 'breaks' one or more of the tests, all work stops until the code is fixed, and all the tests pass again. The unit tests provide a safety net to protect the programmers from themselves.

Finally, Extreme Programming calls for programmers to write no more code than is necessary. They attempt to keep things simple by being focused and specific. On the Extreme Programming web site,[6] Don Wells nicely describes this notion of simplicity:

> A simple design always takes less time to finish than a complex one. So always do the simplest thing that could possibly work. If you find something that is complex replace it with something simple. It's always faster and cheaper to replace complex code now, before you waste a lot more time on it. Keep things as simple as possible as long as possible by never adding functionality before it is scheduled. Beware though; keeping a design simple is hard work

Extreme Programming is a much more flexible model than the Waterfall Model, and more complex than we have presented here. Critics of this approach believe that XP is only appropriate for small projects with a short development time; also, they think that this kind of flexible working style better suits experienced, or expert, programmers than it does novices. That said, there are programming courses at universities all over the world that encourage their students to use pair programming, as it is a more social, friendly and supportive way of learning to program. If you feel that pair programming could work for you, be sure to check that your course allows you to work in this way because in some courses it is essential to be able to determine an individual's contribution to coursework.

▶ Chapter summary

Extreme Programming, the Waterfall Model and PSP are all just different ways of managing complexity. By providing organization for the way we go about programming, these approaches help us through the hardest bits of large projects so we can focus on things that are more important. All of this comes down to a rather simple fact that we think is both reassuring and frightening at the same time: writing bigger programs is something anyone can do. That's the reassuring bit. For some of us the frightening bit is that writing bigger programs requires us to be more methodical and careful than we are in our everyday lives. However, if we *are* diligent and methodical, we can write complex software that runs well – and that's about as good as it gets for a programmer!

If you're interested in different programming languages, and how fast the programs written in those languages are, you can check out 'The Great Computer Language Shootout' online.[7] This Internet project compares programs that do similar things written in many different languages, and compares how fast they are, as well as how many lines of code it takes to do those things.

The Waterfall Model was first presented to software engineers in August 1970 at WESCON (West Coast Electronics Show and Convention). In his paper 'Managing Development of Large Scale Software Systems', Winston Royce suggested that implementing large software systems requires two phases: planning and programming. He went much further than this in his paper, however, and it is likely that many people who think that old-fashioned models (like Waterfall) are obsolete or broken have (a) probably never read his original paper, or (b) have learned it wrong.

Another useful reference is B. W. Boehm, 'A Spiral Model of Software Development and Enhancement', *IEEE Computer*, 21 (5), 61–72.

9 Becoming a Detective

By now you've probably written several programs. In creating your programs you have made something original. It probably took a lot of time and mental effort and you should feel pleased with what you have achieved. Programming is a creative activity; that is one of the things that makes it attractive to programmers. People get satisfaction from writing a program.

If you have written several programs you will have become familiar with the task of compilation – removing syntax errors. You will also have realized that programs that compile successfully do not always run without error or produce the required results.

We've distinguished between two main types of programming mistakes: syntax errors, that is, errors in the grammar or structure of the program; and semantic errors – errors in the logic or meaning of the program. We looked in some detail at how to deal with syntax errors in an earlier chapter. Here we will look at semantic or logical errors.

Your error is detected at runtime

Let's take an example where we are asked to write a program that will find the average mark for the students in a class test. The program must work for any number of students. The word 'average' can be used to describe several different calculations. What we are calculating here is known as the *mean* and an algorithm for calculating it is:

- calculate the total of all the marks;
- count the number of students in the class;
- divide the total by the number of students.

The algorithm is correct, but suppose that we make a mistake when coding it: we do not calculate the number of students correctly so that it gets left at zero. Then when we come to divide by the number of students we are actually dividing by zero. Although our design is OK, our program is not.

Because there is no meaningful answer to an attempt to divide by zero, the computer will not continue after such an attempt in a program. Here's the kind of error message we might get:

```
java.lang.ArithmeticException: / by zero
        at CalculateAverage.main(CalculateAverage.java:6)
```

This gives us information about the nature of the error and also the location where it is to be discovered. An `Exception` is a form of error. `'/byzero'` is a description of the error: divide by zero. `CalculateAverage` is the name of the program, and the error was found on line 6 of the source code of the source file.

However, knowing *what* went wrong and *where* it was discovered might still not be enough to allow us to correct the error immediately. We now have to make use of those clues to find out *why* it is dividing by zero when this is not what we intended. We'll follow up on this later in the chapter.

Your error remains undetected at runtime

If the program runs without error and produces likely-looking output, how can we find out if it is correct or not? Sometimes it is obvious. Maybe the program is designed to find out how many people passed an exam but it gives a negative result, say -5. We know this cannot be correct.

However, often it is not obvious that the results are incorrect. For example, I am the examiner for a course where several hundred students are enrolled. I programmed a **spreadsheet** to show how many of them obtained a 'distinction' grade by getting 70 per cent or more in the exam. The first time I used the spreadsheet I got a result of 20 students. This was a likely-looking answer, but it turned out not to be correct. The problem was that I had counted only those whose result was more than 70 per cent. I had made a logical programming error and left out those who obtained exactly 70 per cent. So in this and similar ways, we can easily get plausible but wrong results from a program.

Therefore part of the program development process involves testing a program to check that it works correctly under different circumstances. If testing shows that the results are inaccurate then we have some detective work to do in finding and eliminating the errors. There will be more on this in the section 'Looking for the unexpected' later in this chapter.

▶ Using what we've got

first things first – make sure you understand any error message. Messages are often short and use technical vocabulary. Although that can be a stumbling block for beginners, as you learn more about the subject it becomes progressively easier to understand them. In the example above, the word `Exception` is a technical term that is used to describe errors or unexpected situations occurring in a program. As soon as you have seen the word once and understood it, you will be in a good position to understand it when it crops up in other messages. If you think you might not remember a new word and what it means, you can use your logbook to record it.

Learning new words

If you come across new words in error messages then you will need to investigate their meaning. It is important to decode messages because of the valuable information they contain. Don't be tempted to ignore a message just because its meaning is obscure at first reading. You might ask someone for help at this point. Other computer users are sympathetic to the problems of learning something new in the subject and will generally be very happy to help you. The textbook or reference manual for the language may also be helpful. It must be admitted, though, that some books are reluctant to describe specific messages. You might also look up unfamiliar words in a computing **glossary**. This will give you the specialized meanings of words as used in computing. Dictionaries are not usually as useful because they give the meanings of words in general use. If they include specialized meanings at all, these may not be up to date.

Error messages will generally give you more than just a description of the error. You may get details of the place where the error was detected. In many cases this is where the mistake was made and this may be enough information for you. Looking again at your program and figuring out what it is doing, you will find your own mistake. If it's a simple slip in the coding then correcting it can also be simple. You amend the code to make it actually do what you always intended that it would, and then rerun the test to confirm that you were right.

But sometimes the mistake was made in a part of the program that is a long way from the place where the error shows up. This is known as the **cause–effect chasm**. These sort of error manifestations can make debugging difficult. The techniques described later in the chapter will help you in these difficult cases – and you'll feel especially pleased when you do isolate the problem.

▶ Tracing the action

Almost all techniques that we use to debug programs involve **tracing** the action of the code. We need to work out, statement by statement, what the program is doing and which statements are being executed. There are different ways we can do this, from simple hand tracing to using a sophisticated debugging tool, but all of the approaches are geared to showing us exactly what is happening at each step. When a program is running we cannot normally see which statements are being executed nor the values of data stored in the variables. But often we need more information than is visible. Maybe the error message is not detailed enough. Maybe there is no error message. When this happens we need to dig around and search for information. We must actively probe the program to make it reveal what is going on.

Hand tracing

Not tracing *of* a hand but tracing the program execution *by* hand! That is, we work through the program statements one by one and note the **state** of the program at each step. You will need to write things down as you go along. It does not work if you try to remember everything in your head. Let's look again at calculating the average mark (figure 9.1).

	total	count	i	mark	mean	Comments
Public Sub CalculateAverage()						Start of the subroutine
total = 0	~~0~~					
count = 0		0				
For i = 1 to 3 Step 1			~~1~~ ~~2~~ 3			Loop three times
mark = InputBox("Next mark")				~~5~~ ~~1~~ 3		getting marks from user
total = total + mark	~~5~~ ~~6~~ 9					and adding into total
Next i						End of loop body
mean = total / count						Calculate the mean
End Sub						End of the subroutine

Figure 9.1 Tracing a subroutine

To do the hand tracing, start by printing out the source code. Alongside the program statements make columns for the variables that are used in this section of code. Read each statement in turn and update the value in any variable that changes. As a variable is set to a new value, strike out the previous value in the column. This will make clear to you exactly what the state of the program is at each point. (Note: by the state of the program, we mean the **set** of all its variables' values taken together. So when the statement Next i is reached for the first time, the state of the program is that count has the value 0, i is 1, mark is 5 and so is total.) If you do this carefully enough you will find the point at which the error comes in. Of course, this assumes that you know what the program is *supposed* to be doing.

You may feel that this approach, using pencil and paper, is cumbersome and rather old-fashioned. But it is a very effective and often a quick way of getting at the root of the problem. Many experienced programmers will try this first before doing more elaborate things. However, if the program is very long and complicated, it may not be feasible or necessary to treat the whole program in this way. It may be that you can look at just part of the program, working from the point where the error is detected, and solve the problem that way. But if not then there are other things that can be tried.

How printing can help

Another technique is to alter the program so that it prints out more information. We print not just the final results that we are looking for, but also intermediate values used in the program. We can also print messages to show which statements are being executed – the flow of control. The printing is only needed during the debugging phase. Once we are convinced that the program is working we can remove the extra statements.

Let's look again at the example that calculates the average mark over several students. Because we are having problems calculating the average, we should add in extra statements to print out the value of the total and the value of the count just before the calculation of the average takes place. This will show us that (as we probably suspected from the error message) the count has a value of zero. We need to choose what to print carefully so that this extra output is easy to understand. So it would be useful to print the name of the variable as well as its value. Then if we are monitoring several variables at a time, we can easily connect the values printed with the variables.

```
Debug message: total = 10
Debug message: count = 0
```

Next we need to find out why the value is zero at the point we are using it. Did we fail to count properly? Or did we count accurately and the reset the value to zero before using it? We can add in more print statements to clarify action of the program further.

It is important to choose carefully the points where the extra printing is done. If you have an error message, this is likely to give you an idea of which part of the program was being executed when the error was detected. You will then suspect that the error has been made near that place, although sometimes it can have been made much earlier.

Choosing to print from a point just before the location of the suspected error is useful. Start with statements just there and print out the values of variables that are being used at that point. Study the output. If you're still stuck then add more statements at other points. These could be where you feel sure that you know what the values ought to be. Check that what is actually in the variables is what you think ought to be there.

You might also be adding print statements just to prove that one part of the program is being executed. For example, an **if-statement** generally has two clauses, only one of which is executed on a particular run of your program. You may think you know which one is being used but adding print statements – delivering suitable messages – will prove it to you. Make it clear that any message is simply for debugging, and clarify where it is coming from.

```
Debug message: entered the routine findMaximum
```

Adding these extra print statements and running the program while doing the hand tracing can be very effective. You are working out by hand what you think the program is doing and then confirming your ideas by getting the program to print extra information. You may feel puzzled and surprised if the values you get are different from what you expect. But from a debugging point of view, this is good! It means that you may be close to finding the source of the program error.

If you are dealing with a long program you may find that you are generating a large amount of output. This may not matter, but if it is becoming confusing then you can always remove some of print statements. Decide which ones are giving the most useful information at this stage and remove the others. (It is best not to delete them from the program but to turn them into comments; then you can easily get them back if you need them. The way that comments work is different in the different languages but in many cases you can add some characters at the beginning of a line which will cause the rest of the line to be treated as a comment. See also the section on 'Commenting out' below).

Using a debugger

Some of the interactive development environments (IDEs) include a tool to assist with debugging: a **debugger**. Such a tool will make it easy to see the values in variables and also to follow the flow of execution of the program. This is done by displaying the source code together with additional information.

Breakpoints

In order to inspect the program state just before the error is generated, the program needs to be halted. Debuggers allow you to control the place where the program will stop. You can choose a particular line in the source code and set this as a **breakpoint**. Then if the program is run, it will continue normally until it reaches the breakpoint. There it will stop and the debugger will display the values in any variables active at that point. When using **VBA** (**Visual Basic for Applications**), a breakpoint can be set by clicking in the margin at the left of the code. The breakpoint is highlighted (figure 9.2).

Inspecting the state

Once stopped, values in the variables can easily be inspected. Often this is done in a separate window. However, in VBA the values are displayed whenever the cursor hovers over the variable name in the source code.

Stepping into the code

The programmer can follow the flow of execution by stepping through the code line by line at a rate determined by key presses or mouse clicks. As

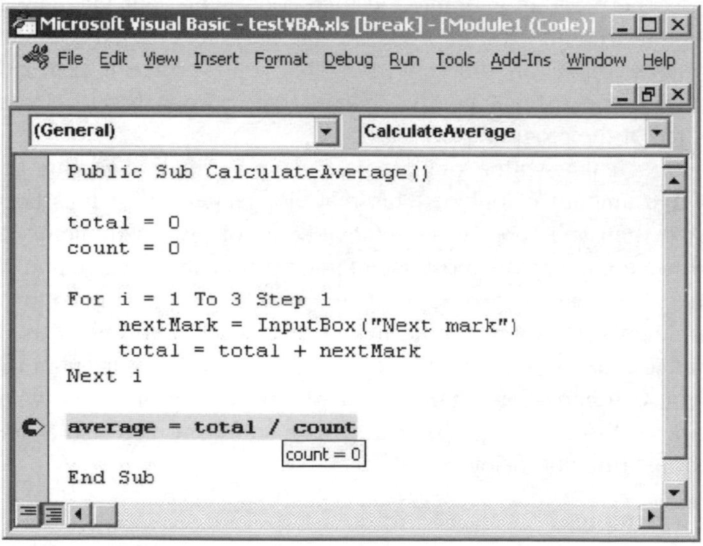

Figure 9.2 Visual Basic code showing a problem in the code

each line is executed, changes in the state of the program are displayed. This can be especially useful after a breakpoint. The program runs to the breakpoint and then its execution is inspected in detail.

These and other features can make a debugger an attractive tool for programmers. They can help beginners but are not always taught on introductory courses. You need to learn about the debugger itself and how to use it effectively. Some debuggers have very many features, making the interface complex. Many programming teachers find that this is an extra burden for the students and so they teach debugging through hand tracing and use of print statements instead.

▶ Keeping it simple

Small problems are easier to solve than large ones. Short programs are generally easier to debug than long ones. When starting to program it is natural to think that you must write code for the whole program and then make it work. This is not always the best strategy.

Programs can be easier to handle if you write just small amounts of code and make them work, adding more once the first parts are working correctly. This can mean adding as little as a line of code at a time, compiling and running the program after each addition. As you become more knowledgeable and practised you will be able to add small sections at a time. You will find that most often the errors occur in the code you have just added; working in this way they are easy to find and correct.

However, sometimes you are in the situation where you have to debug a large and complex program; for example, if you have to take over a program written by someone else. It can help here if you are able to focus your attention on just parts of the program. It is not usually a good idea to remove unwanted parts permanently but it can be helpful to turn them into comments so that they can be recovered easily once the problem has been solved.

Commenting out

If you are having trouble locating an error, then your best strategy may be to look at the code in small sections, even as small as a line at a time. There is a technique for doing this without wasting the effort you have already put into writing the program. What can be done is to remove unwanted parts temporarily and get them back when needed. This is done by taking advantage of the *comment* facility.

Usually comments are included to document what the program is doing. It is text for humans who read your program. But when a program is compiled, the comment lines are ignored. So we can get the effect of removing program statements by pretending that they are comments.

Most programming languages support *single-line comments* and *multi-line comments*, which are entered in different ways. For single-line comments, one or more special characters at the start of a line will indicate that the rest of the line is a comment. So you can turn one line of code in your program into comments by adding comment characters to the front of the line. A block of several lines can be treated as a single comment by surrounding the block with special opening and closing comment symbols. For example, in several languages multi-line comments open with the character pair `'/*'` and close with `'*/'`. Whole blocks of code can be turned into comments in this fashion.

To make use of this technique, identify the first line that is generating an error message. Remove all lines after that one by turning them into comments. When you have solved that error, adjust the position of the comment characters so that one or more statements are added back into the program. Repeat this as many times as you need in order to make the whole program work.

▶ Getting unstuck

It can happen that you are still stuck even after trying the techniques described above. It is tempting at these times to make experimental changes to the program in the hope that the problem will go away. This is not a good idea. Really, it isn't. Problems always need to be diagnosed by following the logic of the program. The good news is that there are still lots of things you can do when you're stuck, and they are all more productive than guessing at the problem.

Take a rest and talk to the dog

Persistence is a positive trait in computing – it's good to stick at a problem. However, there does come a time when you feel that you are going over and over the same ground and so then it is better to stop. There is good reason for the advice, 'Sleep on it!' Going away from a problem, physically and mentally, can be very helpful. Sometimes you get inspiration while doing something completely different, or when you wake up in the morning after a long sleep.

I was once talking to a student as she described how she struggled through her first programming course. One particular day the group had been asked to write a program to produce a fibonacci sequence. She pondered and puzzled, but couldn't work it out. Later that day, as she was cooking supper, she suddenly 'saw' the solution. 'I just knew what I had to do,' she said, 'And at that point I burnt 18 fish fingers.'

Another useful tip is to explain the problem to someone else. This does not have to be a programmer. The very act of describing the problem in detail can make you realize your own mistake. A student of mine found that he solved one tricky problem by explaining the program to his dog: as he was talking out loud he realized the source of the problem.

Use your colleagues

More formal ways of talking through a problem are the **code walkthroughs** used by professionals. The way these work is that you 'walk' through your code in detail in front of a group of colleagues, or one of your colleagues reads your code and describes what it does. That avoids the natural tendency we all have to believe that our programs are correct even when we can see that there's an error. It takes skill to read your own program accurately, but doing this in front of other people lets them challenge you whenever you're not clear. We are inclined to read what we feel *ought* to be on the page, and not what is actually there. For instance, if we should be using a 'less than' sign '<' it is easy to type a 'greater than' '>' instead. Then when we come to read our program we 'see' the correct sign and not our mistake. Your colleagues are not as close to the code as you are and so will not be as easily misled.

Professionals use code walkthroughs because they work. But they are time-consuming and costly. It's a bit like what happens when I lose my keys. first, I don't believe it, and flap around. Then, I look in all the likely places. Then I look in all the places I had them yesterday. If I still haven't found them, I crank up the big guns and, preferably with someone else by my side, start at the door and systematically walk through the house looking in every possible place (however likely or unlikely) until I find the keys. It's a time-consuming and costly process, but it works.

Ask the experts

There are generally people around who know more than you do about a particular subject, even when you're an expert in some things yourself. If you are on a course then your teacher or class supervisor can be consulted. If you are in a large institution, such as a university, then you may find that there is a helpdesk service. Other students may also be very knowledgeable and willing to help.

When you are in a work situation, you need to be aware that people's time is precious. So you must do all you can for yourself before turning to others. Be really clear about what you have done to try and solve the problem. If you have been simplifying the program, perhaps by commenting out sections, then take along the simplest version that still demonstrates the error. This will make it easier for someone else to understand the problem and help you. Thus they will be happy to help you again next time you need them.

▶ Looking for the unexpected

When your program is free of syntax errors and runs to completion, it is tempting to believe that it works. But do not put confidence in it until you have tested it carefully.

What is testing?

Testing involves running the program with specially chosen sets of data to check that no errors can be found. Different sets of data are likely to cause the program to execute different sets of instructions. For example, consider a program that calculates how much tax you should be paying. If your income is below a certain level then you pay no tax at all. But if your income is very high, then you pay some tax at the standard rate and some at a higher rate. The program will execute different instructions depending on the level of your income. So you need to construct at least three sets of data, one for low incomes, one for medium incomes and another for high incomes. You need three test cases that test the three different *classes of test*.

There is a skill in knowing how many test cases are needed, and in choosing suitable data for each one. You will need to learn how to test effectively, in addition to learning how to program.

It is essential that the tester (the person carrying out the tests) knows what results are expected. How can the tester know what the results should be before the program has processed the data? Well, the tester needs to calculate the results by some other method first. This might be done by using pencil and paper, or a calculator. The point is that the results are calculated both with and without using the program, and the two sets of results are compared.

Testing should first verify that expected results are generated from valid input data. What we mean by 'valid data' is data that the program has been designed to handle. For instance, maybe the program is designed to handle exam results that are whole numbers in the range 0 to 100. Test first that it can do this accurately. Later you may want to see that the program gives appropriate messages if invalid data, such as negative values, are supplied.

It is rare that one **test case** is sufficient to cover a whole test class. Normally several sets will be needed to test for different circumstances. For example, candidates in an exam will often get results that are spread through the possible range but occasionally all candidates will fail, or all will get full marks. Data sets need to be prepared to test that the program can handle these and other cases.

How to choose test data

For many programs we cannot try out all the values and combinations of values that the program is required to deal with. We need to check using values that are typical of sets of values. So, when checking my spreadsheet that counts the number of distinctions (see above), I need to test it using a variety of values within the range I am looking for. I might have included one mark of 70 and one or two marks above 70, and one or two marks below 70. As long as I know what output to expect, this would be a useful test of the program.

One point to understand straight away is that running the program with a sample set of the real data it has to process may not be the best way of spotting errors. It can be better to use specially designed test cases, with small sets of data chosen to include typical and also unusual circumstances.

It is also important to check for **boundary conditions**, as programs are vulnerable to errors there. In the spreadsheet example, the error cropped up because the value 70 per cent was excluded from the count. I should have tested that the program worked correctly for values inside the range 70–100 as well as at its boundaries, 70 itself and 100. I should also have checked that the program gave a sensible result if no candidates were in that range, and if they all were.

Boundary conditions

It is not generally feasible to test all possible combinations of all the values that a program needs to handle. So we pick a small number of the values within a range, where we expect that all values in the range will be treated in the same way. So if we are processing data in the range 10,000 to 99,999, we would run tests for some values in that range but not all of them. By testing a small number of values we can reasonably expect that the remainder will also be processed accurately.

However, the values at the ends of the range – the boundaries – are special. It is important that the program reliably either includes them or excludes them, depending on the program specification: it is here that things can easily go wrong. They must be included in tests. In our example this means explicitly using the value 10,000 and also 99,999.

There are other special cases too, such as when there is no data, or when the maximum limit is reached. The program must not give an error if no candidates were entered for an exam, or if a file to be read is empty.

Black box and white box testing

These terms refer to contrasting approaches to testing. In **black box** (or **functional**) **testing**, the tests are designed to verify that the program produces the correct output, according to its specification. The tester knows what the program is supposed to do but does not know how it does it. The tester treats the program as a 'black box' in that they cannot look at the source code, but they know what it's meant to take in and they know what it's meant to give out. The tester may well not be the programmer.

In **white box** (or **structural**) **testing**, the tests are designed to show that all the code is used, and that the program execution follows the correct paths through the code. The tester reads the program source code to verify that it is structured to give correct results. With white box testing, a minimum set of tests should ensure that every statement in the program is executed at least once. For complete testing, both black box and white box testing need to be done.

Warning: testing does not prove your program works. The purpose of testing is to show up any errors and not to prove accuracy. When tests run cleanly we can say, 'No known bugs', but not that the program is bug-free. This limitation on the role of testing ought to make us ponder. If testing cannot prove that a program works, how *can* we be sure that it does? This is a most important matter when we consider that programs are used in safety-critical situations such as the auto pilot systems in aircraft.

▶ Guarding against errors

Some of the research work in computer science is concerned with the writing of more reliable and robust programs. Better design and more time in the design phase can help. Modern computing languages can also help, and coding with an awareness of the problem can mean that errors are detected early and close to their source.

Guarding against bugs

Some programmers favour adding extra code into their programs to guard against errors. This may seem a strange idea if you are a beginner and struggling to put together even small amounts of code that work. However, it can be remarkably effective and make the debugging process quicker if it is done with an understanding of where the errors are likely to occur.

Anticipating invalid data

Suppose that a program has been written to process exam results that are marks in the range 0 to 100. What will happen within the program if a value over 100 or below zero is supplied? Programs are vulnerable if they are used in a way that does not match their design specification. So a programmer may decide not to assume that all values given are within the required range but to check each one. Using this approach, if invalid data is found it can be reported.

This type of problem occurs not only with data supplied from outside the program. Sometimes, a logical error elsewhere in a program will cause internal calculations to go wrong and pass invalid data to other parts of the program. Defensive programming techniques will allow the presence of these problems to be identified.

Protecting against too much data

Most programming languages provide structures, such as **arrays**, for holding fixed-size collections of data. There will be a maximum number of data items that can be held in such a structure. For example, we might have an array that can hold the exam results for up to 300 candidates. What will happen if the user tries to process results for 301, or 498 candidates? Sometimes there are checks within the language for such misuse of data structures, but some languages do not check. If the program goes on adding data into a structure that is full then the additional data may overwrite other parts of the program and so cause errors. Adding your own checks on the use of data structures can greatly reduce problems.

But don't go overboard

Programming in this manner is something that you will be in a better position to do the more experienced you are. You need to have an understanding of the places where the errors are most likely to be generated and this comes with study but also with experience.

The approach is useful for guarding against common errors but cannot be used to prevent all errors. The number of additional checks that you build in needs to be chosen with care. A good rule of thumb is that if you are increasing the lines of code by more than about 25 per cent then you need to question your approach.

▶ Tips to take away

- Use the error messages – even if they are difficult to understand at first.
- If there's not enough information available, generate some more.
- Work it out – don't guess!
- **Software tools** can be great – if you've got the time to learn how to use them.
- Test your program thoroughly to reveal undetected errors.
- The more tests your program passes, the greater the confidence you can have in its correctness.
- Choose test data that exercises different classes of test.

▶ Chapter summary

In this chapter we have looked at how you can use information from the system to help you find and remove errors in your programs, and how you can generate additional information if necessary. We have seen that there are things we can do to find bugs in our programs, from using simple pencil and paper techniques to the use of sophisticated software tools such as debuggers. It helps to be persistent but it's also good to know when to stop, and when to look for outside help. Programs can have additional code included to guard against common errors and misuse. finally, testing is a skill that needs to be learned and practised.

▶ Code explained

```
Public Sub CalculateAverage()

total = 0
count = 0
```

```
For i = 1 to 3 Step 1
   nextMark = InputBox("Next Mark")
   total = total + nextMark
Next i

average = total / count
End Sub
```

Visual Basic code from Figure 9.2

The problem with this code, as shown in figure 9.2, is that it involves division by zero. The variable count was initialized to zero and its value has not changed. As you can also see, the problem has been identified by the computer, which has brought the information to your attention.

Part Four

It All Gets Interesting

10 Grappling with Design

As programs increase in size and complexity, so the amount of work increases between having a problem specification and producing a solution. In particular, an increasingly large proportion of the process becomes **design**. Design is time spent planning, anticipating, gathering information, making choices and assessing what could happen or what has happened. Because design involves choice and uncertainty it is essentially a human activity and, like other human activities, there are no rules that guarantee a good solution! Nonetheless we can learn from what has worked well in the past.

▶ When design isn't needed

There is a type of exercise we have all encountered at some time in the past: these problems are frequently puzzles, and often they are of the sort that are called 'bath-filling' problems, or word problems. ('Turnips were brought into this country from Hanover, in Germany; they are now much cultivated in Norfolk. If twenty bushels cost two angels, how much is that a peck?'[1]) While we are often told that this is 'problem solving', the skills of being able to spot what parts of the problem to use and what parts we can safely ignore are usually quite simple. For example, it doesn't take us long to realize that *where* turnips came from is irrelevant, and that fact that they are grown in Norfolk is just a distraction. We may not know what a bushel, angel or peck are but we do know that the calculation we are going to have to perform is to convert bushels into pecks, and multiply angels by the result. Design isn't needed to deal with these sorts of exercises.

> The word **design** has many uses in computing. **User interface design** refers to the process of designing the boundary at which a user and a computer get together. **Information design** refers to the process of structuring information so that it is most useful. In this chapter, 'design' refers to a process of strategic thinking that guides larger-scale projects.

At the start of studying programming, the focus is on learning a programming language. The exercises you work on have been very specifically geared to practise the ways in which the language works. When you have finished working on one part of it, you move on to a new feature, which may not have much in common with the ones that went before. But there comes a time when you start to use the language to build programs and devise solutions to more real problems. At this point, you need to develop new skills – integrating skills that bring together your knowledge of different parts of the programming language with your understanding of the world.

▶ Recognize that a design process is needed

The first step is to recognize that design is needed to help you solve the problem. One clue is that the number and range of issues that need to be dealt has become large. If it is hard to get a clear picture of all the factors that play a role, you will almost certainly need to do some design; problem spaces requiring design are larger and more complex than the textbook problems.

Frustratingly, though, when we encounter a design situation, we often find that the information provided doesn't tell us how to proceed. For example, we will not be told to, 'Write some code that uses this algorithm to transform x to y.' More likely the description will be something like, 'Build a system that will . . .' and rarely will anyone tell us how to get from that starting point to the goal of a complete piece of software. Instead, we must devise our own starting point (which will require us to do some research on what is wanted and what is available), and we must determine what the end goals of our project will be: when and how will we finish?

Unlike simple textbook problems, design situations do not have right and wrong answers, only a range of possible solutions. Some solutions will be better than others, although no one solution is likely to be better in every respect than all others.

▶ What's your design block?

There are three common types of block that people encounter when they're doing design: *I don't know what it's meant to do*; *I don't know where to start*; and *I don't know how to build it*. We'll look at ways that have been devised to help you with each of these. They're not the only ways that these areas can be approached, and they will suit people differently; design is a human activity, and people will always devise their own paths to it. But here are some things that others have found useful.

I don't know what it's meant to do

> When I build a tool to save other people grief on their computer I feel a
> real connection with them.[2]

In software design, we have to figure out what the program we are to build
has got to do. Sometimes this is stated in the requirements specification,
sometimes this is obvious, sometimes we have to work with the people who
are going to ultimately *use* the systems to find out what they want and expect
it to do. When studying programming, assignments can be like requirements
specifications. Sometimes they may be clear and direct statements of what
is expected; at other times there will be gaps in our understanding that need
to be filled in.

Requirements
Requirements outline what the users want the software to
do. It is up to the designer to find out ('elicit') the requirements and build a system that meets them. Quite often
users don't know what it is possible – or impossible – to
build with software, so you may have to *negotiate* the
requirements with them, too. If some requirements are
missing in the finished product, then the product isn't
finished.

For example, if you undertake a project to write a system for a local hair-
dresser to keep track of their clients, what would you think the system has
to do? Well, some of it is clearly stated – 'keep track of their clients' – and
some of it is obvious – it's going to have something to do with how often
they have their hair done and what they have done to it. But beyond that,
what is this system meant to do? The only way to be sure is to ask the users.
Sometimes you will see this process of asking referred to as **requirements
elicitation**.

There are difficulties with requirements elicitation and things to look out
for. One of the difficulties is that you are always working outside of your area
of expertise – we are software designers, not hairdressers. Nor are we finan-
cial experts or train controllers. And yet we write software in all these
domains, and more.

Another difficulty is that, when we talk with different users, they may have
only partially overlapping areas of knowledge – sometimes with separate and
conflicting vocabularies. For instance is an 'order' in the shipping department
the same thing as an 'order' in the sales department?

To get the information you want and to make sure you've got the right information, you need to ask the right questions. Fortunately, there are some basic ways to ask the right question. You can ask *fishing* questions, 'Tell me about the widget', and then you can ask questions which give you an idea of their quantity and relatedness, 'How many types of haircut are there?' and, 'How does the widget relate to the gizmo?'

> ### Gizmos, widgets, foo and bar
> Programmers often express ideas in a shorthand way. They just want to say, 'I need one of *those* there,' when it doesn't really matter what the 'thing' is – it doesn't represent anything in the world, it just holds a place in the program. So, in this section, it doesn't matter what **gizmos** and **widgets** are (actually, they aren't anything): they just stand in for the idea of 'stuff in the workplace'. *Foo* and *bar* are frequently used by programmers in the same way, as a quick name for programs, files, variables or processes. Because of this usage programmers rarely use these names for anything important or permanent.

When you think you have an idea of what the system has to do, you need to check out your understanding with other sorts of questions. 'Can you ever have a perm without a cut and blow dry?' 'Would the gizmo still work if we took away the widget?' These sorts of questions have sometimes been called 'Without' questions, and they often help you isolate distinct **objects** or ideas. Walking between questions help find other relationships that may not be used often: 'What else is related to/connected to the gizmo?' What 'if questions' enable you to explore possibilities and to get a better idea of the range of ways the system can be used and misused. Finally, Other ways questions often reveal ways in which users bend or get around the current system: 'Is there any way you can get to a Form B without first having a Form A?'

When eliciting requirements in this way it is also important to keep feeding back to the users you are talking to: 'Let's see if I've got this right . . .', and to keep summarizing what you think you know: 'We have a gizmo. It's connected to . . .'

We've gone into some detail with the real-world example, in part because at some time it is likely that you will develop programs in a real-world situation, but also because aspects of the real-world situation apply directly to what happens when you are learning to program. Your instructor is a bit like a client for whom you are building a piece of software: Do you understand what is required? Does your understanding of what your program should achieve match with the teacher's? Just as with a client, you may need to ask the right questions and to check your understanding. You don't want to submit a brilliant solution to an assignment, only to find that you missed what was actually being asked for.

I don't know where to start

George Polya, an accomplished mathematician, was fascinated with how mathematicians and logicians arrived at solutions. What was the process of 'solving'? Over the course of half a lifetime of thinking, observing and questioning he distilled what he had learned into a book called *How to Solve It*. In this he structured a four-stage process: understand the problem; devise a plan; carry out your plan; reflect. For each of these stages he produced a series of **heuristics**. We use here the overall structure of his advice and some of his development of that to set out steps that may lead to solutions in programming:

Heuristics

Heuristics are short descriptions of methods or approaches to problem solving. They don't guarantee that a solution will follow if they are used, but they are good 'rules of thumb' we can follow when we initially encounter a new design problem to help get us started. Heuristics are strategies for thinking (the word 'heuristic' is based on the Greek word *heuriskein* which means 'to find') and these heuristics are especially valuable when we first approach a design situation, seeking a way to move forward, off the 'blank page'.

Famously, Archimedes yelled 'eureka!' ('I have found it!') when he realized (in the bath) that two objects of equal weight will displace different volumes of water when immersed unless their densities are equal.

Table 10.1 is an adaptation of his work to programming.

In this way, we can work at problems so that we get off the blank page, and get started in our design and our design thinking, in a way that moves us forward to a reasonable solution. Painters call this process of getting off the ground 'killing the white', and in programming, too, drawing and **prototyping** are key skills. The sooner you can make a sketch of your design, the better. Designers' whiteboards are covered with sketches – not in an artistic sense, but in an exploratory and explanatory sense: 'This goes here', 'This must be linked by that'. Sometimes more formal notations (like UML) may be used, but often they are more like diagrams or doodles. Designers use these for clarifying their own thoughts, for communicating their thoughts

Table 10.1 *How to Program It*

	Understanding the problem
• First *understand* the problem. • *Name* the program or function. • What is its *type*?	What are the *inputs* (or arguments)? What are the *outputs* (or results)? What is the *specification* of the problem? Can the specification be satisfied? Is it insufficient? or redundant? or contradictory? What special conditions are there on the inputs and outputs? Does the problem break into *parts*? It can help to draw diagrams and to write things down in **pseudo-code** or plain English.
	Designing the program
• In designing the program you need to think about the connections between the input and the output. • If there is no immediate connection, you might have to think of auxiliary problems which would help in the solution. • You want to give yourself some sort of plan of how to write the program.	Have you seen the problem before? In a slightly different form? Do you know a *related* problem? Do you know any programs or functions which could be useful? Look at the *specification*. Try to find a familiar problem with the same or similar specification. Here is a problem *related* to yours and solved before. Could you use it? Could you use its *results*? Could you use its *methods*? Should you introduce some *auxiliary* parts to the program? If you cannot solve the proposed problem try to solve a related one. Can you imagine a more accessible related one? A more *general* one? A more *specific* one? An *analogous* problem? Can you solve *part* of the problem? Can you get something useful from the inputs? Can you think of information which would help you to calculate the outputs? How could you change the inputs/outputs so that they were *closer* to each other? Did you use all the inputs? Did you use the special conditions on the inputs? Have you taken into account all that the specification requires?
	Writing your program
• Writing the program means taking your design into a particular programming language.	In writing your program, make sure that you check each step of the design. Can you see clearly that each step does what it should? You can write the program in *stages*. Think about the different *cases* into which the problem divides; in particular think about the different cases for the

Table 10.1   *How to Program It (Continue)*

- Think about how you can build programs in the language. How do you deal with different cases? With doing things in sequence? With doing things repeatedly or recursively?

- You also need to know the programs you have already written, and the functions built into the language or library.

inputs. You can also think about computing parts of the result separately, and how to *put the parts together* to get the final results.

You can think of solving the problem by solving it for a *smaller* input and using the result to get your result; this is *recursion*.

Your design may call on you to solve a more general or more specific problem. Write the solutions to these; they may *guide* how you write the solution itself, or may indeed be *used* in that solution.

You should also draw on other programs you have written. Can they be used? Can they be modified? Can they guide how to build the solution?

Looking back

- Examine your solution: how can it be improved?

Can you *test* that the program works, on a variety of arguments?

Can you think of how you might write the program *differently* if you had to start again?

Can you see how you might *use* the program or its method to build another program?

© Simon Thompson, 1996. Acknowledgements to *How To Solve It* by G. Polya, upon which this table is based.

with other designers and for communicating their thoughts with the users. Building models like this helps you understand the problem, because you can't build a model without understanding what it's got to do. As a model develops it becomes more and more obvious what you don't know – and sometimes, what your users don't know, either.

One step on from the sketch is the prototype. Again, the sooner you can mock something up that looks like (or demonstrates) the system, or part of it, the better. It's an excellent way to expose problems and issues, to act as a concrete focus for discussion, and to share thoughts and ideas. In fact, this approach has proved to be so powerful that IDEO (probably the leading design firm in the world) have a slogan in their offices: 'Never go to a meeting without a prototype.'

I don't know how to build it

One of the most interesting parts of building programs is making them work – bringing the idea of *what* they have to do together with how they have to do it.

A colleague reported this story:

> I once asked a student to look up the phone number for S.A. Reddington. They opened the phone book in about the middle, looked at the column headings, realised they'd gone too far, fanned rapidly backward, checking the column headings again, realised they'd gone too far the other way, paged slowly forward to 'R', then slower still to 'Red' then used their finger to trace down the correct column for the number.
>
> When I asked them to describe *exactly* what they did to look up that phone number they said, 'Well, first I found the R's. Then I looked up Reddington'.
>
> The student smiled happily, clearly feeling that that about covered it. This student had focussed completely on the *what*, not on the *how* and it reminded me of some interactions I have with beginning programmers.[3]

Bringing the *how* and the *what* together can be made easier (or more difficult) by the way you **decompose** the problem in the first place. Decomposing a problem in this sense means breaking it down into programmable parts; a difficulty here is that there are many ways of breaking down a problem, but different programming languages, and different language families, are structured in different ways and there are ways that are more (or less) appropriate for the language you are working in.

Top-down and Bottom-up

Two terms that you will often hear in respect of software are **top-down** and **bottom-up** design. They refer to broad-brush ways to approach a problem: if you approach a problem 'top-down' then you start by formulating an overview of the whole system, without going into detail of any part of it. If you approach a problem 'bottom-up' then you start with the detail of the system, possibly having to build some parts from scratch. In practice, software is most often designed with a combination of these approaches.

Suppose you're playing a game of Monopoly[4] and you are on the wrong side of the table to move your piece (the Boot) to the next property (Vine Street). You might say to one of the other players, 'Please move me onto Vine Street', and they would do so.

On the other hand, instead of saying, 'Please move me onto Vine Street', you could try, 'Please remove your right hand from your glass, move it to the left until it contacts the Boot, grasp it, lift it from the table, move it in a natural arc towards your left, stop when it is over the property marked Vine Street, lower the piece to the board and when it makes contact with the board, release it.' This would probably work as well, though it might also result in a quiet phone call from your friend to the local hospital.

This example illustrates the difference between the levels of **abstraction** at which it is possible to describe the solution to a problem. At a high level we might say, 'Move me onto Vine Street', whereas at a low level we might have to describe every step of getting that piece across the board.[5] The level at which we have to work depends upon which stage of development we are at and, in the case of an implementation stage, what level the particular programming language we are using allows us to work at. If we were using an object-oriented programming language to help play our game then we could naturally decompose the world into **entities** (things in the world), **attributes** (data associated with the things) and relationships between the entities. So, we might have recognizable entities such as Player, Piece and Property, where Property may have attributes such as *number of houses* and *rental value*. Relationships between entities might allow us to indicate that a Piece 'is on' a Property, e.g. 'Boot is on Whitehall'. To make a particular move we would find out which piece was associated with the requesting player, find out which property the piece was currently associated with and then change that association to Vine Street. If we were using a different type of programming language, we might be able to work at a higher level of abstraction, or be forced to work at a much lower level.

We see that, amongst other things, 'building it' means knowing something about both ends of the design process – knowing something about the scope of the problem in the world, and also knowing something about what we are going to do with the information, and how we are going to model the world in our program. So we decompose the parts of the problem into the right sort of chunks to fit the solution. We need to be thinking about both the *how* and the *what*.

▶ Things to take away

- You can't build a solution unless you understand the problem.
- You can't understand the problem if you don't know what the system's meant to do.
- You can find out what the system is expected to do by talking to the end users who will benefit from using it.

- A system that does not fulfil its requirements is incomplete.
- You have to think about the *how* and the *what*

► Chapter summary

As the size of the programs you write increases, you will have to change the way you go about creating programs. In particular you need to go through a *design* stage, which might end up taking much of the time that you give to writing the program. This process becomes more complex still when you have several people working on a program; not only do you have to have a clear design for the program, but you need to have a shared understanding of that design and a well-understood breakdown of the various programming tasks. In this chapter we have skimmed the surface of this vast area; software design is one of the most complex and important areas of computing.

11 Writing Your *n*th Program

What does it mean to 'Write your *n*th program'? When we use '*n*th' we are saying that we don't particularly mean either the first, or the last, or any especially distinguished point in between. It's just one more program in a long series. It may be our twenty-fifth program or our seventy-sixth; who knows? We're certainly not counting. So (because we know about programming) we use a variable, *n*, as a placeholder.

*n*th programs are no longer 'toy' programs – that is, programs that are small and have a reasonably short, well-defined answer. Most programs we encounter in the early stages of a course on introductory programming are likely to be toy programs. Real-world complexity starts to creep in around our *n*th program: design challenges, tying components together with scripting languages, or just sitting down to create a program of your own invention. More often than not, this real-world complexity shows up in the *data* that our program operates on, and the lesson that we need to come to terms with is that the structure of our code follows the structure of our data. In this chapter, we'll look at the several forms data takes; how we recognize those forms; and then how those forms are represented in code.

▶ Four kinds of data

When we find ourselves dealing with small to medium-sized problems, we can make the task at hand simpler by remembering one simple rule: start with the data. By asking ourselves what kind of information our program will need to manipulate, we can go a long way towards understanding the extent of the challenge we face. No matter how complex the problem we're facing may seem, we have an ace up our sleeve by starting with questions about the kind of data our program will manipulate. Why?

There are only four kinds of data in the world.

No matter what a program does, whether it is a program for a physics laboratory that calculates the slope of a line defined by a set of points, or a script to send email from a web page, there are only four kinds of data a programmer will ever need to deal with in their programs. We don't mean to make it sound too simple – it's not – but when we've written *n* programs (and will write *n* more) we should start looking for the similarities in what we're doing.

Atomic data

The simplest kind of data we can find in any programming language is data that has no *structure*. Another way of saying this is that the data is **atomic**: it cannot be broken down into any smaller constituent parts. For example, in the Java programming language, an example of a piece of data that is atomic might be the number three.

That's it – just the number three. It is a simple piece of data. You cannot break the number three into smaller pieces. Yes, it is the sum of $1 + 1 + 1$, but it is also the result of an infinite number of other arithmetic expressions: $27/9$, $-4 + 7$, etc. None of these 'break down' the number three into smaller parts – they are simply different ways of expressing the same thing.

Atomic data plays an important role in many programs, but it is easy to overlook. In many programs we find the need to express some constant value that never changes – like gravity (Code 11.1):

```
/**
 * Calculate the distance travelled
 * by an object dropped given the amount of time
 * it has been falling.
 * @param time The time it has been falling (in
 * seconds)
 */
public double calcDistance(double time) {
    return 4.9 * time * time;
}
```

Code 11.1 Calculating distance travelled by a falling object

This equation in Code 11.1 is correct, but hides one critical assumption: that we're on Earth. The problem is that the equation for distance travelled due to the acceleration of Earth's gravity is

$$d = t^2 \cdot g/2$$

and the value of 'g' is a **constant**, where its value for Earth is 9.8. In the `calcDistance` code, this value has been multiplied with 0.5 to get 4.9. No physicist looking at our code is going to immediately recognize it for what it is – and, worse yet, our code no longer works for other planets, so it shouldn't be used in a Mars lander, for instance.

Using a variable to hold the constant 'g' allows us both to name a significant piece of data (Code 11.2), and to come back later and change the value of 'g', without having to rethink what '4.9' is, or 'undo' the multiplication we've already done.

```
// The gravitational constant for Earth
double gravity = 9.8;

/**
 * Calculate the distance travelled
 * by an object dropped given the amount of time
 * it has been falling.
 * @param time The time it has been falling (in
 * seconds)
 */
public double calcDistance(double time) {
   return .5 * gravity * time * time;
}
```

Code 11.2 Naming a significant constant value

We will revisit these examples again in this chapter, but for now, note that the variable `gravity` has no structure – it is a single number, atomic and indivisible, with no component parts.

Structured data

We know that most things in the world have a number of parts to them, and therefore most data is not atomic: interesting data is rarely atomic. For example, if we were writing a program to keep track of a collection of books we might decide to capture the author of a book, its title, and the number of pages in it. Or, when writing a program that represents a character in a game, our character might have some vital statistics (energy, age), and perhaps some descriptive fields as well. So 'book' and 'character' each contain several pieces of atomic data. We need to represent the values of these data and how they relate to each other in our programs.

Every programming language represents **structured data** in different ways; we'll look at two. In Code 11.3 is some Java code which represents our notion of 'book':

```
public class Book {
    private String title;
    private String author;
    private int numberOfPages;
```

```
public Book(String t, String a, int nop) {
    title = t;
    author = a;
    numberOfPages = nop;
}

// . . . code to set and get values goes here . . .
}
```

Code 11.3 Representing a book in Java

To create a Book object that we can work with, we might write in our program Book ourBook = new Book("Studying Programming", "Us", 42);

If we were to create a structure to represent a book in Scheme, it would look different. The code

```
(define-struct Book (title author numberOfPages))
```

defines the book structure, and the code

```
(define ourBook
  (make-Book "Studying Programming" "Us" 42))
```

creates a new book structure and stores it in the variable ourBook.

In both languages, however, the effect is the same: Book (called a 'class' in Java and a 'structure' in Scheme) gives us a way of gathering up several smaller, atomic pieces of data into one place that has more meaning than the pieces would all by themselves.

Structures within structures

We see structures within structures all the time in the world. When you give someone your address, they ask for your name – but a name isn't a single string: usually names are represented as a first name and a family name. When we receive an email with an attachment, there is a structure representing the whole message, and within it is a structure representing, say, the picture from our friend.

With structures within structures, we can represent things like a boxed set of DVDs, or a trilogy of books. For example, we might create three Book objects like those described below (Code 11.4):

```
Book h2g2 = new Book(
    "Hitchhiker's Guide to the Galaxy",
    "Douglas Adams", 216);
Book rest = new Book(
    "Restaurant at the end of The Universe",
    "Douglas Adams", 245);
Book life = new Book(
    "Life, the Universe, and Everything",
    "Douglas Addams", 232);
```

Code 11.4 Creating three Book objects

These three books could be captured in a new structure that we might call a Trilogy (Code 11.5):

```
public class Trilogy {
    private Book first, second, third;

    public Trilogy(Book o, Book t, Book th) {
        first = o;
        second = t;
        third = th;
    }
    // . . . more code for manipulating the trilogy . . .
}
```

Code 11.5 A class structure for a Trilogy

This is a perfectly good way to collect three books up into one place:

```
Trilogy firstThree = new Trilogy(h2g2, rest, life);
```

Now we have all three of our favourite Douglas Adams novels in one place. However, convenience isn't the only reason for using structures. If we look at the way a Book is defined, we see that the author is a String. And, worse yet, we misspelled the name 'Addams' in the last book. So, to help eliminate the duplication of data in this example, we can use a variable for the author of the books, and reuse that in much the same way that we used a variable for gravity earlier.

```
public class Author {
    private String firstname, surname;
```

```
public Author(String f, String s) {
    firstname = f;
    surname = s;
}

    . . . other code goes here . . .
}
```

Our whole book example can now be pieced together as follows:

```
Author dna = new Author("Douglas", "Adams");
Book h2g2 = new Book(
   "Hitchhiker's Guide to the Galaxy", dna, 216);
Book rest = new Book(
   "Restaurant at the end of The Universe", dna, 245);
Book life = new Book(
   "Life, the Universe, and Everything", dna, 232);
Trilogy firstThree = new Trilogy(h2g2, rest, life);
```

We can see that we now have quite a complex combination of structures (figure 11.1) but they were built up from simple, atomic pieces of data. We could have done this the other way around: start with a Trilogy, and figure out how to represent all the parts of that trilogy. However, we might not have seen that we need to group together several pieces of data into a Book, and we might not have seen that we can break the 'Author' out into its own structure. We have, effectively, engaged in a bottom-up design; although there is nothing to say that top-down wouldn't have worked as well.

We still have one more kind of data to examine – probably the most important of the four types of data we encounter in the programming world.

'One or more' structures

Almost every language has a way of representing 'pods' and 'gaggles' – groups of dolphins and geese, respectively. A pod of dolphins might have three, four, five, or perhaps 20 playful, air-breathing mammals in it. If we were helping a biologist to develop software for tracking these dolphins, our program would have to be able to handle many contingencies. We clearly do not want to spend our time building a new data structure every time the pod gains or loses a member. Instead, we need a data structure that can grow and shrink flexibly, in response to the ever-changing population.

There's no end to the number of places we might find pods and gaggles of information. **Databases** of student records, musical scores, lists of phone

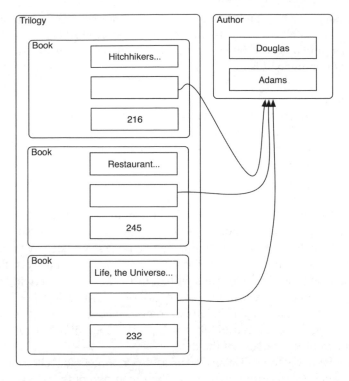

Figure 11.1 Structures within structures

numbers and addresses, playlists of MP3s – these are all things that clearly need some way of tracking 'one or more' pieces of information. And in almost all cases, we don't just need to track a 'flock' of atomic information (say, a bunch of numbers), but we need to track a whole 'cartload' of structures (perhaps representing book authors), or perhaps a 'drove' of structures within structures (representing all the trilogies of books that we own).

While it's true that there is a whole 'herd' of words for representing groups of animals (and we're sure there are a few more we could use), our point is clear: 'one or more' is everywhere. Every programming language lets you represent these 'one or more' in different ways. In fact, when programming we often extend these sorts of structures to be 'zero or more' structures, allowing us to conveniently represent **empty lists** as well as occupied **lists**.

In some languages, for example C, you have to build these flexible structures yourself. While this gives the programmer a great deal of control, it also gives a programmer a great deal of rope with which to hang him- or herself: common C errors are responsible for most of the security holes on the Internet today. In languages like Scheme and **LISP**, lists of things are the primary way of representing zero or more pieces of information. Java, on the other hand, gives the programmer Sets, **Hashtables**, ArrayLists, Vectors, and a *host* of other tools to represent, say, a *cete* of badgers or a *charm* of hummingbirds.

Data first

Learning to see the relationship between the programs we write and the data those programs operate on requires practice. What makes our nth program different from our first program is the experience we gain along the way. We see our nth program in a different light: we are no longer concerned with the details of getting individual programs to work, but instead are concerned with ourselves as programmers developing fluency and style.

The nature of data has a strong influence on the structure of the code we are writing. The style of code we write to support a particular sort of data will also be influenced by the programming language we use. Java programs end up taking on a structure of their own, which looks and feels different from Scheme programs. Programs written in Python have a certain look, as do Haskell, Smalltalk, Visual Basic, and programs written in a host of other languages. Each language is unique in some respects, and has its own idiosyncrasies and foibles. But in all languages the code of a program *follows* the data and the structure of the data.

There are many tools available to us as programmers for reflecting on the way we and others write programs. We'll look at two of them here: the role of variables and software patterns. Both of these rely on a programmer having some experience of having written and read n programs; they rely on seeing things that are not on the surface of a program, things that programs have in common with each other.

▶ The roles of variables

Imagine we walk into a movie halfway through – a movie we've never seen before, and know nothing about. On the screen we see:

* a man leap from a plane into the sea; and
* swim though a pod of trained killer porpoises.

At this point we know we're watching an action film. Next

* the hero strips off his wetsuit to reveal a white dinner jacket;
* he walks into a casino and orders a Martini, 'Shaken, but not stirred.'

Now we know we are watching James Bond. Even if we don't know the name of the actor playing James Bond, we recognize the *role*.

Similarly we have to learn to see in our own programs – and when we read

others' – that every variable has a purpose. Jorma 'Saja' Sajaniemi, a profes-
sor of computer science at the University of Joensuu in finland, would instead
say that each variable plays a role.

We like Jorma's work because it does two things for us as programmers:

1. Thinking about variable roles helps us to reflect about our programs.
2. Variable roles force us to think about the data in our program, and how
   the structure of that data affects the structure of our program.

The challenge to us as programmers is that in order to recognize these different roles, we have to learn to look beyond the name of the variable,
beyond what we *think* a variable does, to the behaviour it is displaying. Let's
explore some of the roles commonly played by variables.

One role: fixed value

Let's reconsider the gravity example from the first part of this chapter (Code
11.6).

```
// The gravitational constant for Earth
final double gravity = 9.8;

/**
 * Calculate the distance travelled
 * by an object dropped given the amount of time
 * it has been falling.
 * @param time The time it has been falling (in
 * seconds)
 */
public double calcDistance(double time) {
    return .5 * gravity * time * time;
}
```

Code 11.6   Gravity is a variable with a fixed value

In this example, gravity is a variable. As we discussed earlier, we wanted to
keep the value of the gravimetric constant of Earth separate from the equation
for calculating distance travelled over time, so that it would be easy to modify
the program to perform the same calculation for the Moon or Jupiter, for
example. Here the variable gravity plays the role of a *fixed value holder*.
Such variables are often called 'constants', which is strangely contradictory
– how can something be a constant if it is a variable?! Some languages allow
us to indicate that a variable's value is fixed once set. For instance, **C++** uses
the word const for this purpose and Java uses the word final.

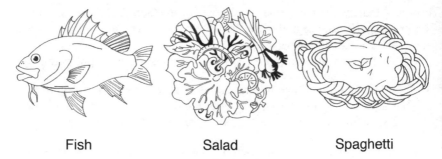

Fish   Salad   Spaghetti

Figure 11.2 Our shopping list

Another role: stepper

A very common structure we encounter in the world is the *list*. A list of items. Nothing more, nothing less. Lists are another name for the 'zero or more' structures we discussed earlier. We all use shopping lists and make 'to do' lists. We'll start with our shopping list from this week (figure 11.2). While we're at the supermarket, we need to get some fish; to go with it, we'd like a salad, and tomorrow we'll have spaghetti. We might imagine writing some Java code that will print out the items on our list (Code 11.7):

```
public boolean printShoppingList(
        List<Item> shoppingList){
    int index = 0;

    while(index < shoppingList.size()) {
        Item currentItem = shoppingList.get(index);
        System.out.println(currentItem);
        index++;
    }
}
```

Code 11.7 Printing a shopping list

In this example, we'll look only at the variable index. On line two, it is initialized to zero. On line four, we check to see if its value is still less than the number of items in the list (we want to make sure we don't try to print items that don't exist!). On line seven, we add one to it, so that the next time we go through the loop, we will be looking at the next item in the list.

This behaviour is associated with the variable role stepper. A stepper variable is typically a number that is incremented every time we go through a loop.

A third role: most-recent holder

We can see another role variables can take in the shopping list in Code 11.7. The variable `currentItem` holds the value of the list item we are currently interested in, and is updated every time we go through the loop (on line 5). On line 6, we print out the value it is currently holding, and so, item by item, print out the entire list. The variable `currentItem` is behaving in the role of most-recent holder, where it contains the latest in a list of values we are interested in.

Saja has identified many different roles that variables can take in a program, and collected them at the *Roles of Variables* home page.[1] The skill of identifying how variables behave and thus what role they are playing in a program helps us develop as programmers, to read beneath the surface features, and find the structure of the solution that the program is expressing.

▶ Software patterns

As our *n* becomes larger and larger, we come to realize that our situation simply cannot be unique and that *someone must have coded this before*. (As we write more and more programs, actually, we come to realize, 'Oh, *I've* coded this before.') Sometimes the solutions we come up with are good, sometimes OK, sometimes poor. It would be nice to have someone tell us which are the good solutions, which are the solutions that are known to work, which are the solutions that experts use. This is what software patterns are constructed to do.

Patterns define a solution to a problem in a particular context. They are abstracted from many successful examples, and are not specific to any given programming language (although sometimes they are specific to a programming approach – such as object orientation). Although many pattern authors vary the way they present their material you can pretty much recognize a pattern from its distinctive form:

- A **name**, which allows for quick reference.
- The **problem statement**, which tells you in what situations this pattern might be useful.
- The **solution statement**, which tells you what to do in order to utilize the pattern.

Suppose we have a shopping list:

> fish, salad, spaghetti, sausage, custard, strawberry yoghurt, steak and kidney pie, pizza ('Veggie Supreme').

We want to remove all of the products from the list that are not appropriate for vegetarians. So we want to end up with a list that looks like this:

salad, spaghetti, custard, strawberry yoghurt, pizza ('Veggie Supreme')

How would you do this?

In our experience, many students write one loop to find where all the meat products are, and then another loop to remove them. This opens up possibilities of many common errors: **off-by-one bugs**, problems with loops running off the end, and problems with boundary conditions (e.g. first meat item, last meat item). This is just one example of a common problem situation; it occurs in many places. Owen Astrachan from Duke University in the United States has written a pattern that contains the essence of a *successful* solution to this problem (a 'linear structure' is another name for a 'zero or more' structure):

Name: One Loop for Linear Structures

Problem: Algorithmically, a problem may seem to call for multiple loops to match intuition on how control structures are used to program a solution to the problem, but the data is stored sequentially, e.g. in an array or file. Programming based on control leads to more problems than programming based on structure.

Solution: *Therefore*, use the structure of the data to guide the programmed solution: one loop for sequential data with appropriately guarded conditionals to implement the control.

Code 11.8 shows a method to remove meat items from a shopping list based on this idea. Note how we only update the stepper index if the current item is not removed from the list.

```
public boolean removeMeatItems(List<Item> shoppingList)
{
        int index = 0;
        while(index < shoppingList.size()) {
            Item currentItem = shoppingList.get(index);
            if(currentItem is a meat item)
                shoppingList.remove(index);
            else
                index++;
        }
}
```

Code 11.8 Removing meat items from a shopping list

Reading pattern collections and familiarizing ourselves with these best practices improves our sense of what is familiar and common across examples, and also increases our 'toolkit' of successful approaches.

► Chapter summary

What we have seen is that:

*   not every situation is unique;
*   not every problem is unique;
*   not every solution is unique.

In fact, we can express this more strongly and say that few problems we will have to solve are unique, and as we write our *n*th program we are almost bound to be working on something similar to what we have worked on before.

As we become more experienced, we start to see commonalities and structures. These insights reflect the fact that we are becoming better, more expert, programmers. We've looked at three examples of this: data in the world, the roles that variables take and software patterns.

► Code explained

About Codes 11.1 and 11.2

```java
/**
 * Calculate the distance travelled
 * by an object dropped given the amount of time
 * it has been falling.
 * @param time The time it has been falling (in
 * seconds)
 */
public double calcDistance(double time) {
    return 4.9 * time * time;
}
```

Code 11.1   Calculating distance travelled by a falling object (Java)

```
// The gravitational constant for Earth
double gravity = 9.8;

/**
 * Calculate the distance travelled
 * by an object dropped given the amount of time
 * it has been falling.
 * @param time The time it has been falling (in
 * seconds)
 */
public double calcDistance(double time) {
    return .5 * gravity * time * time;
}
```

Code 11.2 Naming a significant constant value (Java)

As you will recall from the discussion in Chapter 11, while both are correct, in the sense that the code does exactly what it should, Code 11.2 is definitely to be preferred because it is easier for us to understand what is happening (in the first code the number 4.9 could be quite a mystery.)

Comments in the code say a great deal about what it is going on here. You can spot the comments: anything on a line following // (two slashes) is a comment and anything between /* and */ is one as well.

The word **double** in Java refers to numbers like 8.9 or −2.4 or 0.3 or .9 (what are usually called 'decimals').

The line in Code 11.2, double gravity = 9.8, sets the term 'gravity' as a double, the value of which is 9.8.

The code fragment:

```
double calcDistance(double time) {
    return .5 * gravity * time * time;
}
```

describes what a method calcDistance does. Give some value to time expressed as a double, the code returns one-half gravity multiplied by the square of the time.

About Code 11.3

Expanding and filling in omissions in Code 11.3:

```
public class Book {
    private String title;
    private String author;
```

```java
private int numberOfPages;
public Book(String t, String a, int nop) {
      title = t;
      author = a;
      numberOfPages = nop;
}

public void setTitle(String t) {
       title = t;
}

public void setAuthor(String a) {
      author = a;
}

public void setNoOfP(int nop) {
      numberOfPages = nop;
}

public String getTitle() {
      return title;
}

public String getAuthor() {
       return author;
}

public int getNoOfP() {
      return numberOfPages;
}

}
```

Code 11.3(a) Representing a book in Java (more
fully spelled out)

This code provides a simple picture of a book. A book has a title, an author
and a number of pages. The terms **public** and **private** scattered through
this code are a way of the programmer controlling what is and what is not
accessible from other programs: if something is `public` other programs can
access it and use it; if it is `private` they cannot.

About Code 11.4

```
Book h2g2 = new Book(
   "Hitchhiker's Guide to the Galaxy",
   "Douglas Adams", 216);
Book rest = new Book(
   "Restaurant at the end of The Universe",
   "Douglas Adams", 245);
Book life = new Book(
   "Life, the Universe, and Everything",
   "Douglas Addams", 232);
```

Code 11.4   Creating three Book objects

Each line of the code condenses a number of operations. A sequence such as Book h2g2 declares the variable h2g2 as one representing a book. The Java keyword new does the magic of 'creating' a book object.

Book("Hitchhiker's . . . 216) sets the value assigned to the particular book.

12 Juggling All the Pieces

In popular mythology, programmers are wild-eyed individualists, hunched over their keyboards in dark, lonely rooms, surrounded by empty coffee cups and half-eaten pizzas. In such a world, the act of programming is like a voyage of the soul; it can only be undertaken alone.

We hope by now that you have been able to appreciate that reality is a long way from this popular view. Programmers who participate in a project of any significant size are just one part of a multi-skilled team who need to communicate with one another and co-operate to get a job done. Most courses will include some work that is done in groups to give you a flavour of what life on those sorts of projects is like. So, in this chapter, we are going to explore some of the issues that arise as we move from small- or medium-scale programs that can easily be designed and coded by an individual, to much larger programs that really need several people to work on them. Larger teams have both pros and cons – many hands make light work, but too many cooks might spoil the broth. Potentially, you can get a lot more done if there are more of you, but you need to work at working together. In addition, you will also have to tackle the problem of how to locate errors – is it your code that is wrong or someone else's? – and how to report errors so that the person responsible fixes them. You also need to ensure that every member of the team is working to the same specifications and guidelines – if you don't, then your program could lead to a catastrophic failure, just like the Climate Orbiter.

▶ Working as a team

It is often said that 'Two heads are better than one', and one of the easiest ways to make a start on multi-person programs is to work with another person. What is usually known as 'pair programming' has been found to be particularly beneficial in eliminating 'obvious' errors at an early stage of a program, and thereby to make us more productive. Trying out pair programming can be a good way to experience some of the ideas introduced in this chapter while you are still learning to program. Check your assessment guidelines carefully, however, to ensure that pair programming doesn't fall under the heading of 'plagiarism'.

Even if working on large-scale, multi-programmer projects isn't your end goal, there are useful techniques and lessons to be drawn from the ideas presented here for your own smaller, individual work.

Working on bigger programs

When two people work together on a program, the lines of communication are simple; A talks to B and B talks to A – that's one pair of conversations. Add a third person and things get a little more complex. A talks to B, B talks to A, A talks to C, C talks to A, B talks to C and C talks to B – that's two more pairs of conversations. Add a fourth person and you don't just get two more but three more – that's six pairs of conversations (Figure 12.1). Imagine how many conversations could take place with a team of 12, 20 or 100 people! That's not a programming project, that's a party. Without some ground rules, no work is going to get done!

In big projects, the people involved always split up into teams – often quite small teams – in order to keep the communication manageable. But if you stop people talking to one another, how are you ever going to get the work done? Well, just as we have rules for pair programming, we have rules for multi-team projects. The most basic rule is that *different teams work on different parts of the project*. If we are using a waterfall model of development, one team might work on the analysis of the problem, another on the design and another on the implementation. We might also subdivide these phase teams into module teams, each working on just one part of the analysis, design or implementation.

If we are using an **evolutionary** or **iterative** style of development, then teams are less likely to be rigidly assigned to a particular phase of the development, but to work through multiple phases of a component part of the whole.

Whatever way the project is broken up, another basic rule is that *lines of communication between the teams must be clear and simple*. We say that the *interfaces* between the teams must be well defined. In that way, the potential complexity we described when lots of people get together is brought within manageable limits. If teams are kept small enough, the lines of communication will be simple within the team, and simple lines between teams prevent rapid explosion of the number of lines throughout the project. Figure 12.2 shows one way of simplifying the communication between six teams, A to F. Teams A, B and C communicate in the same way as three people in the example above, as do teams D, E and F. Then teams A and D communicate the results of their three-team discussions.

If different teams work on different parts of a program, one of the obvious hurdles to be overcome is how to join all the different pieces together.

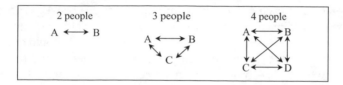

Figure 12.1 Interactions between individuals

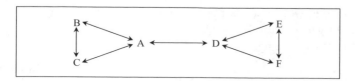

Figure 12.2 Simplifying the lines of communication

Particularly important for successful integration is that the rule about keeping communication interfaces clear and simple will also apply to the pieces of code that the different teams write.

▶ Implementing to an interface

In broad terms, an **interface** can be defined as a shared boundary, a physical point of demarcation between two things. We could think of the door dividing two rooms as an interface: the door is a shared boundary between the rooms; it allows you to pass from one room to another. An interface can be what you see when you look at your monitor: the collection of words, pictures, buttons, menus and other stuff that lets you do things. This is often called a **GUI**, or **graphical user interface** – it is the boundary or access point between a human user and a program's functionality.

Just as we can reduce complexity in team communication by limiting who needs to speak to whom in the different teams, we can reduce the complexity of coding large applications by applying these principles to the interface between pieces of code. If different teams are responsible for writing different **components** of the program, each team will usually focus only on the source code for its own component, and not interfere with (or even see) the code for any other component. It is only when one component needs to interact with another that communication between the teams responsible for those components becomes necessary. This communication actually takes place before the teams start coding. They plan how the different components will interact with each other, and define the interfaces between those components. Each team can then go away and work on implementing their own component, with a reasonable degree of confidence that it should be straightforward to link the two completed components together via the defined interface. What we mean by an interface here is a set of agreed commands and statements that lets the pieces exchange information with each other. Each team must be completely clear about what the interface describes, otherwise the components will turn out to be incompatible. It is a little like two teams working on the design of adjacent rooms in a house. As long as they can agree where the door between the rooms will go, each should then be able to get on with designing their own room without worrying about what the other is doing.

► How do I do it?

So, you know the different sorts of interface that exist on a programming project and you are working as part of a team. What do you do now? How do you ensure that the pieces of code fit together properly? What are some of the other issues that might arise within your team? For instance, how do you stop two people from editing the same piece of code at the same time? What happens if you edit your code and the changes activate a previously hidden bug in someone else's code?

Let's take this step by step to get an overview of what is necessary. Then we will go back through and discuss in more detail some of the key ideas.

You obviously need to know the specification you will be working to: a clear and accurate description of the **technical requirements** including both the description of the subject and aspects of the implementation that affect its representation. Since you are working as part of a team, there is a possibility that several people will be working on the same piece of code. To prevent problems of different developers making incompatible changes what you will need is called a **code management system**.

Once you have some code you need to debug and test it and we have talked about doing this on a small scale already. You will be familiar with the need to trace and eliminate all **compile-time** errors, and to identify and correct as many **logical** errors as you can. But your code not only needs to be self-consistent and work on its own; it will need to be integrated with other code. Before you attempt to integrate it with the code produced by other groups, it will need to work in relation to an entire set of tests, contained in a **test suite**. These tests may well have been created by another member of the team, prepared directly from the specification of the system – or at least your part of it. The test suite might be held in a **test harness** that supports the automation of the testing process.

When your code has passed these testing hurdles, you can integrate your code with that of others to try to make a larger component. Larger and larger components will gradually be integrated until the system as a whole is complete, and thoroughly tested at all levels of integration.

Code management system

One way to manage the physical activity of multiple people working on code within a team is to use some form of code management system. **CVS (Concurrent Versioning System)** is one particular widely used code management system that provides a mechanism to track, manage and (if necessary) undo changes to source code. It is good for groups because there is a facility to lock files so that only one person may alter them at a time. As well as a facility to email all members of the group every time a change has been made, there is an **audit trail** so that you can trace who altered the file when. If you have ever shared Microsoft Office documents, such as Word files or Excel spreadsheets, you will know that if a person you are working with is already editing the file you can only access a 'read only' version, you can't make any changes to it. Once the other person has finished editing the file you can open the updated version and apply your own edits. CVS allows you to do this with all your shared files.

Test suite

You know what a test case is – verifying that the code conforms to its specification for one particular set of data. Any sizeable program will need a large number of individual test cases to provide any reasonable level of assurance that it is performing as required. A test suite is a cohesive collection of related test cases. A test suite usually relates to a particular group of features, e.g. testing one particular module, or testing all the boundary conditions for a particular subset of the program's data. Suites are combined into groups and these are often collected into a test harness.

Test harness

A test harness is a software component or software tool that automates the testing process by holding collections of test suites. It allows you to apply the tests in a similar way to a mechanic's testing bench. Mechanics can test and tune a car engine on the bench before fitting it into the cramped engine bay of the car it belongs to; it not only makes the testing easier, it also allows for easier access when fixing any problems that are encountered.

Integration

Integration is basically the process of bringing separate parts together. Often these parts will have been developed independently. It involves co-ordinating separate elements into a balanced whole, and ensuring that the combination of parts works well together. For a large software project that has involved several teams producing different components it implies that the combined software, from the user's point of view, should work as if it were a single unit. Integration is usually only attempted once testing of the individual components has been completed. That way, we would expect any subsequent errors to relate to the way in which the components interact. A key part of integration is integration testing.

We said earlier that complexity is often reduced in large projects by having teams work independently on their own components, implementing to an interface. One problem with this approach is that each component that needs to be integrated with another will, necessarily, be incomplete; therefore its testing as a stand-alone component will be incomplete. The way a component team will often try to deal with this is to produce a 'mock-up' of the complementary component, and simulate integration before the proper integration happens. This can help a lot in finding interfacing errors before full integration, but it is never quite the same as the real thing. So the testing focus when components first come together is on integration testing – ensuring that both teams have correctly interpreted the agreed interface, and that the two components work together smoothly as a whole.

Producing a program, however complex, is not a **one-off** thing. You don't make your piece of code work, then combine it with other working bits and expect the entire program to simply run correctly. There will be problems and things that need to be changed. These changes may affect the ways in which the program runs – they may even make it stop working. In order to check for this you need **regression testing**.

Regression testing

Regression testing is basically the retesting of a previously tested program following modification. This is done to ensure that faults have not been introduced or uncovered as a result of the changes that have been made. Regression testing helps to ensure that changes made to the code do not break other previously working parts of the software. It is important to perform regression testing frequently while writing code, because the code as a whole may easily 'regress' to a lower level of quality after a change has been made. Regression testing is necessary, even though a change appears to be working correctly and is believed not to affect the rest of the software. A key principle with testing is that whenever you find an error, you ensure that one or more, test cases are added to the test suite to cover that error, in order to ensure that it doesn't recur during later code modifications.

▶ Working with alien code

Alien code isn't something produced by monsters from outer space – although it might as well be! It is code that somebody else wrote, perhaps for another purpose, that you need to integrate into your program or that you need to alter to keep working. Imagine yourself having to alter a section of code that was written 30 or 40 years ago (maybe a Y2K bug fix). Would it make your job easier if the original programmer had commented the code well, or if they hadn't provided any comments at all? Keep this in mind when you write your own comments!

Legacy code

You will encounter code from earlier releases of a piece of software. Some of this code will be fragile but still key to the operation of the project you have been assigned to. These pieces of code are called **legacies**. The common meaning of the word legacy is 'A gift passed down in a will', and legacy code can be thought of as prewritten code that is being passed down to you. Sometimes **legacy code** can simply be integrated into the new program and used as it is, but often it needs to be adapted to suit your current needs. This adaptation is a process akin to evolution (a process in which something passes by degrees to a different stage), so such sections of a program are known as **evolving code**.

In Chapter 3 we found out what happened to the rocket Ariane 5 when the programmers reused some of the code from Ariane 4. The code produced for Ariane 4 worked for that rocket and conformed to the specifications of that particular rocket, but was not designed for any other rocket in the past or future. The programmers worked to their specification and made assumptions about maximum velocities and all kinds of other things based upon the known limits at the time. Programmers working on the systems of Ariane 5 wanted to do the same things, but used sections of the legacy code as it was – they did not adapt them to suit the new specification, so the system did not evolve as it should have. This highlights the importance of proper testing. If the entire program had been fully tested, rather than relying on a previously proven piece of software simply working in a new environment, the 'bug' might have been caught and fixed before the rocket blew up.

When you use legacy code – whether you simply use it or adapt it – you need to remember the importance of testing; particularly regression testing. Just because the code worked as expected in its old program, it doesn't mean that it will work as expected for you. Have you checked that the boundary conditions haven't changed? Have you checked that you can store enough values? Does your code highlight a bug in the old code that wasn't a problem before?

Legacy systems

A **legacy system** is an existing computer system that must be accommodated when building new systems in a modernization programme. Such a system often continues to be used because the cost of replacing it outweighs the benefits that replacement might bring; it is often unwieldy and difficult to modify. When such a system runs only on particular hardware then, eventually, the costs of maintenance (for both the software and the hardware) is likely to become large enough to outweigh the cost of replacement, but all legacy systems will be affected by modernization to a greater or lesser extent.

▶ Chapter summary

This chapter has introduced the concept of working on large projects that require many people. We have shown you that the ideas and methods that you are learning as a beginner are important to large projects. The tasks may become more complex, but the methods required to solve them remain the same – you just require more of them. A particular issue when working as part of a large project team is the need to ensure that interfaces between subgroups are well defined, and that each group can do a lot of its work relatively independently of the other groups. When one group's work needs to be combined with another, integration testing will be important to ensure that the increased independence hasn't led to the programs moving away from the specification to which everyone is supposed to work.

Part Five
Other Languages

13 Why Do We Have Different Programming Languages?

This book is not about programming in a particular programming language, but about programming in general. We have used several different programming languages throughout to provide examples. You might be wondering why so many *different* programming languages exist? Why isn't there just one programming language, sufficient for all programming tasks, that everyone could use?

There are several reasons behind the ways things are, and there are different *sorts* of answer to the questions. We need to consider:

- how programming languages help us solve problems;
- how different programming languages address different problems;
- why there isn't just one programming language for each problem-type;
- how (and why) programming languages develop.

But before we move on to why we have different programming languages, we should first consider what it is that a programming language actually *does*.

A programming language is a way to describe solutions to problems. The structure and formality of programming languages helps us to write a description (a 'program') that allows a computer to implement a solution. Different programming languages have different features. A particular programming language has features that make it a more (or less) suitable way to talk about particular sorts of problem. For example, think about doing the following multiplication using Roman numerals (don't convert it into Arabic numerals in your head!):

$$\begin{array}{r} \text{XIV} \\ \times \quad \underline{\text{IX}} \\ \text{?????} \end{array}$$

The particular features of Roman numerals that mean they are useful for keeping tallies with primitive writing materials (make a mark for one, make another mark for two, make two marks at an angle joined at the bottom for five) mean that they are very difficult to use for arithmetic that depends on positional value. In a similar fashion, some programming languages make certain sorts of problem easy to describe, and therefore make it easy for certain sorts of software to be built.

▶ Some problems programming languages need to address

There are many categories of problem that we need to solve with programming languages, but we have chosen four major ones here: **data processing**, glue, **numerical applications** and safety-critical systems. There are languages that are good to use when solving one type of problem that would not be good to use when solving a different type. There are some languages that are useful for addressing more than one type of problem, but most fill a distinct **niche**. Here we describe the four problem categories we have chosen and provide examples of languages that are used for working within them. The example languages are occasionally old, but this does not mean that they are not useful. When a language has been adopted by large numbers of programmers it becomes difficult to change to a newer language even if it is better – think about how difficult it would be for the UK to swap from driving on the left-hand side of the road to driving on the right.

Data processing systems

One sort of problem that programs help solve is characterized by the need to move a lot of data around, but not do much with it on the way. Examples of this family of problems are call centres, where people are seeking and searching for information on a product or service. Most online (and, increasingly, in-shop) purchasing falls into this category – buying books, music, holidays or a basket of shopping from the supermarket. Also, what we call directory services: for example, finding out what time the trains will run, or getting directions for driving from Bath to Edinburgh. You can immediately see that there is not much benefit to be gained in these situations from the extra effort of defensive programming and the overheads of proving a program correct. So the sorts of languages that support this category of programs are good at manipulating large amounts of data and have built-in support for searching, moving and querying.

Example languages

   COBOL (1960) – **COmmon Business Oriented Language** – defined its
   primary domain in business, finance, and administrative systems for

companies and governments. A committee that was appointed by the US Department of Defense designed it. COBOL was developed within a six-month period, and yet is still in use over 40 years later.

SQL (1970) – **Structured Query Language**. An industry-standard language for creating, updating and querying **relational database management systems**. Developed by IBM in the 1970s, access to it is often embedded in general-purpose programming languages. The first SQL standard, in 1986, provided basic language constructs for defining and manipulating tables of data.

Glue

As well as building systems 'from the ground up' there is an increasing need for programs that 'glue' other applications together, to take advantage of existing large pieces of software. The programming languages that have been devised to help solve this category of problem are often referred to as scripting languages. 'Scripting language' is a fairly loose term, but in general it means a **high-level language** that is interpreted (rather than compiled to machine code), has powerful string-manipulation features and has few data structures. The emphasis is on programming speed and programmer power. These characteristics don't necessarily distinguish 'scripting' languages from general-purpose programming languages, though, and it is likely that any distinction will become smaller and more slippery over time. Perhaps a more reliable indicator is how closely integrated the language is with the supporting environment: with scripting languages you get a lot of support.

Example languages

Visual Basic (1991) – A popular event-driven visual programming system from the Microsoft Corporation for Microsoft Windows. VB is good for developing Windows GUIs.

Perl (1987) – Designed by Larry Wall from a huge variety of influences, C, Lisp, Unix shell languages among them. Perl was designed to be a practical language to extract information from text files and to generate reports from that information. Larry says, 'Perl is designed to make the easy jobs easy and the hard jobs possible.' However, the language's highly flexible syntax and concise regular expression operators make densely written Perl code indecipherable to the uninitiated.

PHP (1997) – A language that allows web developers to write web pages that have dynamic rather than purely static content. PHP is one of a number of languages developed with this purpose in mind as the **World Wide Web** grew in popularity from the 1990s onwards.

Numeric applications

Typical numeric applications are associated with scientific data processing, especially what we might call Big Science – areas like astronomy or particle physics – which generate really large sets of data, or which require complex calculations to be performed efficiently. However, there are other sorts of problem that share the same characteristics: weather forecasting, electronic games and cinematic animation, for example. They might not, on the face of it, seem to have very much in common with each other, or with science and scientific data. But in all these areas, getting to something sensible means dealing with massive amounts of numeric data, and doing very complicated things to it.

Example languages

Fortran (1967) – Formula Translator – The first and, for a long time, the most widely used programming language for numerical and scientific applications. The name is often written 'FORTRAN', reflecting its origins in the days before computers were able to use lower-case letters.

C (1972) – A programming language designed by Dennis Ritchie at **AT&T Bell** Labs in California. Partly due to its distribution with the Unix operating system, C became immensely popular outside Bell Labs after about 1980 and is now the dominant language in systems and microcomputer applications programming. It has grown popular due to its simplicity, efficiency and flexibility. C programs are often easily adapted to new environments. C is often described, with a mixture of fondness and disdain, as 'a language that combines all the elegance and power of assembly language with all the readability and maintainability of assembly language'.

C++ (1985) – One of the most widely used object-oriented languages, a **superset** of C developed primarily by Bjarne Stroustrup. Bjarne writes: 'Programmers are smart people. They are engaged in challenging tasks and need all the help they can get from a programming language as well as from other supporting tools and techniques. Trying to seriously constrain programmers to do "only what is right" is inherently wrongheaded and will fail. Programmers will find a way around rules and restrictions they find unacceptable. The language should support a range of reasonable design and programming styles rather than try to force people into adopting a single notion'.[1]

Safety-critical systems

The name we give to this family of problems gives more than a clue to their central, defining feature. They are 'safety critical', which means that if they stop operating safely, dangerous things happen. Examples of this kind of system are nuclear power plants, air traffic control systems, car braking systems. These must work, and they must work reliably, predictably and in all circumstances. This is a difficult problem. In programming it is addressed (broadly) in two ways. One way is with the engineering techniques used to construct the software, but the other is with the programming languages themselves. These languages share common features: statements written in them can be **formally proved**; this means that we have an extra safeguard that the code will do what we expect it to.

Example languages

Erlang (late 1980s) – Designed for developing robust systems of programs that can be distributed among different computers in a network. Named for the Danish mathematician Agner Krarup Erlang, the language was developed by the Ericsson Computer Sciences Lab to build software for its own telecommunication products.

Ada (1979) (named after Ada Lovelace) – A language, designed by Jean Ichbiah's team at CII Honeywell and made mandatory for US Department of Defense software projects by the Pentagon.

occam (1983) – A parallel programming language that builds on Communicating Sequential Processes (CSP), a formally defined algebra for describing interactions.

Proving correctness

When it is important to be sure that a program runs the way we intend and expect, a programmer can use additional steps, tools and procedures to make sure that there are no **'nasty surprises'** in their code. One of these tools is proof. 'Proof' here means **mathematical proof** – the application of a set of tightly and precisely defined steps (logic) which guarantee that, if the statement you started with was true, then that truth is preserved to the following statement. You can only prove programs in languages that are designed to support this activity: some of these are programming languages, and others are **specification languages**. A specification language (a good example is the language called **Z**) is used in the analysis and design stage of a project, and its output must include a lot more detail before the solution it describes can be implemented. Proving a program is a time-consuming and costly business: well worth it in safety-critical areas.

We've looked at the four main types of problem, but these are not hard-and-fast categories. For instance, banking systems have elements of 'data processing', but I'd like details of my account and transactions to be secure, please. Flight control systems have to be safety critical, but they also have to deal with enormous amounts of numeric data. We've just picked out four areas that are distinct enough to illustrate different programming approaches, and given a thumbnail sketch of some languages that are used within them. This leaves us with the question, 'Why isn't there just one programming language for each problem type?'

One of the reasons we have different programming languages is based on the history of computing itself. Originally, each machine had just one (low-level) language, no matter what type of problem the programmer was asked to address. Later, each type of machine (or each manufacturer) had its own language for each sort of problem. This was good for manufacturers (you had to keep buying their machines), but bad for buyers and programmers (same reason). If a company wanted to switch manufacturers, it also really wanted to take its programs with it, so they really wanted the language their programmers used to work on the new machine. This consumer pressure meant that pretty soon there were large numbers of languages, across machines.

New languages are developed in response to new problems (and new ways of understanding old problems), and 'old' languages survive. Sometimes they do a particular job particularly well, sometimes there's a large set of programmers who use them. The complicated human reasons that mean we have different approaches to situations in many areas of life also apply to programming languages: language designers like to make new languages, programmers like to use languages they like (or are especially good at using). All this means that there are many, many programming languages in the world.

Luckily, although there may be 10,000 languages, there are not 10,000 different languages. Because languages have evolved to solve similar problems, they talk about problems in similar ways ('families'), and, no matter how inventive, nobody creates a language from scratch. Language designers usually base their ideas on an existing language, or on features that they like in existing languages. This means that much of our detailed knowledge is portable. For example, let's look at some code which just adds up numbers:

BASIC (1960 to present)
```
FOR I = 0 TO 10
     SUM = SUM + NUMBERS[I]
NEXT I
```

BCPL (early 1970s)
```
FOR i = 0 TO 10 STEP 1 DO $(
     sum := sum + numbers!i
$)
```

C (1970s), C++ (1980s), Java (1990s)
```
for (int i = 0; i <= 10; i++) {
     sum += numbers[i];
}
```

Code 13.1 Code samples over thirty years

The similarities at the code level are quite striking.

It seems unlikely that the number of programming languages will reduce very much. As old ones drop slowly out of use, new ones are being developed. Yet they all bear a relationship to each other that makes our job of studying – and practising – programming easier.

▶ Chapter summary

Why do we have different programming languages? Firstly, because computers are used to tackle different sorts of problems. Therefore, languages have been designed with different sorts of problems in mind. Also, there are different languages because language designers have found new ways of solving problems, so they have invented new languages. However, the older languages remain – programmers often favour languages with which they're familiar.

And last but not least . . . having different programming languages *is a good thing*: "a carpenter who only has a hammer thinks that a hammer is the best tool for all jobs. A knowledgeable carpenter has a complete toolbox, knows how to use all the tools, and understands which to use under what circumstance. You'll find that each language encourages a different approach and mental model, which has the effect of stretching the mind – a good thing'.[2]

So, when you learn your next language it is a good thing to choose one from another 'language family' – a toolbox containing a spanner and a screw-driver is more useful than one containing two very similar screwdrivers.

▶ Code explained

Basic (1960 to present)
```
FOR I = 0 TO 10
SUM = SUM + NUMBERS[I]
NEXT I
```

BCPL (early 1970s)
```
FOR i = 0 TO 10 STEP 1 DO $(
    sum := sum + numbers!i
$)
```

C (1970s), C++ (1980s), Java (1990s)
```
for (int i = 0; i <= 10; i++) {
    sum += numbers[i];
}
```

Code 13.1 Code samples over thirty years

These are all examples in different programming languages of what programmers call for-loops, and they all do the same thing in their respective languages.

These for-loops have been written to *loop* around some code doing something *for* as many times as it takes for i (an index) to get from 0 to 10. Each time through the loop i is increased by one. Each time through they get a number that has been stored somewhere corresponding to the index and then add that number to the sum.

You start at zero (by now you've probably seen this happen a lot in programming), find the number that is being held in the array numbers, add that number to sum, and keep going; stop after you've done your stuff with first ten places. If the numbers array looks like this (we've pictured the numbers array as having 13 slots; we don't know how many it might have – there would be an error generated if there were less than 11):

0	1	2	3	4	5	6	7	8	9	10	11	12
n_0	n_1	n_2	n_3	n_4	n_5	n_6	n_7	n_8	n_9	n_{10}	n_{11}	n_{12}

the final result of the code would be that sum_at_the_end_of_the_process equalled sum_at_the_beginning + n_0 + n_1 + n_2 + n_3 + n_4 + n_5 + n_6 + n_7 + n_8 + n_9 + n_{10}.

14 Exploiting Your Programming Skills

You are probably learning how to program by studying one particular language yet you know that there are actually hundreds and thousands of different programming languages used all over the world. So you might be asking yourself what you are actually gaining from learning this particular language. How will you make use of your newly acquired knowledge and skills once you have completed your introductory programming course? This chapter looks at the wider world of software applications and identifies ways in which studying programming in even one particular language gives you new skills that you should be able to exploit.

Learning how to program gives you many things. The most obvious is the ability to write programs that do what you want, reliably and correctly. Perhaps you have already begun to see things in your study, workplace or leisure activities that could benefit from having a program written for them. If so, great! Go for it! You have an immediate payoff for all your hard work in learning the language and you will go on learning with every new program. You might even come up with a genius idea that could make you a lot of money! However, for most people, this is not the most valuable thing they gain from learning to program in one language. In fact, many people never write a stand-alone program in their first programming language once they have finished studying programming. So, given the number of different languages you could be learning, is learning to program in a single language too limited? Absolutely not. The most valuable thing you will be able to do, once you have learnt one language, is to *learn to program in other languages.*

A quick look at some job advertisements shows that programmers do need to use a mixture of languages, not just one.

Job adverts
Essential skills are a minimum of 2 years SQL Server 2000, Visual Basic (VB6), Access 97 & 2000 from within an investment banking background. Candidates who have a good knowledge of VB.Net, ASP, Java, JSP or workflow and

imaging applications would have an advantage in securing this role.

Typical applications development environments may include PHP, ASP, Visual Basic, Perl, Linux, MySQL, Java, **JavaScript**, HTML and **XML**, with many solutions being delivered across the web. However a flexible and adaptable approach is of greater importance than specific skills.

High proficiency in C++ is expected, and a working knowledge of other languages, such as Perl and Java, will be an advantage. Experience with Oracle programming interface ProC*/OCI, as well as Oracle RDBMS, are desirable.

Candidates should be able to demonstrate an aptitude for developing applications within a Microsoft based environment, developing in .Net, C# and/or VB.Net. They should have an understanding of SQL and XML. Knowledge of UML documentation would be beneficial but is not essential.

Applicants should be proficient in a scientific language such as Fortran or C and have experience of web-based programming.

They also need to keep up to date with programming languages as they develop. Fortran was first developed in the mid-1960s but has gone through many changes since then. The current version is vastly different from its progenitor. Similarly, languages like Visual Basic change every year or two, to meet developers' needs to keep up with current trends in application design. One reason why learning a second, third, or nth language is not such a difficult task is that programming languages are often very similar to each other. Most programming languages allow you to define variables, make choices between different courses of action, repeat blocks of code, group together related code into modules, and so on. Although the exact words used or the order of words differs from language to language, if you know how to write a loop in Visual Basic, say, you will quickly be able to learn how to write a loop in other languages.

Even if you are not going to be a programmer, you will find it useful to know how to program in other languages. One reason is because the most commonly used software **packages**, such as word processors and spreadsheets, can be customized using built-in programming languages. Although these are designed to be used by people who do not consider themselves to be programmers, you can get the best out of them by studying them in the same way that you would study Java or C++, say.

▶ Programming in spreadsheets

Spreadsheets are packages that are widely used in office environments. You can use them to develop 'rough and ready' applications very quickly. Many spreadsheets are developed by individuals for their own use, often in order to help with occasional tasks. Suppose that you have to perform simple calculations on fairly large amounts of data. The data is entered into **cells** on one of the **worksheets**, and then processed using formulae entered into other cells. If you are the only user you will know what the spreadsheet does and where to find the results, so it will be tempting not to make the application look especially good, nor to document it extensively. On the other hand, it is remarkably easy to make errors in setting up a spreadsheet application. If, for example, you have built an application to help you plan your finances, an error that misleads you into thinking that you have more money available than you actually do could be costly as well as embarrassing. It is therefore a good idea to use testing techniques to ensure that the spreadsheet is giving the correct results.

When people find out about your application, they may ask if they can use it too. At this point you would certainly have to do some additional work. You must document it so that others will know how to use it and what its limitations are. You will also need to emphasize where data is to be entered and where the results are displayed. You also need to build in additional checks so that the application cannot be misused. Perhaps additional functionality will be needed – the new users' data may have different filenames from the one you use and so you may need a facility for allowing them to specify these. You may want to automate some of the processes so that the user is more likely to make accurate use of the application. How are you going to tackle this task? You will need to talk to the other users about the layout of the data entry and results areas to make sure that they will understand them as well as you do. You will also have to check much more thoroughly than if you are the only user to make sure that the application will give the right answers. Other users will not know how to fix bugs; worse, they may blindly trust your spreadsheet and not even notice if there are errors. All of this involves programming activities – design, implementation and testing – despite the fact that you are doing it in a spreadsheet rather than a general-purpose language. As a result, you will need to think about all the things described in Chapters 7, 8, 9 and 10, just as if you were programming in any other language. The good thing is that these techniques will already be familiar to you – you don't need to learn them afresh just because you are using a different language from your first language. You have developed what are known as *transferable skills*.

Spreadsheets make a lot of use of program-like things called **macros**. Macros are small programs that can be used to help with some of these tasks. Some packages allow you to generate macros by recording keystrokes, rather than by typing in the source code. This means that you can automate a task that you perform frequently by recording the keystrokes you make. Then the macro can be run by using a single keystroke or by clicking on a button. For instance, Microsoft Excel macros are written in VBA (Visual Basic for Applications). When you record a macro, the system stores appropriate VBA code to match the effect of your keystrokes. You can then associate the macro with a particular key combination to run it. While recording is a good way of making a start with the power of macros, there are limitations to what can be achieved in this way. You will soon find that you want to edit and enhance the recorded macros, or even write complete macros from scratch. At this point, you will need to learn at least a little about how the VBA programming language works. VBA macros can also be used in Microsoft Word, so you can also benefit from your programming skills when using a word processing package. Once again, the skills you have learned in writing subroutines, functions or classes in one language will have simplified the effort you need to expend to learn how to write macros in a spreadsheet or word processor.

▶ Code generators – letting a program write your code

Generating a macro by recording keystrokes is just one example of the use of a **code generator** to create the text of a computer program. When the macro is executed the stored code is interpreted line by line to carry out the required operations. Many other code generators have graphical user interfaces that allow the user to concentrate on design and reduce the amount of time that they have to spend on coding the solution. For example, GUIs are very laborious to program from scratch. They are constructed from standard components that we are all familiar with, such as boxes for entering text, pull-down menus and buttons. These can all be implemented using standard code. The important part of building a GUI is working out where to put these components on the screen. Tools such as Visual Basic provide a drag-and-drop mechanism for this and have a **library** of code for boxes, buttons and so on. This enables them to generate a complete program once the design is right.

What are the plusses and minuses of letting a program produce the code? On the plus side, it is a quick and easy way of generating the large amounts of code that are often needed. Remember that this is what compilers do for you, in effect, whenever you write a program in a high-level language. On the minus side, a generated program may not do exactly what you want and it might be quite inflexible – can the code cope if you want to allow users to resize the GUI window, for instance? As a programmer who knows how to learn programming languages, you will be able to take the generated code as a starting point and modify it to meet your requirements. This is analogous to early programming exercises in which you are given a program to change.

Building from components

One way to produce software that carries out a complex task effectively is to write a single large program. An alternative approach is to use several separate programs, each of which does part of the task. Let's look at a simple example to illustrate this. Suppose that I am a club secretary and I have a file that gives the names and addresses of all the club members, together with the date on which their membership expires. My file might look something like Table 14.1.

One job I might need to do is produce a list of people who have not paid recently so that the club committee can decide whether to terminate their memberships. The committee might expect a report looking like the one shown in Table 14.2, with the members sorted by expiry date first and within that by surname. One way I could do this job would be to write a program that reads through the file, selects records with expiry dates before the current date, sorts them into the required order and then prints the report in the specified format. This is not hugely difficult but it would take me a

Table 14.1   A database of membership details

Name	Address	Expiry date
Smith, Jim	1 High Street Anytown	2004/12/31
Patel, Aysha	Elm Cottage Ambridge	2006/10/30
Brown, Mary	23 Coventry Road Warwick	2005/04/12
Jones, Simon	44 Strand Street Whitstable	2006/10/30
Cheng, Jian	3 High Street Anytown	2004/12/31

Table 14.2   Overdue membership report 2005/10/10

Expiry date	Name
2004/12/31	Cheng, Jian
2004/12/31	Smith, Jim
2005/04/12	Brown, Mary

Figure 14.1 Linking existing independent components together

reasonable amount of time to design the program, write it, test and debug it. Alternatively, I might think to myself, 'I already have a little program that can select lines in a file that meet a specified condition. I also have a program that does sorting very quickly and efficiently. There's also that **report-writing package** that can lay out and print my report.' The end result is that I don't actually need to write a program at all! I just need to make those three programs link together (Figure 14.1).

The three separate programs are examples of what we call software tools or components. They could be programs that I have written myself, but they are more likely to have been supplied with the operating system of my computer, bought as a set of tools, or downloaded from the Internet. The advantage of this **component-based approach** is that I can benefit from other people's expertise in writing programs to sort, select and lay out data. I can also reuse the components quickly and easily when I have another task that involves selecting, sorting or report writing.

On the face of it, it should be possible to use components to achieve results without having studied programming. In practice, you are likely to find it much easier if you understand how programs are designed and built. There are several reasons for this. Firstly, you will understand what the components do much better if you have tried to write your own programs to do some of these tasks. Secondly, the documentation for the components tends to be written by programmers for programmers, so knowledge of programming will enable you to understand it. Thirdly, the design process for building a system from components is pretty much the same as the design process for writing a complex program from scratch. The problem has to be analysed to identify the activities needed to solve it, whether or not these are implemented in a single program or using components. Finally, the components used to build the system may require commands that look like bits of programs to tell them how to work.

How e-commerce sites use components
E-commerce exploits the Internet to give consumers access to a wide range of information and facilities. The different styles and complexities of e-commerce sites nicely illustrate the ways in which components can be used to create applications with different levels of sophistication.

The simplest sort of e-commerce sites just give fixed information about a physical company; for instance, what type of business it is, where its premises are located and what its opening hours are. This involves web pages with predominantly fixed content that are delivered from the business's web server to a browser on the consumer's computer. The web server and the browser are software packages that, together with the networks of the Internet, form components of an e-commerce system. We can represent this as Figure 14.2. If the company wants to enhance its web presence, it can add more components to this basic model. By linking in a database containing a catalogue of all the items it sells, their prices and descriptions including pictures, the web site becomes dynamic. The web pages are built on demand with completely up-to-date information, instead of having fixed contents (Figure 14.3). At a

Figure 14.2 A static business web site

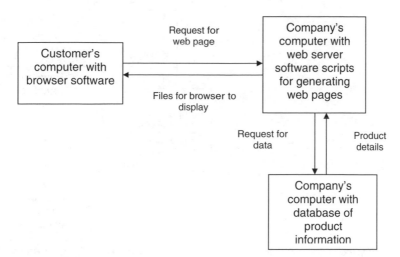

Figure 14.3 A dynamic e-commerce web site

later stage, the company might choose to add more components so that they can take orders online and process credit card payments.

E-commerce relies on ready-made components – browsers, web servers, database management systems to hold catalogue and order details, and payment handling software – in order to build systems quickly and cheaply. It also needs programs to make each site unique. These programs are typically written in languages such as HTML, SQL, Java, JavaScript and PHP: the languages named in several of the example job advertisements above. E-commerce software package vendors provide all sorts of easy-to-use packages that help novices to generate this code but they produce rather standardized web sites. To build a really effective e-commerce site needs some expertise in these languages (Figure 14.4).

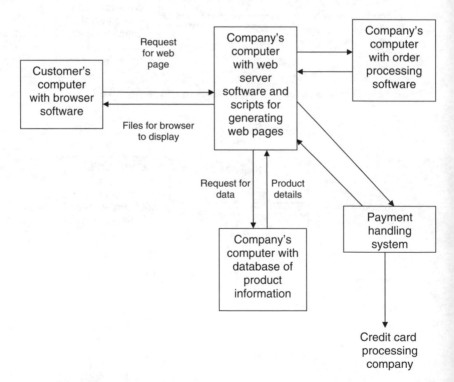

Figure 14.4 A highly integrated e-commerce business

► Special-purpose and incomplete languages

Even if you are not involved in e-commerce, you may want to develop your own web pages and web site. Knowing a bit about the special-purpose languages used for these can be helpful.

Word processors (and other software packages) give their users the opportunity to save documents as web pages. They produce a file written in a language called HTML, short for 'Hypertext Markup Language', which is used to specify the design of web pages. Is this a programming language? The Wikipedia has a '*Hello, world*' program written in it that certainly looks much like a computer program (Figure 14.5). Closer inspection shows that it has no variables, commands or control structures, so perhaps it is not a programming language after all? Nevertheless, the file of HTML statements acts, in effect, as a series of instructions that have to be interpreted by a web browser in order to render a web page on a computer screen.

HTML is an example of a special-purpose language that can be used in building a component of a computer program but which, unlike Java, C or VB, cannot be used to program a conventional computer. Despite this, it is a fundamental part of the World Wide Web when used in conjunction with components written in other programming languages.

Another special-purpose language that is widely used in building web sites (and many other applications) is SQL, 'Structured Query Language'. This is used to give commands to computer packages called **relational database management systems** (RDBMS for short) such as SQL Server, MySQL and Oracle. SQL also cannot be used to program a conventional computer, so HTML and SQL have to be glued together using a scripting language such as Perl or PHP, or some other suitable programming language such as VB.Net or Java. Using three languages rather than one sounds very complicated but actually it works extremely well. Each language just does a few

```
<!DOCTYPE HTML PUBLIC "-//W3C//DTD HTML 4.01//EN"
   "http://www.w3.org/TR/html4/strict.dtd">
<html>
  <head>
    <title>Hello, world!</title>
    <meta http-equiv="Content-Type"
    content="text/html; charset=UTF-8">
  </head>
  <body>
    <p>Hello, world!</p>
  </body>
</html>
```

Figure 14.5 'Hello, world' in HTML

things, so it can be simple to learn and simple to write. By splitting the program up into components it can be made to run across the Internet, potentially using computers on several continents to do its job. This is exactly what is needed for web sites and e-commerce applications.

▶ Programming into the future

In studying programming you will have learned a language. You will also have learned techniques for doing standard things with that language, like reading in data, manipulating data in various ways, displaying results and interacting with the program's users. At a higher level, you will have learned ways of tackling problems for which a computer program is a solution (or part of the solution). You will have gained experience of designing software, and of implementing and testing it. Over and above all that, you will know what is involved in studying programming and that it can be a creative and rewarding experience.

This chapter has illustrated some of the diverse ways in which all these skills can be exploited. Developments in code generators, software components, **embedded systems** and ubiquitous computing are changing the way in which computer programs are written all the time.

Interpreters

An **interpreter** is a computer program that reads in source code and executes it. For example, a web browser such as Netscape or Internet Explorer can read a text file containing HTML code, interpret it and display the results on a computer screen. Scripting languages like Perl, JavaScript and PHP are also usually interpreted. Interpretation is appropriate for short pieces of code or code that is seldom used.

Interpreters perform the combined tasks of compilers and runtime systems. The difference between a compiler and an interpreter is that an interpreter does not produce a file of code that is executable directly on a particular machine. General-purpose languages such as Pascal, C++, Java, Fortran, etc. are usually compiled.

▶ Chapter summary

Most programming jobs are not about sitting down and writing programs from scratch in a single language. They are about taking programs that other people have written and modifying them. They are about taking programs in old languages and writing new interfaces to them, or rewriting them in new languages. They are about taking several languages and building a 'program' that has aspects written in each. They are about combining programming languages with other tools such as spreadsheets and web pages.

What it means is that programming is just the beginning; to combine languages together, or modify programs, requires a fluent knowledge of programming in all the relevant languages.

15 Taking Programming Further

If you are taking an introductory programming course at university, are you perhaps thinking about taking it further – possibly even thinking about becoming a professional programmer? People have different motives for considering this path. Maybe your friends or parents are suggesting it to you because they realize that you are good at it. Perhaps you like programming and think it would be great to get paid for doing something so enjoyable. You might even see it as a way of earning a lot of money, possibly by setting up your own company at some point. Or maybe you are considering it as just one of several career choices.

▶ Getting ready to decide

Let's look at some issues that you will need to consider when deciding whether or not it would be right for you to pursue programming and related subjects in other courses that are available to you.

Programming is a practical activity. You need to try it in order to find out what it is and whether you enjoy doing it. You will probably have done some by the time you are reading this chapter, either as part of a programming course or by programming independently. How did you feel about it? Was it challenging? Interesting? Boring? Rewarding? Too time-consuming? Too hard? Absorbing? Fun?

Use your experience to consider for a moment what things characterize programming for you. What does it have in common with other subjects you are studying, and what makes it different from them? Clarifying your own ideas will help you to see if you agree with what we suggest in following paragraphs.

If you have not yet done any programming, then the most helpful thing you can do now is make a start. You can use this book together with a text-book that introduces you to a specific language, or you can enrol on a course. Bring your own experience back to this chapter later.

▶ Exploding the myths

To help you decide whether programming is really the right choice for you or not, try taking the simple test below. You should score 2 points for each 'Yes' answer, 1 for each 'Not sure' and 0 for each 'No'. You will need to score at least 6 points to make it as a successful programmer.

	Yes	Not sure	No
I'm very good at maths			
I'm a bloke			
I'm a bit of a nerd			
I have no fashion sense			

Ok, it's not really a serious test – but there is a serious point to be made here. Because of a few commonly held myths, some people are put off a career in computing before they even give it a chance. So let's begin by debunking some of the more pervasive myths.

1.   It is not necessary to be really good at maths
One of the most common misconceptions about programming is that you need to be an ace mathematician to be able to do it. This is because, historically, programming was built on a mathematical foundation. The very first computer (built in the early nineteenth century) was Charles Babbage's[1] Difference Engine, for the automatic compilation of mathematical tables.

All programming, at the lowest level, is about instructing a computer to perform logical and mathematical operations. The first programs were written in a language called 'machine code', which told the computer to perform instructions such as storing values in memory locations, adding/subtracting numbers and jumping to other parts of the program. These instructions had to be written as strings of binary numbers so that the computer could understand them – for example, an excerpt of machine code to add together two numbers might look like the left-hand column of Figure 15.1.

Programming in a language like this required considerable mathematical rigour and, consequently, in the early days of coding, programs were nearly all written by scientists (people such as physicists whose experimental data necessitated intensive computational processing). Since then, however, computer languages have evolved a very long way – nowadays we could write the three-line machine code program shown in Figure 15.1 by simply saying:

```
A is B + C
```

Instruction	Meaning
10000010 10000000	**load** a value from a specified memory location
00000000 10000001	add a value from another memory location to the value just loaded
00000101 10000000	store the result in the first memory location

Figure 15.1   Machine code instructions

Whilst being a skilled mathematician can help with the sort of problem solving and abstract thinking required of a good programmer, mathematical training is *not the only way* to acquire these skills – and furthermore, mathematical skills do not always translate directly into programming skills. People acquire the skills they need in their own ways – it's really not that important how they do it.

A maths failure's story . . .

I didn't get on with maths at school and much preferred humanities subjects to science ones. I went on to do A-levels in modern languages and then to university intending to pursue a career as a linguist – but the university I attended made all students take a subsidiary subject from a different faculty as part of their degree course.

There was a subsidiary course in maths for people like me who didn't have maths A-level – being older and wiser I thought I'd give the subject another go, tried it and found I still detested it! Next I swapped to geology, but that was so dull I only lasted three weeks. I had to find a science-based subsidiary course quickly or risk failing my degree, so in a panic I plumped for Computer Science (there wasn't much left to choose from at this stage).

Not being mathematical I expected to hate it, but as soon as we started learning how to program I was hooked – I couldn't believe how creative and how much fun the subject was. When I graduated I chose a career in computing rather than modern languages and haven't looked back!

It is undoubtedly true that certain programming tasks do require a good grasp of mathematics – scientific programming, signal processing, geometric modelling and the like – but most programming jobs are not like this. You don't need to have a first-class honours degree in Pure Maths to create a database for a car manufacturer, or a dynamic web site for a supermarket chain, or an expert system for diagnosing tropical diseases, or a design package for a kitchen-installation company. The truth is that if maths isn't your thing you can still earn just as much money programming as someone who is a maths whiz (and you'll probably be working on projects that you find much more interesting!)

2. It is not necessary to be a bloke

Whilst it is still true that in the UK the majority of programmers are male (women make up between 20 per cent and 35 per cent of the IT workforce depending on which survey you read), this is *not* because men make better programmers than women. There are two main reasons why women are under-represented in this field.

The first reason is historical – the fact that the IT industry has always been male dominated is off-putting to some female applicants. Unfortunately this means that the imbalance has been self-perpetuating, but now employers are realizing that this alienation of a huge proportion of their potential work-force is a bad thing, and many companies and universities are actively doing their best to turn the situation around.

The second reason is that women seem to naturally gravitate towards customer-facing roles (currently nine out of ten women work in the service industries), and traditionally computing jobs are not seen in this way. Many females perceive computing as a 'masculine' subject – all about engineering, tinkering with hardware, something non-creative, and in the past this was perhaps partly true – but the industry has changed rapidly in recent years. IT staff now need to have more customer awareness than ever before and things like communication skills and being a good team player are becoming increasingly important. Good programmers need to be able to communicate with users to find out what they need from software, and they need to be able to express themselves effectively. The industry is becoming more diverse and, as it does, women are beginning to realize that the opportunities are more exciting than they thought.

The ratio of males to females in the IT workforce is also partly a cultural matter. In India, for example, it is a preferred career for women because it is seen as a 'clean', non-manual job – women comprise some 45 per cent of the IT workforce in India. The same is true of Singapore and Malaysia where half of the students on computing courses are female. With the current Northern European/American trend to outsource programming work to countries where labour is cheap, there are plenty of IT jobs to go round in those parts of the world. This explosion in IT jobs in developing countries has led to equal employment opportunities for women, the like of which have never been available before. Interestingly, computing is also seen as a good career for women in many southern European countries, while in Northern Europe, Australia, Canada and the USA, the numbers of female participants in the industry is still low. If you're female, how about helping to put this right?

> ### Rear-Admiral Grace Murray Hopper (1906–92)
> Rear-Admiral Grace Murray Hopper is one of the most influential people in the development of programming. She was both a brilliant US Navy Officer and a pioneer in the field of data processing.
>
> After joining the Navy in 1943 Grace Hopper was assigned to Harvard University's Computation Lab, where she worked on the Mark-I – the first ever large-scale American computer. During the 1950s and 1960s, at the Eckert-Mauchly Computer Corporation, she devised the first ever compiler, and was jointly responsible for creating the FLOW-MATIC language – upon which the specification for the COBOL language was based. This is a highly significant achievement because since its creation in 1959 COBOL has enjoyed widespread use and COBOL programs are still used today in many large commercial enterprises and financial institutions.

3. It is not necessary to be a nerd
Another commonly held misconception about computing is that you have to be some sort of geeky social misfit to be any good at it. **Wikipedia** – the online encyclopaedia – has this to say on the subject:

> Traditionally, a nerd is a very intelligent but lonely and socially awkward person who is fascinated by knowledge, especially science. . . . Beginning in the late 1990s, many nerds on the Internet reclaimed the word *nerd* as a badge of pride, and began using it as a positive description . . .[2]

All subjects attract nerds (except possibly drama . . .) and it *may* be true that computing attracts a slightly larger nerdy element than some other subjects, given its historical (although not particularly accurate) image as a solitary pursuit, but most computer scientists are not nerds. These days, if you wandered into an average student bar, you'd be hard pushed to tell the computer scientists from the other students.

Of course, you need to be prepared to work reasonably hard to become good at programming – but then this is true of any skills-based course. This may be where one of the differences lies between a computing course and, for example, a history course. Whilst it's not advisable, some people do scrape through Humanities courses by largely avoiding their lectures and then indulging in panic swotting when an essay or examination looms. But with a skills-based subject this approach doesn't work – if you are learning to program, it's important to practise what you are being taught regularly, so that you have a good grip on particular skills before you move on the next ones. It's not so very different from, say, learning to snowboard – you wouldn't get very far if you missed all your lessons, virtually never got on your board to practise and then tried to cram the theory on the last day of your holiday, hit the slopes, and become king of the mountain (actually, you might get further than you thought – but probably not on your feet!)

The 'Nerd Pride movement'

Incidentally, in case you do consider yourself a nerd, and are proud of it, you might like to know about the 'Nerd Pride movement'. It was started at the Massachusetts Institute of Technology by professors Hal Abelson and Gerald Sussman. The latter was quoted in the *New York Times* (29/08/1994) as saying:

> My idea is to present an image to children that it is good to be intellectual, and not to care about the peer pressures to be anti-intellectual. I want every child to turn into a nerd – where that means someone who prefers studying and learning [rather than] competing for social dominance.

Admirable stuff – but, more importantly, as a paid-up member of the movement you could purchase 'Nerd Pride' baseball hats, badges and even pocket protectors, which are little plastic liners designed to contain leakage from faulty writing implements.

4.   It is not necessary to lack fashion sense

Well, quite frankly, have you seen what some drama students wear?

▶ What makes a good programmer?

The opinions expressed in this section are those of the authors, based on their experiences of being programmers and working with programmers. There is no standard formula you can apply to decide what makes a good programmer. However, some characteristics are commonly held to be helpful.

A positive attitude to problem solving

Programming is an intellectual challenge. It is about solving problems and is attractive to people who naturally enjoy problem solving. Some people solve problems just for fun, for example crossword puzzles or other challenges that can be found in newspapers. Programming involves thinking things through, and sticking with a problem until a way around it is found. If you enjoy this sort of activity then you will probably make a good programmer.

The ability to think logically

Programmers must be able to think logically. They need to be able to follow sets of conditions to their logical conclusions in order to design efficient algorithms; and they need to be able to understand patterns in program code in order to find fixes for annoying bugs. This requires an analytical sort of brain. If you are the type of person who operates using the 'stab in the dark' approach to problem solving then programming probably won't be for you.

The ability to think logically and laterally

Some programming problems will seem unsolvable, however logically you have thought about them. If all logical approaches have failed, a programmer needs to be able to think laterally – to gain distance from a problem and see it from new angles. As a programmer it is important not to keep thinking in circles once it becomes apparent that you are not getting anywhere. You need to be flexible and creative in your approach.

An elegant approach to crossword numbering

Suppose you had been asked to write a program to automatically number the appropriate white squares in a crossword puzzle.

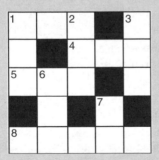

Your code should only number the *first*-occurring white square in any succession (horizontal or vertical) of two or more white squares – and this would usually mean making sure that the square to the left of (or above) any square to be numbered was black. Look at '4 across' or '6 down' in the example.

But what about white squares at the extreme left or top of the crossword (like '2 down' or '5 across')? In such cases you apparently need a separate rule to determine whether to number the square or not (because squares such as the one between '1 across' and '5 across' should not be numbered).

However, if you think about this laterally, you could have an imaginary extra row and column in the crossword (that just didn't get printed). If you write your program to assume that there is an imaginary top row and left-hand column, which consist of only black squares, then any white squares at the actual left or top of the crossword will be subject to the same rule as any other white squares – i.e., that they should be numbered if they are the start of a succession of two or more white squares and *the square to the left of (or above) them is black*.

A methodical approach

In programming you have to pay attention to detail. You need to be able to read code carefully and spot details of the syntax. At least some of the job will involve trawling through hundreds (perhaps thousands) of lines of code looking for errors or trying to make improvements in speed or functionality. The skills needed here are similar to those used by professional proofreaders.

You also need to be able to work out whether an algorithm is correct – whether the method you are going to use will actually solve the problem you are having to address. People who take pride in getting things exactly right, and are even a bit fussy about the details, are likely to enjoy programming more than those people who like seeing the broad view but are irritated by having to get the details correct.

Good programmers also write programs that are easy for other programmers to read and maintain. It is important to be methodical and rigorous with your commenting and layout, and to write your programs in a coherent and well-structured fashion.

Design skills

The analysis of a problem or situation and subsequent design of software to alleviate, ameliorate or automate it is often a large part of a programmer's job. As a software engineer you may find yourself designing whole systems from scratch. For instance, a programmer given the job of producing a dynamic web site for a client company could find that the responsibilities included analysing the company's needs, designing the physical and aesthetic layout of the site, building the back-end databases, writing the software to support the site and perhaps much, much more. These types of tasks are creative in different ways and require a software engineer who can design solutions using appropriately creative methods.

Forward planning

As well as paying attention to detail, the programmer needs to be able to look ahead – to think about the consequences of solving a problem in a particular way, to anticipate any problems that might occur and think about ways round them. This means looking beyond the immediate problem. It may involve considering how other people will use your program, predicting any unorthodox ways in which users might behave and making sure your program is robust enough to deal with them. Or it might involve thinking about unusual ways in which the hardware might behave or what errors it might generate. Looking outside the immediate problem and solution helps to ensure that high-quality software is produced.

Unpredicted user behaviour

The very common instruction 'press any key to continue' has apparently been a source of confusion for a great many software users. In fact at one stage the well-known firm Compaq allegedly considered changing the command 'Press any key' to 'Press the Return key' because of the flood of calls to their helpdesk asking where on the keyboard the 'Any' key was! The 'Frequently Asked Questions' section on the Hewlett Packard/Compaq website[3] gives the following information:

> The term 'any key' does not refer to a particular key on the keyboard. It simply means to strike any one of the keys on your keyboard or handheld screen.

Flexibility and willingness to learn

Bad programmers stick resolutely to what they already know (languages, algorithms, methods) and use them whatever the task demands. Good programmers are able to pick up new trends and learn new languages when appropriate. A university computing degree won't necessarily teach you the latest languages and tools but it will give you the skill set you need to be a good programmer – because it will teach you how to judge for yourself what is the best tool for a particular task. As mentioned in Chapter 14, the more languages you learn, the easier it becomes to learn new ones.

The ability to work on your own *and* as part of a team

Even if you are working as part of a development team, it is likely that a large proportion of your job will consist of sitting in front of a keyboard writing code, or poring over program listings. You need to be the type of person who is happy in this sort of task. That is not to say that you will necessarily be on your own – these days most programmers work in open-plan office spaces or at least shared offices, so isolation shouldn't be an issue. But you will need to be able to organize your own schedule effectively given that you will have ultimate responsibility for the way you divide your time between tasks, and will need to ensure you meet the deadlines set by your clients or managers.

The ability to work and communicate with others

Unless you work for a very small firm it is likely that you will be part of a team of developers working on the same project and will need to be able to work comfortably – and communicate effectively – with the other team members. You may also need good communications skills for liaising with clients and users, so that you can be sure of correctly interpreting their needs and delivering appropriate and well-designed software.

Other personality issues

Finally, it has to be said that some particular personal characteristics are helpful in this field. Programmers need patience and determination. They need to be prepared to work hard and stick at a problem, not give up easily. Sometimes it may take hours of work to find a bug or spot where to make an enhancement. You may spend lots of time making improvements and then find the code still doesn't work correctly. A good programmer will be tenacious enough not to give up. On the other hand, good programmers also need to be prepared to seek advice from time to time. Keeping going is good, but so is knowing when to stop. As you can probably tell, programming can be very frustrating, but also very rewarding.

► Know yourself

Now, assuming that you have read the thoughts under the previous headings, how do you think you measure up? Consider your own strengths and weaknesses in the areas described. Be honest with yourself. Some people find it helpful to write down a list of their strengths in one column and weaknesses in another. You can then use this character profile to help in making your choices.

You might also want to consider your approach to reading this book. Did you work through the examples given? Did you enjoy looking for syntactic details and spotting errors? Did you find the process engaging/challenging/motivating?

But above all, given the exposure you have had to it so far, ask yourself if you actually enjoy the act of programming. Good programmers enjoy what they are doing. For them it is like combining a hobby with a job. So if you feel that way too then it is certainly worth thinking more about taking the first steps towards becoming a professional programmer.

What if I don't take to programming?

Not everyone will take to programming. Some students have a good go at the subject, and indeed might get decent marks in a first programming course; yet at the end of it all they know is that they do not find programming 'easy' or 'natural' and would rather not follow this route further. Some students in this position will turn away from computing entirely and choose other options as part of their degree. Others may stick with computing (perhaps as a subsidiary part of their degree), but avoid those courses that involve large amounts of programming.

Remember that programming is one of the core skills for technical computing work. If you do not take to programming then it is unlikely that jobs such as software engineering, computer networking, and computer systems administration will appeal to you. We are often surprised that some students battle on with programming and other technical aspects of computing, despite those subjects not being the natural strengths of those students. At the end of this they then want a job in computing; more of the same! It is important to realize that if you find something like programming difficult at university it is not just a matter of 'sticking with it' until you have learned 'everything' about it; programming is a growing subject and you will need to continue to learn new aspects of programming once you are in a job.

Nonetheless there may be ways of making positive use of your experience in having done a programming course, even if you don't go into technical computing. You may find yourself in a position where you need to work with programmers, or employ programmers, or even manage them! In this situation having some programming experience is useful, so that you can talk to programmers and other IT experts with an understanding of what they are doing; this is valuable in administrative and management jobs concerned with computing. One common complaint from working programmers is that the people who are managing the projects often have no knowledge of computing or programming, thus making it very difficult to communicate effectively about the project, so if you have some knowledge along those lines it is likely to be to your advantage.

It is also highly probable that you will find yourself needing to use computers as tools in your job, even if you do not program them. Having a good understanding of the sorts of things that can be accomplished with computers will be a great help in deciding how they can best help you – there may be things you do in a job which would lend themselves well to computational solutions, but which you might never consider if you were ignorant of the possibilities.

▶ Taking it further – programming at university

At A-level, students can usually choose to study ICT (Information and Communications Technology) or Computing. The former has more practical content, while the latter is more theoretical and its content is closer to what you might expect in a Computer Science degree. But no matter which of the two options you might have been exposed to, studying Computing at university is actually quite different to studying it at school. Indeed, having an A-level in a computing-related subject is not necessary if you want to pursue a computing course at university.

If you choose a Computer Science course at degree-level you will probably be taught in depth about things like programming language theory, programming paradigms, compilers, algorithm design and data structures. You will also be taught formally how to program (probably in several different languages). However, a computing degree is not just about programming. You may end up studying a very diverse set of topics. In addition, perhaps even as a by-product of your main courses, you will learn about things like teamwork, commercial awareness and project management.

> ### Possible degree-level computing topics (a small sample)
> **Artificial Intelligence**, **Computer Architecture**, Database Systems, E-Commerce, **Graphics, Human–Computer Interaction**, Networks & Communications, **Neural Networks**, Operating Systems, Web-based Systems

You might decide that you don't want to be a hard-core computer scientist but would like computing to form part of your degree. There are many degrees available which focus on computing in a less technical way, as well as many universities which offer 'joint honours' programmes, where you can opt to study Computing alongside another discipline – Business, for instance. In addition to this, many institutions will allow you to take one or two subsidiary courses which may or may not relate strictly to your main degree – this would be another way to get some degree-level computing under your belt.

Here is a definition of a joint honours degree, where half of the programme of study involves computing. It is taken from the web site of the University of Kent:[4]

The joint honours degree programmes emphasise how computers can apply to business, commerce and the World Wide Web. They focus on the uses of computers rather than on their technical aspects; our graduates are more likely to be systems analysts than software engineers. The degree programmes have a large practical element, which means you have to analyse problems and reason logically.

You will find that university courses do not focus on the finer details of using particular tools and packages, and may not teach the latest trendy language or operating system – good courses will not be built on information that dates quickly. Instead they aim to give you a sound theoretical base and the ability to make informed decisions.

There is a huge range of computing and computing-related degree courses to choose from, so if this is the path that you wish to follow, make sure that you allow plenty of time for reading prospectuses before you decide on a particular programme of study at a particular institution. You should be aware that courses with the same title can vary widely in terms of content!

▶ Going beyond the first programming course

Assume for now that you have completed a first university programming course, say a course taking up a substantial part of your time in the first year of a degree. Where can you take this from here? Some of you might have no choice: you might be on a degree programme where there is a fixed follow-up course. However, many students will have an option about whether they continue to do programming in some form or other.

Continued study of computer science or software engineering subjects

If you are studying for a degree entitled 'computer science' or 'software engineering', or a degree jointly with one of those subjects, then the usual next step is courses involving topics such as **algorithms** and **data structures**. These are courses that look at patterns that are found in solving lots of different kinds of problems on the computer. A course on algorithms, for example, concentrates on common processes that occur in many different problem areas. You might look at ways of getting the computer to sort a list into order: once you know how to do this efficiently, you can apply it to problems like sorting a list of goods by price, sorting a list of people into alphabetical order, ordering a list of exam scores or sports results into a ranked table, etc. Data structures courses are typically also about generalization and patterns, but this time the focus is on how we organize information on the computer. In this sort of course you might look at patterns of data that occur over and over again: lists, hierarchies and dictionary-like structures. Again, once you are familiar with these, many different problems can be solved using them.

Another kind of course that commonly follows on from a first course in programming is a course on **software engineering**; this kind of course is about how to build bigger programs. As the name suggests many of the ideas in software engineering draw their inspiration from comparisons and analogies with engineering subjects. Some software engineering topics involve breaking down large problems into manageable chunks, and then organizing those chunks so that several programmers can work on them at the same time. Other aspects of software engineering relate to managing the process of creating large projects and knowing how to communicate ideas about software between people working on large projects.

Business-oriented computing courses

A different slant on computing, which retains the technical detail typical of programming but applies it in a different direction, is taken by courses which are oriented towards computing applied in business. Some of these are about applying combinations of existing programs in new ways. However, a number of these courses can involve programming or programming-like activities.

As mentioned in Chapters 13 and 14, computing for business applications such as sales, stock control, e-commerce, etc. is different from the kinds of programming that you typically learn in a first computing course. Instead of writing a single large program in a single language, this kind of computing often requires you to write lots of interacting programs in a mixture of languages, including traditional programming languages, scripting languages, languages to control interactions with users on the web and database languages. Therefore, if you choose to follow up programming along this route you might want to study topics such as dynamic web programming (JavaScript, PHP, etc.), programming for databases (e.g. in SQL), scripting languages such as **Tcl** and Perl, and 'languages' that allow you to add structure to data (e.g. XML).

Other computer science topics that include programming

Students can be surprised that computing topics other than 'programming' can actually involve programming. Programming is *the* key skill in computing; it would be difficult to think of another topic that has anything like the same level of importance across the whole range of computing topics. Therefore courses in computer networks, parallel computing, computer graphics, operating systems etc., are all likely to involve substantial amounts of programming. This occasionally comes as a shock to students who believe that they have 'done programming' at the end of the first-year programming course.

Applying programming to other areas

Another route forward with programming is in applying your programming skills to other subject areas within the university. This may be of particular interest if you are doing a joint degree (computing with another subject), and many students find it interesting when it comes to final-year projects to do some work which applies their programming skills in other areas.

Some subject areas, such as physics, have a long tradition of computational work. When such a subject has a long history, the choice of language can be rather unusual: for example, in the computational physics community there is heavy use of Fortran, which has not been commonly used for general programming tasks for many years. Similarly in the newly emerging area of bioinformatics, which is concerned with processing strings of text describing biological molecules, Perl is heavily used: this came about because Perl has a number of built-in facilities for text processing that do things that are similar to things which are of interest to biologists.

Computing within other subjects is often based around numerical issues. However, there is scope for interesting collaborations with other subjects: for example, some of our students have worked with sociologists on modelling patterns of voting behaviour, and with the drama department on using virtual reality for the theatre.

▶ Programming projects and placements

If you continue to take programming courses throughout your university career then it is likely that you will at some point get the opportunity to work on a substantial piece of programming work – perhaps an industrial placement or a large project in the final year of the course.

Work placements

Work placements are a common feature of computing degrees, whether for a whole year (most commonly between the second and final years; these years are often called 'sandwich' years) or just for the summer. Mostly these involve working with regular employers and being paid (sometimes fairly well!). There are a number of reasons you might want to do such a placement. One of these is that you will improve your computing skills, particularly in programming, as a result of the placement. This extra year of practice can be very useful when it comes to the final year of your studies, which often counts most in determining the class of degree you will get. Moreover you are likely to see your programming experience 'in the large'. Most of what you do on a degree is either individual work or rather artificial group work; in a placement you will get to see all of the ideas about software design and managing software projects in use for real, and see where they succeed and fail.

Occasionally students wonder whether to do a placement as a 'gap year' between school and university, or to do a sandwich year instead. If you specifically want to use your placement to develop your programming skills, the sandwich year is generally better; you will be able to go into it with more technical experience, and are therefore more likely to be given more responsibility for real programming work.

Final-year projects

The other place where you will get to do programming on a larger scale is when you undertake a project in the final year of your degree. Almost all computing degree courses require students to work on a large project in the final year; sometimes this is a piece of individual work, sometimes it is done in groups. Most projects of this kind involve a lot of programming and, in particular, programming on a large scale.

Choosing the right project is important. Depending on how your course works, you might get to make up your own project, or choose one from a list supplied by your university. There are good and bad things about each. Making up your own project means that you will be working on something that really interests you. However, you may choose something that is too ambitious, or, at the other extreme, not significant enough to occupy your time across the year.

▶ Taking it further – programming as a career

If you decide to become a professional programmer you will need to be constantly learning – new languages, new tools and new methods. Different tasks require different approaches and new and better ways to accomplish things are being dreamt up all the time. This is an industry that is constantly evolving, so the career of an IT professional is not one you can afford to sit still in!

If you do decide to take this route there are innumerable opportunities for you once you leave university. Many Computer Science graduates choose to work in the software industry, usually in roles where the majority of their time is spent designing, developing, debugging, enhancing and/or maintaining programs. But there are so many different roles for people with computing qualifications that this does not have to be the case.

It would be impossible to list all the possible jobs on offer to graduates with computing and computing-related degrees, but here is a taster:

> ### Jobs in the computing industry
> Analyst programmer, applications programmer, computer games designer, computer programmer, database administrator, IT consultancy, IT management, IT support, multimedia application developer, network administrator, software developer, software designer, software engineer, software tester, system administrator, systems analyst, systems engineer, systems developer, systems manager, web developer/designer

Advantages of a career in programming

If ultimately you decide that a programming career is the one for you, then you will have chosen a field that offers considerable benefits. If you are thinking about this seriously you might want to pick up a copy of a computing paper and look at some of the job advertisements to see what sort of job specifications are given. It might not be a bad idea to talk to people who work as programmers too – perhaps friends of your parents or friends of friends might have relevant experience.

If you enjoy coding then doing it for a living can be very satisfying. It's an engaging and creative process, and you will gain a great sense of achievement each time you finish a project, or see your work being used by other people. It is extremely rewarding to design and build something from scratch, but also just fixing a frustrating bug in a piece of code can be immensely gratifying!

As a programmer with the right skill set you will be extremely employable and should be able to pick and choose the field you want to work in, the company you want to work with and where you want to work. If you opt for contracting (where you hire yourself out to companies on a freelance basis) this is even truer. Computing is a very broad subject – it opens many doors in terms of future career choices.

▶ Taking it further – programming for fun

Finally, you might not take up programming as a career, but may perhaps want to continue with it for fun. Many people enjoy working on their own programming projects, e.g. writing computer games. Others enjoy working on collaborative projects. There are a lot of large 'open source' projects, many of which are willing to accept new collaborators. For example, a number of our students have been involved in a project called *RoboCup*, which is an attempt to develop software to enable robots (both real and simulated) to play football. Programmers from all around the world collaborate on this, either by supplying new 'teams' of programs that control the players in the game, or by improving the software that simulates the game and allows you to watch what is going on. There are lots of projects like this in all sorts of different areas; perhaps you might want to get involved?

► **Chapter summary**

Having learned the basics of programming, you need to decide whether you are going to take programming further: whether you are going to study it further, take up programming as a career, or carry on programming for fun. In this chapter we have tried to give you a feel for all of these aspects: exploding the false myths about what a programmer should be like, giving you an insight into the ways in which programming is used in the workplace, and discussing ways in which you might remain involved in the world of programming even if you don't become a professional programmer.

Part Six

Here be Dragons!

16 How Languages Differ

'Here be dragons!' We associate this phrase with the unknown. In fact, many people associate it with the edges of ancient maps – a phrase indicating that the world ends, or (as the case may be) perhaps it is the mapmaker's knowledge of the world that comes to an end.

You may be surprised to know that the phrase *never* appears in English on any historical maps. However, the Lennox globe (held in the New York Public Library) is engraved with the phrase

HC SVNT DRACONES

These Latin words are engraved on the 12 cm copper sphere, just off the coast of Asia. It is the earliest, and one of the very few, examples of a map with the phrase 'Here be Dragons' on it.

True to the spirit of the phrase, this chapter takes you into the unknown. It is for the adventurer, the explorer, and the student who wants to know more. Learning to program is not a task for just one semester, term or year. Nor is it a task for one language – programming is a lifelong activity that never ends. Over the course of your years as a programmer, you'll encounter many languages in many settings, and each one will be different. You'll learn their similarities, their differences, and (sometimes) where the dragons are.

Unlike the rare engraver who surely imagined fearsome and fantastical creatures in the chilly waters of the Pacific, we invite you to enjoy this sampler of languages. They're some of our favourites, and we'd like to take this opportunity to share them with you.

▶ All about paradigms

Part of developing good software means being able to assess the suitability of the tools at your disposal and understand their strengths and weaknesses in terms of the current project. The programming language is the primary tool, while others would be utilities such as libraries, debuggers and development environments. Accordingly, a good programmer needs to be in a position to select an appropriate programming language, and to do this must understand that there are different approaches to writing computer programs and sets of languages that are appropriate to each of these different approaches.

We use the term **paradigm** to describe a particular approach to coding. Programming paradigms are a means of classifying languages and grouping them according to the ways languages perform tasks and the sorts of tasks they perform best. These groupings describe the methods of coding and other features the languages have in common. Many texts and web sites group languages into four basic paradigms according to how they perform tasks: **imperative**, **declarative**, **functional** and object-oriented.[1]

In this chapter we will cover these four paradigms, plus two additional ones: the scripting paradigm and the concurrent paradigm. As we will see below, scripting languages are most useful for writing limited programs called scripts, while the concurrent paradigm is useful for writing programs designed to deal with situations in which several things may be happening at the same time.

▶ The imperative paradigm

This paradigm gets its name from the word 'imperative', meaning 'an order or command'. In English, statements such as 'Tidy your room', 'Eat those vegetables', and, 'Don't miss the class on Tuesday morning', are examples of imperative statements. Imperative programs are in essence sequences of commands which tell the computer what it has to do, step by step, to complete a particular task. Examples of commonly used imperative languages include Fortran, COBOL, BASIC, Pascal and C.

Programs written in imperative languages generate a sequence of states when executed, and these states are associations between memory locations and values. The imperative statements that the code consists of are basically concerned with state transformations. Programming commands, such as conditional and looping constructs, along with the assignment operations, determine the transitions between states. For example, assuming that the memory location representing the variable x contains the number 3 and the location named y contains the value 6, we might represent the computational state at that point as $\{x:3, \ y:6\}$. The following line of code:

```
x = y * 2;
```

would then result in a transition to the computational state represented as $\{x:12, \ y:6\}$. The key point to note is that the value of any particular variable (memory location) does not necessarily remain fixed once initialized. Its value at any particular point in the program is dependent upon the state changes represented by preceding statements.

The task of converting a distance from miles to kilometres lends itself well to the linear, sequential style of coding that we associate with the imperative paradigm, because it involves writing an explicit series of steps to achieve the end result:

- Ask the user to enter a number (representing a distance in miles).
- Read the number into a variable.
- Multiply the number by 5, divide by 8 and store in a new variable.
- Print out the value of the new variable (the distance in kilometres).

The following lines of code show how these four steps would be written in the C programming language:

```
printf("Please enter a distance in miles: ");
scanf("%d", &miles);
kilometres = miles * 5 / 8;
printf("%f\n", kilometres);
```

Most programming languages implement the imperative style to some extent. Many tasks are linear by their very nature, so programs which belong to a different paradigm will probably still perform some tasks imperatively – therefore languages from non-imperative paradigms often contain constructs of an imperative nature.

To give you a better idea of the structure of an imperative program, here is a more complete example, again written in C. The purpose of this program is to read a file of text and return a breakdown of the number of different types of character in the file (lowercase, uppercase, digits and whatever is left). This is a useful thing to be able to do – many email anti-spam systems use this sort of text classification as part of their arsenal of spam-detection algorithms (because spam emails characteristically do not contain the same ratio of lowercase characters, uppercase characters, digits and other characters as normal emails).

```
/* Include the library of built-in input/output
 * functions
 */
#include <stdio.h>

/* Start of the program
 */
int main(void) {

    /* Declarations necessary for reading the file
     */
    FILE *fp, *fopen();

    /* Declare variables to hold...
     *    ...the current character
     *    ...the count of lowercase and uppercase
     *    characters
     *    ...the count of digits and other characters
     *    ...the name of the file to be processed
     */
    int ch;
    int lowercase = 0, uppercase = 0;
    int digits = 0, others = 0;
    char filename[50];

    /* Prompt the user to enter a filename, read the
     * filename,
     * then open the chosen file so that it can be read
     */
    printf("\nEnter filename: ");
    scanf("%49s", filename);
    fp = fopen(filename, "r");
```

```c
/* Start looping, reading characters from the file,
 * one by one, (until the end of the file is found)
 */
while ((ch = getc(fp)) != EOF) {

  /* If the current character is lowercase, add to the
   * lowercase count.  If it is uppercase, add to the
   * uppercase count.  If it is a digit, add to the
   * digit count, otherwise add to the count of
   * other characters
   */
  if ((ch >= 'a') && (ch <= 'z')) {
     ++lowercase;
  }
  else if ((ch >= 'A') && (ch <= 'Z')) {
     ++ uppercase;
  }
  else if ((ch >= '0') && (ch <= '9')) {
     ++digits;
  }
  else {
     ++others;
  }
}

/* Print out the results - the number of each type
 * of character found in the chosen file
 */
printf("Lowercase: %d\n", lowercase);
printf("Uppercase: %d\n", uppercase);
printf("Digits: %d\n", digits);
printf("Others: %d\n", others);

/* Return a 'success' indication to the runtime
 * environment
 */
return 0;
}
```

This program consists of a succession of clearly defined steps:

- Declare any necessary variables.
- Obtain the name of the file to be read.
- Open the file.
- Loop, reading and classifying characters from the file.
- Print the results.

It is characteristically imperative in style.

▶ The object-oriented paradigm

The object-oriented paradigm has its origins in the 1960s, which was a fertile period for the invention of new programming languages. The language Simula introduced the concept of representing things in terms of their *class*. The paradigm was further developed via the Smalltalk language, which was actually both a language and a programming environment (IDE) combined. Object-orientation (OO) started to become more popular and more accessible (two concepts that are closely connected in the world of computer languages!) through the development of the C++ language as an enhancement of the imperative C language. OO finally reached the masses through the Java programming language, developed at Sun Microsystems in the 1990s.

The essence of object-orientation is that the programs we build often represent *models* of things in the world. You can see this in the way that IT is used in many organizations. For instance, a sports centre that manages its business with IT will have programs that model the day-to-day activities of the sports centre. The programs contain concepts like squash courts, badminton courts, playing fields, pitches, climbing walls, etc. so that bookings can be made. Membership details will be stored and manipulated so that renewal reminders can be sent out and patterns of usage monitored. Each real-world entity that influences the operation of the centre is likely to be represented in some way within the programs they use.

Programming with the object-oriented paradigm is centred on the idea of capturing descriptions of entities in **class definitions**. A class definition describes the way in which typical examples of a particular entity are structured and behave. For instance, if we want to store membership details for members of the sports centre, then we are likely to define a class called Member that stores information such as the member's name, the date they joined the centre, their membership status (e.g. full, student, affiliate, etc.), contact details, and so on. As you can see, the class does not represent any particular member but rather the details held on a typical member. Within an object-oriented program, the class is used to create *objects*, and it is the objects that are filled out with the distinctive details of the individual entities that they represent. For instance, one object created from the Member class might contain details recording that Robert Bocking joined the centre on 3 January 2005 and is a full member; another might contain the details for Louisa Lindo, a student member who joined on 27 March 2005, and so on – one Member object for each sports centre member. Code 16.1 shows some of the details of a Java class to represent Member objects.

An important feature of class definitions that distinguishes them from being little more than database entry descriptions is that they combine both data (name, date, status, etc.) and functionality – which is called **behaviour** in the object-oriented paradigm. Class definitions contain program code that operates on the data the individual objects store. For instance, the Member class will contain code to update the membership expiry date when a person renews their membership. If a person upgrades from affiliate to full membership, then there will be code to change their status. There may be quite sophisticated code within a class to ensure that inappropriate operations are not performed on the objects belonging to that class. For instance, an object might check that the person's membership has not expired before permitting a change of status.

```java
public class Member
{
    // Personal details.
    private Name name;
    private Address address;
    // Status and renewal date.
    private MembershipStatus status;
    private Date renewalDate;
    /**
     * Prepare the details of a potential new member.
     * A membership status of NONE is the default.
     * @param name The member's name.
     * @param address The member's address.
     */
    public Member(Name name, Address address)
    {
        this.name = name;
        this.address = address;
        status = MembershipStatus.NONE;
        renewalDate = null;
    }
}
```

```
/**
  * Set the membership status and renewal date for
  * this member The current status must be NONE.
  * @param status Must not be NONE.
  * @param renewalDate
  * @throws AlreadyAMemberException If already a
  * member.
  */
public void join(MembershipStatus status,
                 Date renewalDate)
  throws AlreadyAMemberException
{
  if(status == MembershipStatus.NONE) {
    throw new IllegalArgumentException(
      "Status cannot be " + status);
  }
  if(this.status != NONE) {
    throw new AlreadyAMemberException(
      this.status, this.renewalDate);
  }
  this.status = status;
  this.renewalDate = renewalDate;
}
/**
  * Renew an existing membership.
  * @param nextRenewalDate
  * @throws NotAMemberException If the current status
  *      is NONE.
  */
public void renew(Date nextRenewalDate)
  throws NotAMemberException
{
  if(status == MembershipStatus.NONE) {
    throw new NotAMemberException();
  }
  this.renewalDate = nextRenewalDate;
}
/**
  * Change the membership status to a different
  * value.
  * @param status The new status.
  */
public void changeStatus(MembershipStatus status)
```

```
{
   if(status == this.status) {
      throw new IllegalArgumentException(
         "Status is already " + status);
   }
   this.status = status;
}
/**
 * Change the member's address.
 * @param updatedAddress The new address.
 */
public void changeAddress(Address updatedAddress)
{
   address = updatedAddress;
}
// The rest of the class has not been included . . .
   . . .
}
```

Code 16.1 Part of a Java class recording membership details

A full information system for a sports centre might consist of hundreds of different class definitions, each modelling a particular entity within the 'world' of sports centre management. From these class definitions, many thousands of different objects will be created, each with its own identity and ability to control its own internal state (the data values it stores).

Object-oriented programming languages typically have associated with them large libraries of class definitions. These represent not application-specific entities, but general-purpose entities or reusable components which prove useful in many different applications; for instance, a List class capable of storing an arbitrary number of objects (such as a list of members), or a Window class for use when building GUIs for applications.

The Java programming language has been particularly influential in supporting the development of e-commerce systems because it is a highly portable language, allowing programs to be run on many different platforms.

▶ The declarative paradigm

Declarative-style coding is about 'what a problem is', not about 'how to solve it'. A declarative programmer is not interested in the sequences of steps involved in a programming task, but rather in simply representing the problem domain.

The building blocks of declarative programs are sets of facts and rules – the programmer produces a 'knowledge base' (basically a database) of facts and rules, which denote the logical relationships between various entities. Thus the relationships in the knowledge base are specified, but the programmer does not say how the rules are applied. Users' queries are put forward in the form of goals that are proved (if possible) using the facts and rules in the working memory. If a goal matches a fact then it succeeds. If it matches a rule, then each of the rule's subgoals must also succeed.

Prolog is a popular and powerful language that comes under the declarative paradigm. It is the most commonly used language in this paradigm (others include Mercury, KL-1 and Gödel) and it inherits its basic structure from the field of logic. When a user submits a query, Prolog's built-in inference engine works through the rules and facts in the knowledge base to see if the query is true.

The Prolog code below is a simple knowledge base designed to assist users in finding holiday deals. Users can specify a maximum price for a holiday, the number of nights required and an activity that they particularly wish to be able to try at the resort. The program then searches through the available options and returns all possible answers if required.

The program has two parts – a 'fact-base' (a number of facts that contain information relating to available holidays and resort activities) and a 'rule-base' – the engine which drives the program and specifies what we are looking for. For the program to be really useful the fact-base would, of course, need to be quite large, but here is a flavour of what it might contain.

The first set of facts in the knowledge base (called deal) shows, for each available holiday, which resort it is in, where that resort is, how many nights the holiday is for and the price per head:

```
%  ─────────────────────────────────────────────────────
% Prolog facts that express information about what deals
% are available at which resorts. For instance the first
% fact denotes a deal in 'Palma Nova' in Majorca for seven
% nights at £379.
&  ─────────────────────────────────────────────────────
    deal( 'Palma Nova', 'Majorca', 7, 379).
    deal( 'Palma Nova', 'Majorca', 14, 569).
    deal( 'Es Cana', 'Ibiza', 7, 289).
    deal( 'Playa las Americas', 'Teneriffe', 7, 259).
    deal( 'Limassol', 'Cyprus', 7, 129).
    deal( 'Bodrum', 'Turkey', 7, 189).
    deal( 'Bodrum', 'Turkey', 14, 329).
```

The second set of facts in the database (called `activities`) shows, for each resort, what activities are available for holidaymakers to try. Since there is usually more than one activity on offer in each resort, the activities are represented as a list (a number of items surrounded by square brackets):

```
%  _____
% Prolog facts that express information about what
% activities are available at which resorts. For example
% the list of activities for the resort 'Palma Nova'
% contains, windsurfing, sailing and paragliding.
%  _____
   activities( 'Palma Nova',
               [windsurfing, sailing, paragliding]).
   activities( 'Es Cana',
               [clubbing, jetskiing]).
   activities( 'Playa las Americas',
               [windsurfing, sailing, diving, clubbing]).
   activities( 'Limassol',
               [clubbing, paragliding, windsurfing]).
   activities( 'Bodrum',
               [sailing, jetskiing, diving]).
```

The next part of the program is the rule-base. In this case it consists of only one rule – concerned with finding the requested holiday deals for the user. This rule has six variables: the first three are input variables, for which the user provides values:

- `MaxPrice` – the maximum price the user is prepared to pay for the holiday
- `NumNights` – the number of nights required
- `Activity` – the desired activity.

The last three are output variables, which, if a holiday matching the user's requirements can be found, will return:

- `Resort` – the name of the resort
- `Where` – the location of the resort
- `Price` – the actual price of the holiday.

The rule has only four actual lines of code (known as subgoals). The code is characteristically declarative because in each of the subgoals we are simply declaring what we want the program to do at that stage, but not saying how we want it to do it – for instance, although we need to repeatedly access `deal` facts, there is no need to set up a loop to do this.

```
%  _____
% The prolog rule for finding holiday deals.  It takes a
% maximum price, number of nights and requested activity,
% and returns a resort, location and price. This rule has
% four subgoals, which perform the following functions:
%
% 1 Find a 'deal' fact in the database which has a
%   'NumNights' value equal to that requested by the user
%
% 2 Check that the price for the deal found is less than
%   (or equal to) the maximum price the user specified
%
% 3 Find the list of activities available in the resort
%   previously located
%
% 4 Check that the activity the user specified is
%   available in that resort - by checking that the
%   activity is a member of the list of activities
%   linked to that resort ('member' is a built-in rule
%   so the programmer does not need to define it)
%  _____
    find_holiday( MaxPrice, NumNights, Activity,
                  Resort, Where, Price) :-
      deal( Resort, Where, NumNights, Price),    % subgoal 1
      Price =< MaxPrice,                         % subgoal 2
      activities( Resort, ActivitiesList),       % subgoal 3
      member( Activity, ActivitiesList).         % subgoal 4
```

The clever thing about this sort of code is that if any of the subgoals fails, the program automatically **backtracks** to a previous goal and generates a different answer at that point before automatically proceeding again.

To explain what is meant by this, here is an example of the program executing. The user queries the rule, stating that what is required is a holiday with a maximum price of £300, for seven nights and in a resort that offers sailing as an activity:

```
|?- find_holiday( 300, 7, sailing, Resort,
                  Where, Price).
```

There are only two holidays (given the limited fact-base) that meet these criteria, and both would be found as a result of this query:

```
Resort = 'Playa las Americas',
Where = 'Tenerife',
Price = 259

Resort = 'Bodrum',
Where = 'Turkey',
Price = 189
```

How is the query solved?

Deals are pulled out of the fact-base in the order in which they occur, so the first deal fact extracted by subgoal 1 of our rule is:

```
deal( 'Palma Nova', 'Majorca', 7, 379)
```

Subgoal 2 is then executed, which states that the price for the holiday just found (£379) must not exceed the user's stated maximum price (£300):

```
379 =< 300
```

This statement fails because 379 is not less than or equal to 300. However, instead of the program stopping here because it has failed, it simply goes back to rule 1 and pulls out the next deal fact. Since the user has set 7 as the value for the NumNights variable, the program skips over the next fact in the database:

```
deal( 'Palma Nova', 'Majorca', 14, 569)
```

because the NumNights value does not match. Therefore the next possible answer pulled out is deal fact number 3:

```
deal( 'Es Cana', 'Ibiza', 7, 289)
```

Here the price and number of nights are fine, so the code moves on to subgoal 3, which pulls out the activities fact for 'Es Cana':

```
activities( 'Es Cana', [clubbing, jetskiing])
```

and then proceeds to subgoal 4, which states that the user's desired activity (sailing) must feature in 'Es Cana's' list of activities. This is not the case ('Es Cana' only offers clubbing and jetskiing), so the program backtracks again. Since no new values can be found by backtracking to subgoals 3 or 2, the program backtracks all the way to subgoal 1 again, and pulls out the next deal fact:

```
deal( 'Playa las Americas', 'Tenerife', 7, 259)
```

This holiday actually satisfies all four of the subgoals (it is less than £300, it is for seven nights and sailing is an available activity), so this holiday is given as the first answer. If the user requests further answers, the program simply backtracks again, looking for the next possible solution. The really clever bit about all this is that the programmer does not have to tell the program how to search the fact-base or how to perform the backtracking – this all comes for free with the Prolog language.

▶ The functional paradigm

In the functional paradigm, we focus our designs on how data is trans-formed. The processes that transform data are known as **functions**. In particular we solve problems by describing how to solve them in terms of other, simpler, functions; in turn these functions are described in terms of other functions. This continues until we have described the problem in terms of standard functions such as doing arithmetic on numbers or sorting lists of words alphabetically.

Scheme is an example of a language belonging to the functional paradigm and it is the one we look at in this chapter. Other functional languages, like Haskell and ML, look very similar.

In Scheme we put the function, the thing that describes what we are doing, first. Then we follow this by the things that we are applying this function to. A typical function we might want to do is to add two numbers together. In Java we would say:

```
3 + 5
```

However, in Scheme we would put the function at the beginning and sur-round the whole thing by parentheses:

```
(+ 3 5)
```

The parentheses enable us (and the computer) to know where a function starts and finishes so, typically, a Scheme program is full of parentheses!

Whenever you see an open **parenthesis** in a Scheme program, it means the thing right after the open parenthesis is a function, and everything else is what is fed into the function. These are called the **arguments** to the func-tion. We can stack these functions inside each other:

```
(+ 10 (- 4 2))
```

When we have a 'nest' of functions like this, we start from the innermost function (in this case (- 4 2)) calculate that (getting the result 2), then apply the next function outwards: after calculating the innermost function we are left with (+ 10 2), which we can calculate to get the answer 12.

Let's make music

Art and music are wonderful places to look when searching for interesting and challenging programming projects. They are creative, meticulous, yet beautiful and spontaneous areas at the same time. Given the nature of the next section, we'd highly recommend the article 'Hackers and Painters', by Paul Graham[2]; he does a wonderful job of capturing how functional programmers often think about programming.

In exploring the functional paradigm, we're going to look at music. We'd like to develop a system that lets us, in a semi-automated way, start using the computer to generate music. In music there are many, many structures we might want to represent: sequences (notes in a row), chords (notes stacked on top of each other), duration (how long a performer might 'hold' or 'sound' a note), volume, instrument type, etc. The number of possible things we could represent is huge. Here, we'll try and do some interesting things with sequences of notes.

To start, we have to decide how we will represent the notes. To keep things simple, we can make some design decisions; this is a fancy way of saying, 'Let's make an assumption or two.' We should note that these decisions may affect us adversely later on, but that's OK. So, for the moment, notes can be represented by numbers, and we'll just number the notes of a scale.

Middle C will be 1, D will be 2, and so on. We're making this simple so that we can get our program working quickly, and then come back and rethink the decisions we've made so far.

Here is an example of how we might write a nested function to do something musically interesting:

```
;; We are going to put two sequences of
;; notes one after another. We
;; will "append" the first to the second.
(append
  ;; This makes the first sequence
  (make-sequence 5)
  ;; This makes the second sequence,
  ;; and then shifts it up by two.
  (shift-seq (make-sequence 5) 2))
```

Which should, after we've written the functions   make-sequence   and shift-sequence,   produce something that looks like:

We could set about writing these two functions in any order we want, but we might as well follow the rules we learned in mathematics. We know we need to evaluate the innermost parentheses first, so let's start with the innermost: a function called make-sequence. make-sequence takes one argument, a number. This number will represent how many notes we want in the sequence. Here, we've asked for five notes. Let us assume that the sequences always end on the note C. We will represent the sequence of notes as a list of numbers. So we would like the Scheme function

```
(make-sequence 5)
```

to produce the list

```
'(5 4 3 2 1).
```

that is, a descending sequence of notes ending on middle C. In Scheme, we define new functions with define:

```
;; We will define "make-sequence" as a
;; function that expects one variable,
;; a number, called "num-notes".
(define (make-sequence num-notes)
    ;; If the programmer asks for a sequence
    ;; of zero notes, or we work our way
    ;; down to zero, return an empty list of notes.
    (if (zero? num-notes)
        '()

        ;; Otherwise, attach the current
        ;; number to the result of calling
        ;; make-sequence with a smaller number.
        (cons num-notes
            (make-sequence (sub1 num-notes)))))
```

Our notes are represented as numbers, and we want to build up a list of numbers. The Scheme function cons does this for us: it takes a number as its first argument, and a list as its second argument; cons attaches the number to the list. In this case, we attach the number we are currently looking at to the list generated by calling make-sequence on a number one smaller. If you work it out by hand, you'll discover that you eventually reach zero, and our program gives us an empty list to attach all our numbers to. Try it out and see for yourself.

Now we need to define a second function that is going to allow us to shift sequences of notes up or down.

```
;; We define a function called "shift-seq"
;; that expects two values, a sequence
;; and a distance to shift that sequence by.
(define (shift-seq seq dist)
    ;; If we are given a list of no notes in
    ;; the sequence, we should return a list of
    ;; no notes.
    (if (empty? seq)
        '()

        ;; Otherwise, we should take the first
        ;; note in the list, and shift it by
        ;; the distance indicated. We'll attach this
        ;; with "cons" onto the list produced
        ;; by shifting the rest of the list.
        (cons (+ (first seq) dist)
              (shift-seq (rest seq) dist))
    ))
```

shift-seq takes a sequence of notes and a distance we want to shift each note – remember, our notes are just represented by a single number. So, we ask if we've been given no notes – a list of no numbers – and if that's true, we should just give back a list of no notes. However, if there is a number in the list (that is, (first seq)), we should add to it the distance, and then shift the remaining notes in the list (which is (rest seq)).

Looking back at our original code, we can see how these pieces fit into place. We had originally written a small program that would combine a sequence with a shifted version of itself:

```
(append (make-sequence 5)
        (shift-seq (make-sequence 5) 2))
```

We can run this program by replacing sets of parentheses from the innermost to the outermost. The innermost (make-sequence 5) can be replaced by some notes:

(append (make-sequence 5) (shift-seq ♪♪♪♪♪ 2))

Then, we shift this sequence up by two:

(append (make-sequence 5) ♪♪♪♪♪)

At this point, we can evaluate the other make-sequence

(append   )

And, lastly, we join these two lists of notes together:

Most programming environments will not insert pictures of notes for you when you are writing programs about music. If you would like to experiment with functional programming, and even try out the Scheme code presented here, you can download DrScheme, a programming environment designed for beginning Scheme programmers, and have a go.

▶ The scripting language paradigm

As we have been learning, different programming languages are suited to different sorts of tasks, and two common programming tasks are the use of 'scripts' to either automate common activities or to connect existing applications together in order to create software with new functionality. Languages that are particularly effective in these types of role are often referred to as 'scripting languages'.

There are lots of scripting languages around; well-known and often-used ones include JavaScript, VBScript, Perl, PHP and Python. You might use Perl or PHP to link a database to a website or create dynamic web pages; you could use JavaScript to add interactivity to a web page; you might use VBScript to tie together an Access database with Microsoft Word; you might use Perl to generate reports from your log files.

Typically these languages enable comparatively rapid code development – although this can be at the expense of run-time efficiency. They also tend to be interpreted rather than compiled languages. For instance, most web browsers come with a built-in JavaScript interpreter, so code written in JavaScript will cause browsers to respond to user interaction. We will first look at some code from one particular scripting language and then go into some of the similarities shared by scripting languages.

A Perl script

Perl is a powerful scripting language that is usually associated with processing text. The following script counts words within a text file, which may be plain text or program code.

```perl
#!/usr/bin/perl -w
use strict;

# "wordcount" is a hash table; it will store
# "keys" (which will be words), and "values"
# (which will be the number of times a particular
# word appears in a piece of text.
my %wordcount;

# This line reads the an entire file into the
# "entire_file" array.
my @entire_file = <>;

# We want to process each line in the file;
# so, we use a "foreach" loop, and temporarily
# store the text of each line in the variable $line.
foreach my $line (@entire_file) {

  # "chomp" newline character off the end of the line
  chomp($line);

  # We use "split" to split up the line wherever
  # there are blank spaces. /[[:blank:]]/ is a
  # 'regular expression'. Look up regexps on the WWW!
  my @possible_words = split(/[[:blank:]]/, $line);
```

```
foreach my $word (@possible_words) {

    # First check: does the word contain at
    # least one letter? If so, we'll work with it.
    if ($word =~ /[[:alpha:]]+/) {

        # Words at the end of sentences have
        # punctuation.
        # I'll remove all punctuation from the word.
        $word =~ s/[[:punct:]]//g;

        # And convert the entire word to lowercase.
        $word = lc($word);

        # Count the number of occurrences of that word
        $wordcount{$word}++;

    }

  }

}


# Now that we've finished processing every line
# in the file, it's time to see how many times each
# word appeared.
foreach my $key (sort keys %wordcount) {
    print "$key -- " . $wordcount{$key} . "\n";
}
```

Perl is a concise language in which a few symbols can have a very powerful effect. This can make Perl scripts impossible to read for those unfamiliar with it. In addition, there is usually a great deal of flexibility available in the way that scripts are written. It is likely that a Perl expert would be able to reduce the size of our script considerably. However, one probable side-effect of the reduction in size would be an increase in obscurity.

As you may have noticed, scripting languages contain elements that are very similar to aspects of other paradigms. You will have probably picked up parts of the code that suggest the procedural paradigm, and possibly some elements may be reminiscent of object-orientation. However, because scripting languages are designed to be easy to use, they typically share certain characteristics.

For one thing, the source code is not usually put through the normal edit-compile-run cycle but, rather, is passed directly to the runtime system. This means that the development process feels a little different. The time between writing the source code and executing it is much shorter, programs also tend to be shorter (hence 'scripting language' rather than 'programming language'), and the programs themselves tend to be more ephemeral in nature.

Scripting languages can dramatically simplify certain design tasks for a programmer by making it possible to define and evaluate functions 'on the fly'. Unlike most of the programming languages we have discussed, scripting languages often dynamically assign types to variables and expressions. For instance, in Perl, the expression "101" will be interpreted either as a string or a number, depending upon the context in which it is used. This 'looseness' makes such languages extremely suitable for rapid development and iteration, but equally involves a loss of the discipline which is essential in programs intended for longevity.

▶ The concurrent paradigm

Every language has its strengths. Some languages are fast. Some languages help you write big, complex programs. The **occam** language lets the programmer write programs about everything at once. By this, we mean that it is a language designed to allow the programmer to reason about lots of different aspects of their program that are supposed to happen **concurrently**, or at the same time.

The best way to introduce you to occam is to give you an example. Because occam is designed to handle lots of things happening at the same time, we need a programming problem that gives us just that situation. As it turns out, robots (and other systems that must deal with the real world, generally referred to as **real-time systems**) are a perfect example. We've chosen to use the **LEGO® Mindstorms™**, a small robotics kit produced by the LEGO Group (Figure 16.1a), as the platform of choice for demonstrating occam's expressive power.

The Mindstorms kit has the ability to take input from three sensors (touch, light and rotation sensors) as well as control up to three motors. In our example (Figure 16.1b), our robot will have the ability to tell if it has bumped into something in front of it or behind it; this way, we can drive around the room and navigate around obstacles by bumping into them, backing up, turning a bit, and trying again.

The only problem with this is when we get into a corner. If we move forward, we hit the wall (Figure 16.1c). This is fine; our bump sensor lets us know, so we start backing up. Let's say that we back up for two seconds, turning along the way. Well, we're certain to hit the wall before the two seconds are up. If this happens, we don't actually finish our pivot, and we'll immediately back into the other wall. So, we need to be able to detect the fact that our rear bumper was hit before we finished backing up for two seconds. Does it sound easy? It's not – unless, of course, we use a language that was designed to help programmers solve exactly this kind of problem. With occam we have the ability to manage communication about events that take place in our programs; in this case, we want to be able to track three different events:

- We need to know when our front bumper is pressed.
- We need to know when a two-second timer runs out.
- We need to know when our back bumper is pressed.

In the real world, we don't know when these events are going to take place; our robot could be running around, and someone decides to hit the rear bumper with their foot: what happens then? What if it gets wedged tight in a corner and keeps hitting its front and rear bumpers very rapidly; will our program be able to handle it? Dealing with the real world is generally the hardest kind of programming there is, because the real world is so unpredictable.

We start by drawing a picture of the communication *channels* that our program will have to deal with, and the *processes* that will handle those communications (Figure 16.2). Only the channels touch1 and touch3 are attached to our robot; they carry the inputs from the touch sensors attached to our front and back bumpers. The two touch sensors we have connected to the bumpers on our robot will communicate what happens to them to a process called controller. This process will deal with the input and, if necessary, communicate over the channel called motors to the process wheels. All the wheels process does is handle sending the correct speed and direction to each of the two wheels attached to our robot. Lastly, all of our channels and processes are wrapped up in a main process that starts everything running.

```
-- This includes a library of code for working with
-- the LEGO Mindstorms.
#INCLUDE "legolib.inc"

-- This defines the kinds of information carried
-- on the Motors channel.
PROTOCOL Motors IS BYTE; BYTE; BYTE; BYTE:

-- How long to backup everytime our front bumper
-- is touched.
VAL INT backup.time IS 2000:

-- The main process; it starts two other processes,
-- and then it quits.
PROC main()
   -- First we declare a local channel for controlling
   -- the motors, and then...
   CHAN Motors motors:
```

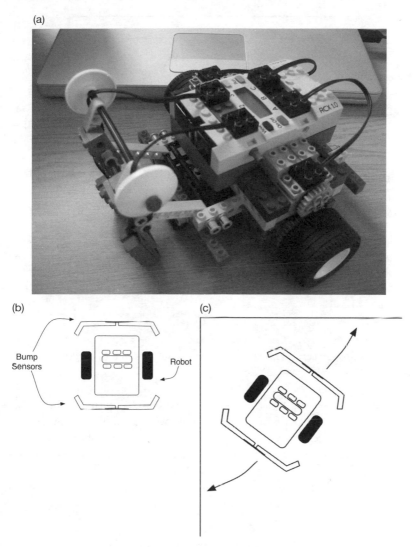

Figure 16.1   (a) The LEGO® Mindstorms™ robot; (b) the bump
sensors; (c) hitting a corner

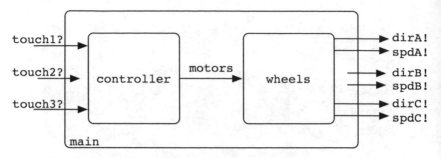

Figure 16.2 Communication channels and processes in the robot program

```
-- In PARallel, we run the "controller" process and
-- "wheels" process. They run forever, but the
-- "main" process is done as soon once they are
-- started up.
PAR
    controller(touch1?, touch3?, motors!)
    wheels(motors?, dirA!, spdA!, dirC!, spdC!)
:
```

The most interesting thing in the code that gets us started is the declaration of the Motors **protocol**. This protocol says that when the controller process communicates with the wheels process, there should always be four bytes (four small numbers) sent; this is how occam programs send structured data between one process and another.

Code is still needed for both the wheels and controller processes; the wheels process is simpler and, generally speaking, unexciting:

```
-- The "wheels" process takes several channels
-- as input.
PROC wheels(CHAN Motors moto?,
            CHAN BYTE dirA!, spdA!, dirC!, spdC!)

    -- Do everything indented under this line forever.
    WHILE TRUE
        -- Local variables for the direction and
        -- speed of the left and right wheels.
        BYTE dleft, dright, sleft, sright:
```

```
-- Do everything under this in SEQuence.
SEQ
    -- First, read in four numbers from the
    -- "moto" channel; the "controller" process
    -- uses these channels to tell us which way,
    -- and how fast, to go.
    moto ? dleft ; sleft ; dright ; sright


    -- Now, in PARallel, set the direction and
    -- speed of the two motors.
    PAR
        dirA ! dleft
        spdA ! sleft
        dirC ! dright
        spdC ! sright
:
```

As you might notice, in occam indention matters. If one line is indented under another, it is similar to using brackets. For example, when we say we want to execute a SEQuence of instructions, we simply indent all the instructions we want to happen one at a time underneath a SEQ. When we want the computer to run several things at the same time, in PARallel, we use a PAR block, and indent all the processes we want to run concurrently under the PAR.

It is this expressive power that makes occam so powerful; with one three-letter word, we can say 'do these four things at the same time'. When run on a single-processor machine (like our LEGO), these things will happen one at a time; however, if the LEGO had four CPUs, then each of these instructions could happen simultaneously, with no effort on our part.

The last, and most interesting, piece of code we need to write to make our LEGO manage its life bumping and wandering around the room is the controller process.

```
PROC controller(CHAN BOOL touch.front?, touch.back?,
                CHAN Motors moto)


    -- Do everything indented under this forever
    WHILE TRUE
        -- First, we declare local variables.
        -- The "clock" variable is a special
        -- channel; whenever we read from it,
        -- we get the current time in milliseconds.
```

```
BOOL touched:
TIMER clock:
INT cur.time:

-- Do everything indented under this in SEQuence.
SEQ
    -- Tell the motors to go foward at full speed.
    moto ! FWD; FULL; FWD; FULL

    -- Next, we wait until the front bumper is
    -- touched; we could wait a long time.
    touch.front ? touched

    -- After it is bumped, we should backup slowly.
    moto ! BWD ; HALF ; BWD ; HALF

    -- Now, we read the current time.
    clock ? cur.time

    -- And, depending on what happens first, we
    -- ALTernatively do one of two things:
    ALT
        -- If the back bumper is touched, we
        -- do nothing, and go back to the start of
        -- the WHILE loop
        touch.back ? touched
          SKIP

        -- If 2 seconds (our "backup.time") go by,
        -- then we will do nothing... and go back
        -- to the start of the WHILE loop.
        clock ? AFTER cur.time PLUS backup.time
          SKIP
  :
```

There are some simple bits of occam's syntax that might help with this example. First, the ? and ! are powerful operators in occam: they control communication. The ? lets us read a value from a channel into a variable:

```
<channel> ? <variable>
```

while the ! lets us send data out on a channel:

```
<channel> ! <value>
```

When we say

```
Moto ! FWD; FWD; FULL; FULL
```

That means we are sending four numbers (defined in the special LEGO library) that represent a forward direction at full speed down the channel called moto. Similarly, when we say

```
touch.front ? touched
```

that means we are reading from the touch sensor into the variable called touched. However, we are (effectively) waiting for the touch sensor to be pressed (in this case), so our program stops here, waiting for the sensor to fire.

The most interesting thing about the controller process is actually the ALT. Up to this point any programming language can manage setting the speed and direction of the motors on a small robot. However, the ALT is a special construct: it watches two or more channels, and whichever one gets a communication first, that ALTernative is taken, and that channel's code is executed. In the case of the controller process, we are either waiting for the back touch sensor to be triggered, or for two seconds to go by on the clock.

The (seemingly) disturbing thing about this is that, regardless of which event happens first, we do absolutely nothing. The SKIP means, 'Don't do anything'. How can this work? The tricky thing about concurrent programming is that there are often a lot of infinite loops; in this case, regardless of which event happens first, if we do nothing, then we go all the way back to the start of the loop (the WHILE TRUE statement). As we continue, we see that the first thing that happens in the loop is that the motors are all set to the forward direction at full power. So, if the last thing we do is go back to the top of the loop, we'll start moving forward again.

Real-time and concurrent programming is often described as being difficult to do. This is because languages like Scheme, Java, C, C++, Perl, Python, and almost all other languages do not inherently support the idea of more than one thing happening at the same time. They were all designed to help the programmer express ideas about functions (in Scheme), or objects (in Java), or just get some small scripts written quickly (Perl). For this reason, occam is a powerful tool in the right context, and understanding how to write concurrent and parallel programs – especially in a world where there are so many computers working together to solve large, complex problems – is a very important skill to have.

▶ Chapter summary

When it comes to the multitude of programming languages in the world, we've found that there are different types of programmers out there. Perhaps you'll recognize something of yourself in one or more of these descriptions.

There are programmers who will tell you which language is best, why it is best, and they'll also tell you why the language you happen to like, regardless of what language that is, is a useless, rubbish tool. We might say these people are closed-minded and, perhaps, uninformed, but that might be a bit harsh. Our goal here is to be encouraging, after all, so perhaps we'll just say that they're Linguistically Challenged and leave it at that.

Certainly, the Linguistically Challenged are not the only kind of programmers you will encounter who have opinions. Many people have a favourite language, and will argue its virtues with you all day long. However, they'll also be open-minded, and acknowledge when different languages have their place. These programmers understand that different problems might be best solved with different languages, all depending on a project's needs and requirements. Because of their open-mindedness, we'll call them the Accepting Faithful.

Then there are the Collectors. These are people who simply love the many programming languages available to them in the world. They revel in finding a new language that has some bizarre quirk, and will almost always have an anecdote about how Language X has some odd feature that would solve your problem in two lines of code. If they have a favourite, they'd probably say it was Io, or Haskell, or maybe ML, . . . ; perhaps Dylan, or Smalltalk, . . . ; then again, they remember with fondness Fortran, and the oddities of PL/1, . . . ; well, you get the picture.

The question is: which do you want to be?

*   *   *

▶ In closing

You've made it to the end of the book; we've considered everything from your very first program to managing the complexities of writing large programs all by yourself, sleuthing errors in your code, working with peers, and preparing for programming in the real world. You've seen some examples from the most common programming paradigms in the world today, and are ready to take on the world. Upon you, the reader, we make no demands, but we do have a request: *keep an open mind*. Computing is a vast and changing field, and the world is yours with the right blend of openness and creativity.

We hope you enjoy yourself. We have.

Notes

Chapter 2

1. Indeed, that is exactly what the first computer programmers had to do, which rather limited the complexity of the problems they were able to solve.

Chapter 3

1. L. Truss, *Eats, Shoots and Leaves: The Zero Tolerance Approach to Punctuation* (Profile Books, 2003).
2. http://semantics-online.org/blog/2003/09/aoccdrnig_to_rscheearch.php
3. http://www.nwrain.net/~newtsuit/recoveries/narrows/narrows.htm
4. http://www.arup.com/MillenniumBridge/index.html
5. http://www.around.com/ariane.html
6. http://marsweb.jpl.nasa.gov/msp98/news/mco991110.html
7. http://www.3m.com/about3m/pioneers/fry.jhtml. Post-it is a registered trademark of 3M.

Chapter 5

1. http://en.wikipedia.org/wiki/Hello_world

Chapter 8

1. In case you don't know, 'tricky things' means things that are hard for other people to understand. Mathematicians often refer to something as 'a nice problem'. This often translates as 'a problem that I can solve and you can't!'
2. http://www.dwheeler.com/sloc/redhat71-v1/redhat71sloc.html
3. http://www.computeractive.co.uk/comment/1156592
4. http://www.sei.cmu.edu/tsp/psp.html
5. http://www.nyx.net/~vputz/psp_index/f10.html
6. http://www.extremeprogramming.org
7. http://www.shootout.alioth.debian.org

Chapter 10

1. Problem number 301 from William Butler's *Arithmetical Instruction for Young Ladies* (1814).
2. Viktors Berstis, Master Inventor, Grid Computing Initiative for IBM.
3. Patricia Haden, Otago Polytechnic, New Zealand (personal correspondence).
4. Monopoly® is a trademark of Hasbro, Inc.
5. This example is derived from the work of Michael J. Quillin, University of Missouri-St Louis.

Chapter 11

1. http://www.cs.joensuu.fi/~saja/var_roles/

Chapter 13

1. Bjarne Stroustrup, *The Design and Evolution of C++* (Reading, MA: Addison-Wesley, 1994), p. 113.
2. David Wheeler, 'My Philosophy on Computer Languages', webpage, available at: http://www.adahome.com/Tutorials/Lovelace/philos.htm.

Chapter 15

1. http://en.wikipedia.org/wiki/Charles_Babbage
2. http://en.wikipedia.org/wiki/Nerd
3. http://web14.compaq.com/falco/detail.asp?FAQnum=FAQ2859
4. http://www.kent.ac.uk/studying/undergrad/subjects/computing.html

Chapter 16

1. These paradigms are not utterly distinct – different programming languages may implement features from different paradigms, but many languages implement features from more than one paradigm (although they will have the overriding flavour of one). Java, for instance, would fall under the 'object-oriented' paradigm, but it would be hard to write a useful Java program that did not include any constructs from the 'imperative' paradigm.
2. Paul Graham, *Hackers and Painters: Essays in the Art of Programming* (Sebastopol, CA: O'Reilly, 2004).

Glossary

This is a list of many of the technical words that we have used in this book, together with their definitions. These words often have a special meaning when used in the context of programming. It is better to use a glossary rather than a dictionary for finding the meanings of technical vocabulary. Although you may find the same word in both, additional meaning has been added to the word when used in this new context. A dictionary will usually only give meanings in common use. Even in cases where a dictionary does include a technical definition this is not likely to be as up to date as in a glossary.

If you cannot find a word here that you want to look up, there are many good online places that you could look. For instance, the Wikipedia (http://www.wikipedia.org/), the Free On-Line Dictionary of Computing (http://wombat.doc.ic.ac.uk/foldoc/), or prefix a search in Google (http://www.google.com/) with 'define:'.

Abstraction   A process of viewing things at different levels of detail. Almost anything can be considered at different levels of abstraction. Typically, the more abstract a view the less detail it contains, and the more it focuses on general principles which can be applied across situations. For example, 'The user logs in' contains little detail about how a user logs in, whereas 'The user enters their name in the top box and presses the Return key' is more concrete, with details specific to one system. The first description is more abstract than the second.

Ada   A programming language named for Lady Ada Lovelace, a mathematician and scientist of the early 1800s. She is recognized as being possibly the world's first programmer in the sense that we know it. Ada was designed to be a safe language for programmers to architect large systems, and has been used extensively by the United States Department of Defense for decades in mission-critical applications.

Agile methods   Techniques for developing programs that are focused on developing working programs quickly, rather than on detailed planning ahead.

Algorithm   A procedure for doing some computation, set out in a precise step-by-step way.

Alien code   Code taken from one program and integrated into a new one.

Application   A program, or collection of programs, designed to fulfil a task. Applications often fulfil a large overall task, such as an e-business application. Such applications will typically be composed of many separate programs that accomplish different parts of the overall task.

Argument   In programming terms an argument is a value that is passed into a program or into a subroutine of a program. For example if 'sqr' were a routine which calculated the square of any numeric value, then in the call 'sqr(3)' the value '3' is the input argument. (The output would be '9' in this case). Arguments are also known as parameters.

Array   A fixed length data structure commonly used in a number of different programming languages.

ArrayList   A Java class that uses an array whose size can be dynamically increased as required. It is an implementation of the Java `List` interface and, as such, permits typical list operations.

Artificial intelligence   Intelligence exhibited by any manufactured system. It usually refers to computers programmed to reason and solve problems in a limited domain. In theory, it can also mean computers that are as sentient as a human being, but researchers are still a long way from achieving this in practice.

AT&T Bell Labs   One of the world's premier telecommunications laboratories. Bell Labs (or Bell Telephone Laboratories) in New Jersey is one of AT&T's research sites and was, amongst other things, the birthplace of the transistor, the Unix operating system, and the programming languages C and C++.

Atomic data   Data that is not usually divided any further at program level. For instance, an integer or a character would be considered as atomic data, whereas an object would not.

Attribute   A property associated with a piece of data – in programming terms, objects and entities can have attributes. Attributes characterize data: for example a car (object) may have the attributes of colour (red) and registration number.

Audit trail   Documentation that records the changes that have been made to a program or an application over the course of its life.

Backtrack   A term for the process that a declarative program performs when a subgoal fails. The program returns to a previous subgoal so that it can then follow a different path.

BASIC   A procedural programming language. It has been around since the 1960s. While it is not used much today, some of its descendants, such as Visual Basic, are still popular. It is pronounced like the word 'basic'.

Behaviour   The functionality of a class in the object-oriented programming paradigm. The behaviour is what the class and instances of it have been programmed to do.

Black box testing   Testing designed to verify that a program produces the correct output, according to its specification. The tester knows what the program is supposed to do but does not know how it does it.

BlueJ   An IDE designed to teach introductory object-oriented programming in Java.

Boolean   A Boolean variable can take only the values 'true' and 'false'. A Boolean expression is one that can only return the values 'true' and 'false'. As Boolean values are not numbers, you cannot use the usual arithmetic operators (addition, subtraction etc.) but you have to use Boolean operators such as AND, OR, NOT. 'Boolean' is named after its inventor, the nineteenth-century mathematician George Boole. It is pronounced 'BOO-lee-an'.

Bottom-up   An approach to system design or building when you start with the low-level detail of the system and work your way up to more abstract levels. See also *Top-down*.

Boundary condition   A value at the boundary (usually one end of) a range of values. For instance, in a program (or subroutine) which grades students' essays as fail (0–39%), pass (40–69%) or distinction (70–100%), the values 0, 39, 40, 69, 70 and 100 are all boundary conditions.

Braino   A sudden lapse of thought causing things you know perfectly well to somehow get muddled up or to disappear altogether.

Breakpoint   A specific place in code where the programmer has intention-
ally arranged to stop the code running. This is done when debugging code
so that details of what is happening when the code is executed can be
checked. It is sometimes done with others looking on to uncover hard-to-
find mistakes.

Bug   An error in a program.

C   A procedural programming language. It is closely associated with the
UNIX operating system, which was written in C, but is a general-purpose
programming language.

C++   An object-oriented programming language. It was mainly developed
by taking C and adding object orientation. It is pronounced 'see plus plus'.

Cascading error   A single syntax error in a computer program that makes
the compiler or interpreter produce multiple error messages at several different places. For example, if the declaration of a variable is omitted in a
language that requires it, there will be an error message every time that
variable is used.

Case sensitive   Some character data has distinct lowercase and uppercase
forms, e.g. 'D' and 'd'. A situation where case differences make a difference
is case sensitive.

Cause–effect chasm   The gap between the root causes of a program's
malfunctioning and the symptoms that show there is a problem.

Cell   In spreadsheet terminology a cell is a space in the spreadsheet grid
that can hold a data item.

Central Processing Unit (CPU)   The part of the computer that decodes
and executes program instructions.

Character   An atomic data type used to represent values in a character set.
Typical values would be 'm', '9', '@', etc.

Class   In object-oriented programming, a class is the way in which a type
of thing in the real world is represented in the program. So, for example, one
class might be *Car*, another *Student*. More abstract things can be classes,
too. For example, the various types of windows and menus in a program
might be represented by their own classes.

Class definition Used in object-oriented languages to describe the way in which typical examples of a particular entity are structured and behave. These are abstract definitions that are used in the program to create objects representing individual entities. For example, a program that processes purchases from a web site might have a class called *Customer* that indicates that a customer has a name and is associated with some purchased goods. When the program runs there might be a corresponding object showing that there is a customer called Abdul Rahman who has bought two CDs and a game.

COBOL A business-oriented programming language that has been around since the early 1960s. It is mainly used now for legacy systems. It is pronounced 'ko bol'.

Code Shorthand for 'source code'. The code of a program is the text that makes up the program. For example, one programmer might say to another, 'Can you show me the code that makes that window appear?'

Code generator A program that generates other programs or parts of programs.

Code management system A system that supports the development of programs by looking after the various versions of a program, making certain that only one programmer is working on each part of a program at once, and bringing together parts of a program that have been written by different programmers.

Code walkthrough Manually going step-by-step though code to see what should be happening as it is executed.

Command An instruction to a program to do something.

Comment A part of programming code that is there only for people. Comments can therefore be written in English rather than being written in a computer language. They are specially separated from the other parts of the code as a signal to the computer to skip over them. Comments have no effect on how a program runs, but they can provide a record of what the programmer was thinking when they wrote the code.

Compilation The process of converting a program that has been written in a computer language that humans can understand into the sequence of instructions that the computer needs to follow in order to carry out the program.

Compiler   A program that turns a computer program written in one language (the source language) into an equivalent program written in another language (the target language). The target language is usually one that the computer can directly execute.

Compile–time error   An error spotted by a compiler. Commonly these are syntax errors you may have missed, or mistyped, a piece of punctuation such as a semicolon. A program with compile-time errors cannot be run.

Component   One piece of a larger program or application. The size of a component varies considerably across different applications. In some, it might be a small piece of one program, such as a GUI button, while in others it could be a complete subsystem.

Component-based approach   Building a computer system by making a number of self-contained programs communicate with each other. A typical example is an e-commerce system where a database, a web server and a browser together enable a user to display and interact with web pages. It can also refer to designing a single program to use existing components (typically functions or classes) from libraries of source code. This is very commonly done in programs written in languages such as Fortran and Java.

Computer   An electronic device that can store data and process data. The sets of instructions for transforming the data (the programs) are not normally fixed inside the computer and so most computers can be programmed to perform a wide variety of tasks.

Computer architecture   Usually the term computer architecture refers to the physical components of the machine (the hardware) and how those parts interact to make the computer work. Sometimes, however, you will encounter a broader use of the term, which includes higher-level software, too.

Computer program   Something written in a computer programming language so that it may be executed on a computer.

Concurrency   A programming technique that permits the simultaneous execution of operations within a program. Single tasks are split into subtasks that can be independently processed and then brought together to form a solution. The term 'parallel programming' is also used to describe this methodology.

Concurrent   Things happening at the same time. In programming languages it is used to refer to things that could happen at the same time or, if they are done one at a time, the order does not matter. An example of a language that allows the programmer to specify that things should happen concurrently is occam.

Concurrent Versioning System (CVS)   A widely used code management system that provides a mechanism to track, manage and (if necessary) undo changes to source code.

Constant   A value that does not change during the run of a program.

Control structure   A programming language feature that composes other programming features and affects the order in which instructions are executed. Examples are if statements and loops.

CPU   *see* **Central Processing Unit**.

CVS   *see* **Concurrent Versioning System**.

Data   Typically numbers and characters, but also images, sounds and other methods of representing information which can processed by a computer.

Database   Special-purpose software for storing and manipulating complex data. The database will contain data, meta-data describing both the data and also how it is organized, and procedures for processing the data.

Data processing   A task characterized by the need to manipulate, or process, a large amount of data. Programming languages such as COBOL and SQL are designed to support the construction of data processing applications.

Data structure   A method of organizing a collection of data items as a single entity, to allow them to be manipulated effectively.

Data type   *see* **Type**.

Debug   Remove errors (bugs) from a program.

Debugger   A program that helps the programmer to find the cause of errors (bugs) in programs.

Declarative   Languages where programs are written by specifying (declaring) a set of facts and rules and then querying them. Prolog is an example of a declarative language.

Declare   In some programming languages before you can use a variable you have to declare it. That is, you have to insert code that says, in effect, this program will have this variable name, which will have a particular type associated with it.

Decompose   Break down into pieces. Large problems are often easier to solve if they are decomposed into several smaller pieces.

Design   The process of strategic thinking that guides larger-scale projects.

Digit   A simple numeral, such as 0, 1, 2, etc.

Double   An atomic data type representing double-precision floating point numbers. There is no consistent memory size associated with a double, but the size is typically larger than that of a single-precision floating point number.

DrScheme   An integrated development environment for the Scheme programming language.

E-commerce (electronic commerce)   The conducting of business communication and business transactions over computer networks. It covers operations such as marketing, buying and selling of goods and services, fund transfers, electronic data interchange and automated data-collection systems.

Edit-compile-run cycle   The process of repeatedly editing a program, running a compiler on the code, and then executing what the compiler produces.

Editor   A piece of software that allows the user to edit files. The term editor is usually reserved for software that allows users to edit plain-text files, to distinguish it from a word processor which is used to edit formatted documents.

Emacs   A powerful text editor that incorporates many features to assist programmers and can readily be customized.

Embedded system A very small computer (often just a microchip) that is enclosed in a larger device. It contributes to the functioning of the larger device, but it is not accessible to be programmed by the user. For instance, controls on central heating systems, or washing machines, often include an embedded system, but the user can only adjust the knobs and dials.

Empty list A list in a computer program that has been created but has nothing in it. This is different from not having a list at all, because the empty list has a name and storage allocated to it.

Entity Part of the problem solution identified in the design phase. An entity generally has attributes and behaviour. The solution design for a complex problem may have many entities connected via relationships.

Erlang A programming language, developed by Ericsson, for the difficult task of handling millions of phone calls that are routed through their switches every day. Erlang combines an interesting set of ideas, as it is a functional, concurrent programming language, and is typically more flexible than occam.

Error message What is printed on the screen for the user to read when a program goes wrong.

Evolutionary development System development that does not try to develop a complete application in one go. Instead, parts of the system are designed, implemented, tested and evaluated, and the experience gained from this cycle is used to evolve the system to its next stage. This process repeats until the full system has been built after several evolutions.

Evolving code Sections of code in computer programs which change over time, due to being modified in order to incorporate new functionality or to fix errors.

Executable code The form of a computer program that can be directly converted into actions by a computer. It is not intended for human readers.

Execute Means the same as 'run' when applied to a program.

Extensible Markup Language (XML) A language (not a programming language) for defining markup languages and defining the structure of information.

Extensibility A property of a program that defines how easily it can be changed. Programs that are in use for a long period of time may need to have additional features added to them. This can be relatively easy to do if the probram has been designed for extensibility.

Extreme Programming (XP) A way of developing programs that concentrates on the development of the program code itself, and is less concerned with planning ahead than traditional ways of developing programs.

Floating-point number Computers do not have decimal places. However, many calculations in the world require decimal points. Computers do this by representing an integer (say, the number '2365585') and a power of 10 (like '−7'). Combining these two gives us the number .2365585, which the computer cannot actually store directly. In practice, the exponent is a power of 2 rather 10.

Flow chart A diagram which shows the structure of a program and how decision-based control flows through it.

Font A term in printing for a set of characters within a particular typeface (a co-ordinated set of designs for letters, numerals and punctuation marks) Fonts combine size (also called *point*), weight (bold, light etc.) and style (regular, italic, condensed etc.). This `word` is set in the Courier New, 16 point, regular weight and style font while this **word** is set in the Comic Sans, 10 point, bold, italic font.

Formally proved A program (or statement) that is consistent within the rules of a formal system – one that is logically or mathematically based. Formal techniques are often used when programming safety-critical systems.

Fortran A programming language used for the complex numerical calculations of the physical sciences. Its name comes from FORmula TRANslator. It has been around since the late 1950s and has been repeatedly developed since that time. It still remains the language of choice for many scientific applications.

Function In mathematical terms, a function is something that computes a value based upon the values of some inputs. A function will always return the same result given the same set of inputs. In programming terms, the word is often used much less rigorously to denote something like 'operation'.

Functional One of the major programming paradigms. Programs are expressed as functions that transform data supplied as arguments.

General-purpose language A programming language that can be used to solve many different types of programming tasks.

Gizmo A made-up name for an arbitrary component or 'thing'.

Glossary A glossary is a list of words that are unique to a subject, or else words that are used in a specialized way within that subject.

Grammatical error An error in the code of a program that prevents that program from running, or from running correctly. It could be due to a simple typing mistake on the part of the programmer, or a misunderstanding about the way the programming language operates. Also known as a syntax error.

Graphical User Interface (GUI) A visual interface to a program that usually includes components such as menus, buttons, windows, etc.

Graphics Computer graphics are taken for granted today: we assume all computers have monitors, and can display text, images, and even video. The displays we commonly use have their roots in the early televisions and displays of the 1950s.

GUI *see* **Graphical User Interface**. It is pronounced 'goo ee'.

Hacking To non-programmers 'hacking' usually means breaking into and attacking computer systems. Amongst programmers the term hacking refers to a particular approach to writing programs. Hackers are knowledgeable programmers who write code quickly with the goal of getting the job done with apparent ease.

Hashtable A way of organizing data – a data structure. Its structure allows quick access to data by mapping from a key to its associated value. The mapping process involves the use of a hashing function.

HCI *see* **Human–computer interaction**.

'Hello, world' program A program that simply prints some combination of the words 'hello' and 'world' to the screen. The first known instance of this program was written in 1973 by Brian Kernighan, one of the inventors of the C programming language.

Heuristic A rule used as a short cut when problem solving. For instance, a heuristic for attempting to avoid losing at noughts and crosses might be, 'Always choose a corner for your first move'. Heuristics are often inexact and don't guarantee to give the result you want, but they are often more efficient to use than an exact computation.

High-fidelity prototype A program that looks quite like the finished product but does not have the full functionality.

High-level language A programming language that has constructs more closely associated with the tasks which must be performed to solve a problem than about the steps which a computer must take to perform those tasks. Translating the task-oriented description (program) into step-by-step instructions which the computer can follow is undertaken by a compiler.

Human–computer interaction (HCI) The study of the interface between computers and the way that humans use them. It is a multi-disciplinary subject involving disciplines such as design, psychology, aesthetics and human factors. HCI studies often provide insights into how to make computer programs easier to use.

HyperText Markup Language (HTML) A markup language used for writing web pages. HTML includes constructs both for describing a document's structure (e.g., paragraphs and headings) and the way it should be displayed (e.g., bold font, centred).

IDE *see* **Integrated Development Environment**.

Identifier A descriptive name chosen by a programmer for something in a program. Variables, methods and classes are all things that require identifiers to be chosen for them.

If-statements In a computer language we often need to do different things depending on the input that a user has given to the program. The kind of statements that deal with these so-called *conditional* decisions is called an if-statement. This is because the statements typically take the form 'if [something is true] do this, otherwise do that'.

Imperative A style of programming which views computation in terms of program states and statements that modify those states.

Implementation   Putting a design into practice. Writing program code to fulfil the specification developed in the design phase.

Information design   The process of structuring information so that it is useful.

Input   Data supplied to a program or part of a program.

Integer   A number with no fractional part. The infinite set of integers consists of the number zero, all the positive natural numbers (1, 2, 3, etc.) and all the negative natural numbers (−1, −2, −3, etc.). Integers are also known as 'whole numbers'. In practice, there is often a limit to the maximum and minimum integer values that can be represented in a program.

Integrated development environment (IDE)   An IDE helps its users to develop programs by bringing together the necessary tools to carry out each of the different steps in writing a program. In a single place you can write the code, compile it, test it and debug it. Many integrated development environments also provide ways of writing code more quickly, ways of visualizing aspects of the code or of finding mistakes in the code more quickly. An integrated development is often refered to as an IDE (pronounced 'Eye Dee Ee'). *See* **BlueJ, DrScheme** *and* **Visual Basic.**

Integration   The process of bringing separate components together.

Interaction diagram   A diagram within UML that shows how objects in an object-oriented design interact with each other. There are two types of interaction diagram: collaboration diagrams and sequence diagrams.

Interface   An interface is a boundary. In programming, the boundary may be between pieces of code or between different parts of a system (sometimes called an API or Application Programming Interface) or between the system and its users (where it may be called a **GUI**).

Internet   An unstructured network of computers that spans different organizations.

Interpreter   A computer program that reads in source code and executes it. An interpreter shares some features with a compiler, but an interpreter usually executes code that is independent of a particular computer architecture.

Iteration   Repetition of an action or sequence of statements. Within a program, iteration is provided by loop control structures.

Iterative development   A style of programming in which code is developed in stages, with each new stage being (hopefully!) a closer approximation to the required solution.

Java   An object-oriented language. It was designed to be able to be run on any platform.

JavaScript   A scripting language. It is often used to provide interactivity on web pages (e.g., buttons that you can push, images that change when the mouse passes over them). Despite its name it is not closely related to Java.

Keyword   A word with a special meaning in a programming language. It is typically not possible to reuse keywords as identifiers. Words such as 'if', 'while' and 'do' are commonly used as keywords.

Language   The word *language* is typically used in this book to refer to programming languages. However the word can also be used to refer to other kinds of computer languages, such as scripting languages, and to the natural languages such as English that humans use to communicate. See: natural language, *programming language* and *scripting language*.

Legacy code   Code retained from earlier releases of a piece of software.

Legacy system   An existing computer system that must be accommodated when building new systems in a modernization programme.

LEGO® Mindstorms™   A small robotics platform developed by the LEGO Corporation in the late 1990s. The LEGO Mindstorms provides a simple and inexpensive way to get into robotics. These little robots are programmable in many languages described in this book: C, Java and occam, to name a few.

Library   Many programming languages have associated libraries. A library contains pieces of code that will perform common tasks – searching or sorting in particular ways, for example. When a language has a library, you don't have to write these things for yourself, but can use the standard code. Indeed, to make your programs robust and reusable you should use libraries whenever possible.

LISP   A functional programming language. Its name stands for LISt Processing. It was invented at MIT in the 1960s and is one of the oldest high-level programming languages. It is still in use today.

List   A way of organizing data – a data structure. A list is collection of zero or more elements. A list (in computing) is quite similar to the ordinary lists of everyday life.

Load   To store some data somewhere. Data is often loaded from one part of a computer's memory into another, or loaded into a variable.

Logical error   A programmer error that does not prevent a program from executing, but is likely to cause it to produce incorrect results because the program's logic is incorrect.

Loop   A programming construct that allows for the repeated execution of a section of code. Examples common to many programming languages are 'for' and 'while' loops.

Low-fidelity prototype   A prototype prepared using simple materials such as pencil and paper. Can be useful as a quick and easy way of showing people your ideas for the program interface.

Lower case   A way of describing an alphabetic character which is not written as a capital letter, e.g. 'a', 'b', 'c', etc.

Machine code   Program code that can be run directly on a particular computer architecture. Machine code consists of sequences of ones and zeros. It is quite difficult for humans to write machine code, so we write code in higher-level languages and the code we write gets turned into machine code by a compiler.

Macro   A means of automating the execution of frequently used sequences of rules. A macro is a name that is equated to a number of actions, into which it is expanded on compilation or running of the program in which it appears.

Markup language   A language (not a programming language) that defines the structure and layout of information. HTML is a markup language.

Mathematical proof   An algebraic demonstration that some conclusion must always be true given a starting set of assumptions.

Memory   Part of the hardware of a computer that is used to store data.

Meta-data   Data describing data. For example, 'A login consists of letters representing a person's initials possibly followed by digits, with a maximum length of nine characters.'

Module   Part of a computer program that performs a coherent subtask. Where a programming language supports the splitting of a program into modules, there are rules about how integration is achieved.

Multi-tasking   Doing several things in parallel – starting them together and working on them at the same time – rather than sequentially – starting one, finishing it and then starting another. In fact, multi-tasking is often achieved by repeatedly performing small parts of several tasks sequentially. This gives the appearance of them all being performed in parallel.

Nasty surprise   In software, nasty surprises often involve crashes of your software at the least appropriate time – typically, when other people are watching, and invariably the error message with rude language that you thought was funny is suddenly the most embarrassing thing in the world.

Natural language   Human languages, such as English or French, are often referred to in computing lectures and textbooks as *natural languages*. This is to avoid confusion with *computer languages;* if you talk about a 'language' in computing, the first thing people tend to think about is a computer language.

Nest   When one thing is inside something we say it is nested. If you have a list inside a list, it is a nested list. If you have an if statement inside an if state-ment it is a nested if statement. Two examples of nested 'if statements would be: 'If the month is December, then if today is the 25th, then today is Christ-mas' or, 'If we had ham, we could have ham and eggs if we had eggs.'

Neural network   A processing device (either software- or hardware-based) whose design is inspired by the way in which animal brains function. The term neural network is used because bioelectrical networks in the brain are formed from neurons, and in computer-based neural networks, individual nodes (which are known as neurons) are connected to form a network of nodes.

Niche   A relatively small specialized area. Some programming languages are designed to enable the solution of problems in specialized areas and these are called niche languages, as opposed to general-purpose languages.

Numerical application   A program to solve a problem (or type of problem) in which non-trivial calculations are required. Because of the limitations of number representation in computers, special techniques are needed to get the best possible accuracy from calculations and to determine the limits of that accuracy. A person who specializes in those techniques is known as a numerical analyst.

Object   In object-oriented programming languages (like Java or Smalltalk) a task is described in terms of interactions between objects. Objects are collections of *state* – information which describes the object – and *behaviour* – things which the object needs to do, and which may require interaction with other objects' behaviour.

Object orientation   A style of problem solving that attempts to model a problem in terms of interacting classes and objects.

occam   A programming language developed in the 1980s by a British computer scientist called David May. Unlike some other languages, occam was designed to be small and simple, making it possible to write concurrent programs on processors with limited resources.

Off-by-one bug   These often occur in processing lists and arrays. The result is that the intended action is applied to the list or array element next to the one it was intended for.

One-off   A one-off is something that you do not expect to do or use again. Sometimes used pejoratively as in, 'You designed that as a one-off but now it's in the production code. I bet you're sorry!'

Open-source program   A program distributed together with its source code. The idea is that the user can understand and make changes to the program if they want to. By contrast, many programs are distributed in 'closed source' form: such programs can only be run, and not modified, by the user.

Operating system (OS)   The software in a computer that runs all of the time and looks after how the other programs run, determines when things like the printers and disk drives should operate, and so on.

Operator   A symbol that is used with other symbols to make an expression. For example, '+' is an operator and we can use it with numerical expressions to make new numerical expressions such as '4 + 5'.

Output   The results or effects produced by a program.

Package   A set of programs designed to be used to solve a particular type of problem. For example, there are commercial packages to help you store, edit and print your digital photographs.

Pair programming   Programming together with another person. Typically one person writes code while the other continually reviews the code for errors.

Paradigm   A model or pattern for how to do something. In programming terminology, a paradigm basically denotes the way in which code is organized. Programming paradigms are a means of classifying programming languages according to the way in which they perform tasks and the sort of tasks they perform best.

Parameter   *see* **Argument**.

Parenthesis   Either of the characters '(' and ')'. Programming languages often use several different types of brackets, so it is safer to talk about round brackets (), square brackets [] and curly brackets { }. We have not found any fancy names for the last two.

Pascal   An imperative programming language originally developed for the purposes of teaching programming. It became quite popular as a working language for a time. It is still sometimes taught as an initial programming language. It's pronounced 'pas CAL'.

Pattern   Something that captures the solution to a commonly occuring problem or situation encountered when programming.

Perl   A programming language devised by Larry Wall. It is particularly suitable for working with text, and is fast and powerful. It is also idiosyncratic in its design and notoriously hard to read. It has been described as the Swiss Army chain-saw of programming languages: 'exceedingly powerful but ugly and noisy and prone to belch noxious fumes' (quote from *The Jargon File*: http://www.catb.org/~esr/jargon/html/index.html).

Personal Software Process (PSP)   A methodology to help programmers track their own work habits and productivity, and so learn from them.

PHP (Hypertext PreProcessor)   A scripting language that allows web developers to create web pages with dynamic (as opposed to static) content. It is an embedded language, with code designed to be placed into HTML documents.

Plagiarism   An offence that is committed when someone takes someone else's ideas, words or images and passes them off as their own. Plagiarism is taken as a serious breaking of trust and repeated plagiarism will lead to being dismissed from university. If you use other people's ideas, words or images in work you submit, you need to cite where you found the material and do so in a way that is clear, proper and accurate.

Platform   The hardware and operating system a program is run on.

Portable   A program is portable if it can be run on different kinds of computers with little or no modification.

Print   To output data, either to a computer screen or a printer.

Private   Used in object-oriented programming to mean highly restricted access.

Processing unit   The part of a computer that carries out basic instructions. It is an essential part of how a computer operates.

Programmer   Somone who writes programs.

Programming language   A formal language in which computer programs are written. Programming languages consist of sets of words and symbols, along with a grammar specifying how the words and symbols may be combined. Programming languages enable programmers to specify actions for computers to take, to enable them to store and process data.

Protocol   An agreed means of communication between two or more parties.

Prototype   An early version of a system such as a computer program. Sometimes a prototype will deliberately miss out certain features; for example, a prototype of the visual interface to a program might be written, missing out any of the program which carries out the actual process, so that the interface can be tested as early as possible. Experience gained with a prototype is often useful in later development of the system.

Prototyping   The practice of making mock-ups of the finished product to test ideas, generate alternatives, and get feedback on the usefulness of the design.

Pseudo-code   Not program code but a structured form of natural language used for expressing an algorithm in a compact and clear way.

Public   Used in object-oriented programming to mean something to which all parts of a program have access.

Punctuation   Punctuation is not a technical term in computing. Punctuation marks, such as full stops (.), commas (,) and semicolons (;) are used in computer languages in a similar way to natural languages. That is, they are used to mark the start and end of different sections within a piece of text.

Real-time systems   These are computer systems which need to react to events that are happening in the real world. For example a computer system that controls a car or an aeroplane is a real-time system. When programming such a system the programmer needs to be certain that when a certain input is given to the system, then it will respond within a certain time: for example when a signal is sent to set off the braking system in a car, it will start braking within 0.1 seconds.

Recursion   The classic definition is 'recursion – see recursion' because recursion means referring to itself. Recursion is a programming technique that involves solving a problem by solving a smaller version of the same problem. For example, if you have to print out the string 'Hello, world!', you could print out the single character 'H' and then print out the string 'ello, world!'. To print out 'ello, world' you print out 'e', followed by 'llo, world!', and so on.

Regression testing   The retesting of a program following its modification.

Relational database   A way of organizing data so that the user can manipulate it as a collection of tables, with each table having a fixed set of columns and rows of data. Data organized like this can be read and updated very flexibly by multiple users.

Relational database management system (RDBMS) A complex software package that holds the data for a relational database. An RDBMS provides facilities for entering data via forms and producing printed and online reports. It controls who can access the data and protects it against accidental loss.

Relationship Defines the roles two (or more) structures have to one another. For example, an 'adult' entity may have a 'parent' relationship with a 'child' entity, or possibly a 'teacher' or 'guardian' relationship.

Report-writing package A set of programs for the production of reports or summaries.

Requirements Descriptions of what a program being written is required to do.

Requirements elicitation Finding out what clients want a system to do.

Return A keyword used in a number of programming languages to mean, 'Give a result back to the bit of the program that called this particular function or method.' A very simplistic example would be a function that was given two numbers and had to return their sum.

Runtime error An error in code that shows up when you run a program. Often when an error shows up at runtime it means that there is something wrong with the logic of the program and not with the syntax of the program.

Runtime system The part of a computing environment that executes programs.

Safety-critical Some programs can have disastrous consequences if they go wrong, e.g., they can injure or kill people or cause considerable damage. Programs such as these are called 'safety-critical'.

Scheme A child of the LISP programming language, developed in the 1970s by Guy Steele and Gerald Sussman. Known for its large number of parentheses, this little but powerful language has found uses everywhere, from web-site scripting to graphical manipulation software.

Scripting language A fairly loose term, but in general it means a high-level language that is interpreted (rather than compiled to machine code), has powerful string-manipulation features and has few data structures.

Semantic   The meaning of something, as opposed to its format or syntax.

Semantic error   An error where the program does something, but what it does is not what was intended by the programmer.

Set   A mathematical term meaning an unsorted collection of zero or more items, in which there are no duplicates.

SloC   *see* **source lines of code**.

Smalltalk   An object-oriented language developed at Xerox PARC in the 1980s. Smalltalk treats *everything* as an object. Numbers, windows, even your cat are all objects in Smalltalk. Like Scheme and occam, this is a small but powerful language.

Software engineering   An engineering approach to the development of software systems.

Software package   *see* **Package**.

Software tool   A program for accomplishing a particular task, such as sorting the contents of a file, or finding all lines in a file that contain a particular string. Software tools can often be used in combination to accomplish very complex tasks.

Source code   A computer program in the source language. Source code is translated by a compiler into machine code so that the program can be executed.

Source lines of code   A count of the number of lines in the program source code that contain program statements. The count excludes blank lines and lines containing comments. It is used to measure the amount of effort needed to write the program.

Specification   A document that details what a system will do. In industrial practice, specifications (also called requirements specifications) can be very detailed indeed, and cover areas as diverse as the purpose of the project, the look and feel of the software and performance measures.

Specification language   A language used to describe what a system or part of a system should do. They are used when analysing what is required from a new system and designing the solution. Some specification languages, such as Z, allow the user to prove that a piece of design is correct while others, such as UML, are more descriptive and help analysts, designers, programmers and end users to communicate with each other. Specification languages are not programming languages.

Spiral model A method for developing large systems by focusing on the most important features first. Once feedback has been obtained from users, additional features are added one at a time. The method was developed by B. W. Boehm.

Spreadsheet A program that manipulates data in a rectangular grid of information. The grid consists of rows and columns of cells. Values in a cell can be automatically calculated from formulae which can involve other cells in the grid.

SQL *see* **Structured Query Language**.

State The state of a program is the set of variable values at a particular time whilst the program is running.

Statement A small piece of a program that does one simple task.

String A sequence of characters. The following are all examples of strings (with the final one being an empty string): 'a', 'green', 'Hello, world!', ''.

Structured data Data formed from pieces of atomic data standing in specific relationships.

Structured Query Language (SQL) A language used to access a database.

Subroutine A section of a program that carries out a specific task.

Superset D is a superset of E when anything that is in E is also in D.

Symbol A character, or sequence of characters, that are part of a programming language. Keywords, operators, punctuation and identifiers are typical symbols used in writing programs.

Syntax The grammar of a programming language. Symbols combined in the wrong order will result in a syntax error. Syntax is checked by a compiler.

Compilers are inflexible programs that understand what you type only if you type it in the exact syntactic form.

Syntax error An error in the grammar or structure of the program.

Tcl *see* **Tool Command Language.**

Technical requirements Technical details of the things a client or customer requires from a system – for instance, that a system must run on a particular operating system, or be able to process 500 transactions per minute.

Test case A specific example that is used to check to see if some code has been correctly written.

Test data A sample of input values for a program that is used to test whether the program is doing what the programmer expects it to.

Test harness A software component or software tool that automates the testing process by holding collections of test suites and test results.

Test suite A cohesive collection of related test cases.

Testing Any method that checks whether a program is doing what it is expected to do.

Text editor A program for entering, amending and storing 'plain text', that is, individually typed characters without any additional embedded code to specify how the text is to be presented. Contrast this with a *Word processor*.

Tool Command Language (Tcl) A scripting language that has long been used in the UNIX world for quickly putting together GUIs and tying together other programs. Today, languages like Visual Basic typically fill this gap. It is pronounced, 'tickle'.

Top-down An approach to system design or building when you start by formulating an overview of the whole system and work downwards. See *Bottom-up*.

Tracing Working through a program step-by-step in order to find errors.

Type   In most programming languages, all items of atomic data are assigned to a specific data type to allow their underlying binary value to be interpreted in a particular way. For instance, the integer type allows data to be interpreted as positive and negative whole numbers, whereas the Boolean type allows data to be interpreted as either a true value or a false value. Structured data is also given a type that describes the category to which it belongs. Most programming languages forbid the arbitrary mixing of distinct types, and some allow data of one type to be converted to a different type.

Typo   A silly slip in typing, where a finger hits two keys or letters somehow get themselves typed in the wrong order.

UML   *see* **Unified Modelling Language.**

Unified Modelling Language (UML)   A collection of types of diagram which are used to record and communicate the design of a program. There are many different diagram types in the language. An example of such a diagram is the 'class diagram' which shows the classes that exist in an object-oriented program and the ways in which information can travel between those classes. Use-case diagrams are also a part of UML.

Unit testing   Testing each component of a program in isolation to check that it does what we are expecting it to do.

Upper case   A way of describing an alphabetic character which is written as a capital letter, e.g. 'A', 'B', 'C', etc.

Use-case diagram   A diagram that shows the way in which actors use or interact with a system.

User interface design   The process of designing the boundary at which a user and a computer get together.

Variable   Something in a program that can store some data or information. Typically, the value stored in a variable can be changed as the program runs. Each variable in a program needs to have a name to distinguish it from all the other variables in the program.

VB   *see* **Visual Basic**.

VBA   *see* **Visual Basic for Applications.**

Version control system   A system that allows programmers to keep track of the various versions of a program that is being developed. For example, it can allow a programmer to go back to previous versions if some errors have been made in the latest version. *see* **CVS**.

vi   A powerful text editor. Its name is pronounced as two separate letters, 'vee eye'.

Visual Basic (VB)   Both a development environment and a programming language. As a programming language, its syntax is derived from BASIC. It is somewhat object-oriented and is a relatively easy way to build GUIs to be used within a Microsoft environment. See *VBA*.

Visual Basic for Applications (VBA)   A programming language for controlling Microsoft applications such as Word, Excel (a spreadsheet application) and Access (a database application).

Waterfall Model   A way of characterizing the process of designing and implementing a piece of software. It separates the software production process into phases, and development proceeds linearly through the phases of requirements analysis, design, implementation, testing (validation), integration and maintenance.

Web browser   A piece of software whose function it is to display hypertext documents and allow navigation of links between them. Normally these documents will be found on the World Wide Web.

White box testing   Tests designed to show that all the code is used, and that the program execution follows the correct paths through the code. The tester reads the program source code to verify that it is structured to give correct results.

White space   Characters that appear as blanks on a page, such as spaces, tabs and new lines.

Widget   A made-up name for an arbitrary component.

Wikipedia   An encyclopedia provided free over the Internet that is compiled and maintained by its readers. Anyone can edit exiting articles, provide new ones or put forward ideas.

Word processor   A program that can be used to create, modify, format (and print) documents. Before the advent of word processors document preparation was usually performed on typewriters.

Worksheet   Part of a spreadsheet. The term is often used when a spreadsheet involves more than one page. In this context, a worksheet would be a single page of a multi-paged spreadsheet.

World Wide Web   The World Wide Web is an information retrieval system that lives in the Internet.

WWW   *see* **World Wide Web.**

XML   *see* **Extensible Markup Language.**

XP   *see* **Extreme Programming.**

Z   A specification language with mathematical foundations.

Index

Note: numbers in **bold** indicate glossary definitions.